D1070972

PUSHING THE LIMITS

PUSHING THE LIMITS

The Remarkable Life and Times of
Vice Adm. Allan Rockwell McCann, USN

CARL LaVO

NAVAL INSTITUTE PRESS
Annapolis, Maryland

Naval Institute Press
291 Wood Road
Annapolis, MD 21402

ISBN: 978-1-59114-485-4 (hardcover)
ISBN: 978-1-61251-334-8 (eBook)
Library of Congress Cataloging-in-Publication Data is available

♾ Print editions meet the requirements of ANSI/NISO z39.48-1992 (Permanence of Paper).
Printed in the United States of America.

21 20 19 18 17 16 15 14 13   9 8 7 6 5 4 3 2 1
First printing

This is for my mother Hilda Irene, child of an immigrant Norwegian
farm family in Port Orchard, Washington.
Her gentle guidance, love of adventure, and support for her three children
inspired them to succeed in life.

A Toast to Commander Allan R. McCann, USN
Developer of the Rescue Bell

God bless you, Commander Allan McCann!
You've won the praises of each Navy man.
The Army, the Navy, and all laymen too
Today sing the praises of no one but you.
Planning, revising, and planning again,
And hoping your planning would not be in vain,
You toiled at the task, on your fine Rescue Bell,
And now we can say that 'You did the job well.'
What a time for a test! With the Squalus below
Hours seemed minutes, and how they did go!
The divers, equipment, and your Rescue Bell
All worked to perfection as headlines will tell.
And all of the days and the months and the years,
You worked on The Bell, to-day bring you cheers.
With patience and study you perfected your plan.
God bless you, Commander Allan McCann.

—Richard B. Gifford
New York World Telegram
May 1939, after the unprecedented rescue
of thirty-three survivors of the sunken submarine USS *Squalus*

Contents

ILLUSTRATIONS

PREFACE

$\mathcal{H}$is family says he was a great storyteller. Yet Vice Adm. Allan Rockwell McCann left no yarns nor recollections, stories that might reveal a deeper sense of his personality and service to the nation. In his four-decade military career, spanning two world wars, he rarely discussed for the record the many historic circumstances that enveloped him. If you were to judge the admiral by his military awards and ribbons, they would not suggest the extraordinary career he led. No Medal of Honor. No Navy Cross. No Silver Star. No Distinguished Service Medal. No Presidential Unit Citation. His signature achievement was the development of a workable submarine rescue chamber. The view I have of Allan McCann is that of an efficient, competent officer who succeeded in all his many endeavors but did not boast of them nor seek self-promotion as many have over the years. Rather, he let the record speak for him.

I came to this project as a result of my previous book for the Naval Institute Press, *Back from the Deep*. That story, about the rescue of survivors of the sunken USS *Squalus* in the Atlantic Ocean off New Hampshire, attracted the interest of Jeff Scism, a U.S. Air Force veteran and California-based genealogist. He suggested I write a book about McCann. He believes the admiral has all but been ignored in naval history. My editor, Lt. Cdr. Tom Cutler, USN retired, wondered where I would get the material to sustain such a book since McCann left no known interviews of any depth. I suggested his life story could be told through the drama he was part of, incredible events that at one time commanded world headlines. If I were lucky, I told Tom, perhaps correspondence with his family might still be around. Bits and pieces turned up, but not enough to reveal the man in full. Still, the admiral's experiences are part of an epoch of the Navy worth retelling. As I got into the narrative, I began to realize that virtually every chapter suggests an entire book of its own. I have done my best to condense the record while keeping the admiral in the picture.

Allan McCann lived a remarkable life. He was born to a Scottish tailor in a remarkable town in the Berkshire Mountains of Massachusetts. In my mind and others', the admiral deserves recognition beyond the rescue chamber that spared the lives of otherwise doomed submariners in 1939. It is my hope that this book will fulfill that purpose.

Among the many people I'm indebted to for their help, two stand out—retired Navy captain Max Duncan and Mr. Scism. Jeff got me curious about McCann's biography and frequently pointed the way to archival information to help close gaps in that narrative. Max, one of the submarine heroes of World War II and a veteran of twenty years of undersea service, reviewed each of my chapters for accuracy and suggested improvements. A resident of Savannah, Georgia, he brought to my project a wealth of experience, including being a former gunnery and torpedo officer in USS *Barb* (SS-220) in World War II and an executive officer of USS *Sennet* (SS-408), which explored the Antarctic polar ice pack after the war. In his career, he commanded two submarines, a submarine division, a submarine tender, submarine base Pearl Harbor, and a submarine squadron. He also taught at the Naval Academy, was on the Submarine Force Atlantic Commanders Staff for the Polaris missile buildup, and completed his service as commander, Naval Support Activities Saigon. Max was a great help in the completion of my previous book, *The Galloping Ghost*, which profiled World War II sub skipper Eugene Fluckey, under whom Max served during the conflict. Max recently accompanied me to the U.S. Strategic Command in Omaha, Nebraska, where we discussed Admiral Fluckey's unique leadership qualities.

Others who offered assistance during my many months of research include the following: Historians Rachel Branch and Paul W. Marino of the North Adams Historical Society were gracious hosts on my visit to Allan McCann's hometown. Rachel drove me around North Adams, pointing out features that would have influenced "Mack" during his youth. Jennifer Bryan, PhD, head of Special Collections and Archives and archivist at the U.S. Naval Academy's Nimitz Library, helped me locate information about McCann's years as a midshipman and a letter he wrote explaining his role in the development of the submarine rescue chamber. Mark C. Mollan, archivist, Navy/Maritime Reference, Archives I—Textual Services Branch of the National Archives and Records Administration, secured for me records of naval inquests into the explosion and rescue attempts on board the submarine *O-5* in 1918 as well as the sinking of the very same submarine in the Panama Canal Zone in 1923. Janis Jorgensen, manager, Heritage Collection, U.S. Naval Institute Press, provided me access to oral histories of those associated with McCann and met my various graphic needs. Thomas O. Paine, the National Aeronautics and Space Administration's former director of the Apollo moon landing program, conveyed to me detailed information about Japan's I-boats and his voyage in I-400 from Japan to Hawaii after the war, when he was a lieutenant in the Navy. Capt. Chris Ratliff, USN, executive assistant to the commander, U.S. Strategic Command, Offutt Air Force Base, Omaha, Nebraska, helped facilitate a personal visit to a modern nuclear boat. Jeffrey Barlow of the Naval History and Heritage Command in

Washington, a leading expert on the so-called Revolt of the Admirals, offered his critique of my chapter on the incident. USS *Iowa* veterans George Graham and Grier Sims gave me insights into the Battle of Leyte Gulf, which they participated in under the command of Captain McCann. My appreciation also goes to Nancy Richards, curator, USS *Bowfin* Submarine Museum and Park, Honolulu, Hawaii, and Cdr. Christy Hagen, APR, public affairs officer, Commander Submarine Force, U.S. Pacific Fleet, Pearl Harbor, for helping me gain a better understanding of modern submarine rescue devices. Dr. Dave Winkler, historian, and Robert Hanshew, photographic curator at the Naval History and Heritage Command in Washington, D.C., helped me secure high-resolution images for this book during my visit to the Washington Navy Yard. Also, a tip of the hat to Laura Kissel, polar curator at Ohio State University Library in Columbus, Ohio, for obtaining images of the voyage of the *Nautilus* in 1930, and to Janice Davis, archives technician at the Harry S Truman Presidential Library in Independence, Missouri, for securing an image of McCann with Truman.

I'm indebted to Commander Cutler, professor of strategy at the U.S. Naval War College and senior editor at the Naval Institute Press, for his patience in providing me additional time to complete my research. His remarkable book *The Battle of Leyte Gulf* illuminated many aspects of the naval clashes that I have incorporated in *Pushing the Limits*. Also a tip of the hat to Julie Kimmel, USNI's copy editor, and Emily Bakely, USNI's production editor, for their diligent work readying this book for publication.

In the McCann family, Bob Crawford, the admiral's grandson, and the admiral's granddaughters—Edie Sims, Janet Kmetz, and Bette Simpson—were helpful. Edie has been especially enthusiastic from the start.

I would be remiss in not giving a nod to Everett "Tuck" Weaver, junior officer in the *Barb* during World War II and loyal supporter of the U.S. Naval Institute. Through his backing, this book got off the ground. I am grateful for his encouragement along the way. Additionally, a note of appreciation to my father, Carl Sr., for looking at my chapter on the Battle of Leyte Gulf. He was there, on board the destroyer USS *Halford* (DD-480), which was part of a special attack group that launched torpedoes against Japan's *Yamashiro* while successfully dodging return fire from the battleship's massive guns in Surigao Strait.

Also thanks to my daughter, Genevieve LaVO Cosdon, a marketing and Web design wunderkind who gave me needed assistance in the photographic presentation for my book.

A final note of profound affection for my beloved wife, Mary Anne, whose father, Albert Ferber Sr., was on board the destroyer USS *Picking* (DD-685), which screened troop landings on Leyte during World War II. Mary Anne supports me in all my endeavors as assistant managing editor for the daily newspapers of Calkins Media in the Philadelphia suburbs and as a writer interested in the world around us. Long hours in the newsroom often were replaced by long hours researching and writing this book at home or away. Her understanding surpasses that of many spouses and allows me the space to fulfill an ambition. My love for her knows no bounds.

—Carl LaVO
Bucks County, Pennsylvania
4 July 2013

CHAPTER 1

ROBOT BOMBS

USS *Vixen* (PG-53)
Washington Navy Yard, Washington, D.C.
8 January 1945

*T*he intelligence was quite disturbing, even to Adm. Jonas H. Ingram, commander in chief of the Navy's Atlantic Fleet. In his flagship, he pondered the latest classified reports about a pending U-boat attack. It appeared that the German Kriegsmarine had issued orders to deploy unconventional submarines to the East Coast of the United States. More worrisome, the U-boats reportedly would carry powerful guided missiles capable of being launched at sea. The admiral, tall and hefty with a flat nose set into a broad, affable face, shot a glance through the wardroom porthole of *Vixen*. Outside, a thick overcast hung low over the icy Potomac flowing past the Navy yard. Ingram contemplated what it would be like if missiles rained down on Manhattan out of such a cloud cover.

"There's no telling what they might do on a day like this," he said to reporters gathered in his wardroom. "The thing to do is not to get excited about it. It might knock out a high building or two. It might create a fire hazard. It would certainly cause casualties in the limited area where it might hit. Yet it could not seriously affect the progress of the war."

The admiral hedged his narrative, however; he was mindful that something more horrible devised by German scientists might happen, events that could hand Adolf Hitler and his fanatical Nazi propaganda minister Joseph Goebbels a stunning triumph. "Think what it would mean to Dr. Goebbels at this stage of the war to announce that 'Today we have destroyed New York'?" The journalists made careful note of the comment.

Citizens in Manhattan the following morning would be jolted by a front-page story in the *New York Times*. An attack on the city, deemed "probable" by Admiral Ingram in his press conference, had seemed improbable to them at this late date in a tedious war that was finally going the Allies' way. In three years of worldwide combat, no attack had occurred on the city, even though U-boats prowled the harbor entrance early in the conflict. The closest thing to an attack was at the British Pavilion of the World's Fair in 1940, when a ticking time bomb in an overnight bag left by suspected German agents exploded, killing two city detectives as they cut open the satchel.

Of course, New Yorkers were aware of developments overseas and the daily missile bombardments of southeast England. Jet-propelled V-1 "robot bombs" had set London ablaze. The pilot-less drones were low flying and noisy, giving advance warning as they glided with a deadly whine into homes, office buildings, churches, hospitals, and schools. Even more fearsome were newly developed V-2 vertical ascent rockets, 13-ton behemoths that fell silently out of the sky at 2,000 miles per hour to detonate 1-ton warheads on impact. A sense of shock pervaded the British public, which had been accustomed to sirens announcing the approach of V-1s. In just twenty-four hours before Admiral Ingram's press conference, more than a hundred V-bombs of both types had pummeled England. Added to all this was a front-page dispatch from Zurich citing unconfirmed reports that the Nazis had developed a V-3 rocket capable of even greater destruction.

Despite these seemingly science-fiction nightmares, the American public had become increasingly nonchalant. U-boats, once a familiar sight off East Coast beaches, had not attacked coastal ships in months. There were recurrent rumors that the Navy intended to disband its antisub patrols because of inaction. In Ingram's mind, the rumors didn't help matters. The threat from Germany was far from over to him and those in the intelligence community. The Third Reich government clearly was rushing new forms of weapons into the fight and racing to create an atomic bomb in hopes of turning the course of the war. Albert Speer, Hitler's minister of armaments and war production, proclaimed in a radio broadcast from Germany in December 1944 that the United States would be attacked by "U-1 and U-2 bombs fired from U-boats." The threat of a new classification of missiles whose range and power could not be deciphered was not to be taken lightly.

At the Navy Department in Washington, many were convinced that the goal was a seaborne rocket salvo on Manhattan, an attack so spectacular that Adolf Hitler might use it to negotiate a peace agreement with the Allies, who had Hitler's forces on the run from enemy-occupied France, Belgium, and eastern Europe. A final, desperate thrust by German infantry on the French Ardennes front and in Alsace had been turned back. Escape routes had been closed off. Allied forces had encircled Germany. Without some sort of military miracle, Hitler was doomed. His best hope now was his array of futuristic weapons and perhaps the submarines being refitted in occupied Norway. What was clear from captured spies and intelligence derived from American and British intelligence services was that seven U-boats dubbed the Seewolf group and two other submarines operating independently were to be deployed amid an unusual degree of secrecy. Ingram's job was to locate and destroy the submarines. The challenge was finding them. That responsibility fell to the mysterious Tenth Fleet, the Navy's "fleet with no ships," and its new chief of staff, Rear Adm. Allan Rockwell McCann.

At age forty-eight, McCann had been recalled from command of a battleship in the thick of the Pacific war to helm the Washington, D.C.–based intelligence unit under the command of Navy admiral Ernest J. King Jr. McCann had taken over for King's chief of staff, Rear Adm. Francis Stuart "Frog" Low.

The Tenth Fleet's purpose was to analyze data about Axis ship movements provided by crypto-analysts in England. With such knowledge, McCann had the authority from Admiral King to direct any U.S. Navy ships and aircraft that he deemed necessary to defeat U-boats anywhere in the Atlantic Ocean. The Tenth Fleet was specifically created in April 1943 by Admiral King, the short-tempered commander in chief of the Navy, to plot a unified strategy to defeat the U-boats that had been so successful in attacks on Allied supply convoys early in the war. Low, McCann's predecessor, had been particularly effective in organizing hunter-killer groups of small carriers, destroyers, and aircraft to corner and eliminate the U-boats. The Allies had been averaging four U-boat sinkings a month. In the Tenth Fleet's first month with Low directing operations, the tally rose to forty-one and soon averaged more than twenty-three a month.

Finding the right kind of man to replace Low was not easy. King set out certain criteria. He would have the authority to commandeer any vessel of the U.S. Navy in the Atlantic whenever and wherever he deemed necessary. He would have easy access to all intelligence services. Foremost, the chief of staff would have to be a highly ranked officer whose prestige and influence was well known, a man with proven decisiveness, ability, and persuasiveness. McCann had that kind of respect and authority in the Navy. He was a pioneering submarine commander known throughout the world. As a hard-driving, brilliant tactician and commander for both submarines and surface ships, he appeared an ideal fit to direct the Navy's "phantom" fleet in perhaps the last U-boat battle of the Atlantic.

While McCann worked behind the scenes to lay down plans to find and destroy the Seewolf sub pack, Admiral Ingram gave the mission its public face. There was no doubt in his mind that the Nazi government wanted to spring a surprise, whatever it was. "I know the enemy," Ingram told the reporters gathered around him in *Vixen*. By age fifty-eight, he had gained profound military knowledge since graduation from the Naval Academy in 1907 and had earned the Medal of Honor in 1914, the Navy Cross in World War I, and a Purple Heart in World War II, the latter for wounds suffered in a tangle with a U-boat "wolf pack" in 1942. As the commander of the Navy's Fourth Fleet, he had implemented new tactics based on Tenth Fleet intelligence that had finally broken the back of U-boat attacks in the South Atlantic. These tactics involved stringing out destroyers and escort carriers in a virtual, oceangoing dragnet in which planes and warships used radar and sonar to locate and eliminate U-boats with bombs, depth charges, and gunfire. The admiral had been remarkably successful using these tactics in the North Atlantic to safeguard troops and matériel being convoyed from U.S. ports to Allied forces in Europe and the Soviet Union.

Ingram, as the voice of the Atlantic campaign, having taken over for Adm. Royal E. Ingersoll, seemed omnipresent as he sailed to naval bases up and down the East Coast and in the Caribbean in his 333-foot-long *Vixen*, a German-made schooner that had been converted by the Navy into a single-stack gunboat with a crew of 279 officers and enlisted sailors. Ingram stayed in constant touch with defensive forces and gleaned as much information as he could about the U-boat offensive. Despite this new threat of a missile strike in the closing days of the war, he was confident to the point of being bombastic about the capability of his ships and planes spread across the Atlantic, which were augmented by intelligence provided by Admiral McCann and the Tenth Fleet in Washington:

> Whatever happens, it won't be a Pearl Harbor. Anything they throw from Norway I'll catch without a glove. And you can broadcast that if you want to. Let the German High Command know we're ready for them. I know of whereof I'm speaking when I say we've got them. In the South Atlantic we credited no unproved victories. The rule was, "Bring back a German ear or a flask of alcohol from a torpedo." We got plenty of both. In other words, the boys of the Atlantic Fleet have won the Battle of the Atlantic, but it isn't over yet. I estimate that Germany still has some 300 submarines. That's all right. Let 'em throw 250 of them at us someday. We'll take care of them.

Still, there was risk that one or more of the Seewolf subs might slip past Ingram's defensive barrier and attack New York: "It may be only ten or twelve bombs but they may come before we can stop them. They may hit before we know they're on the way. And the only way to stop a robot is at the source."

Rear Adm. Allan R. McCann at about the time he headed the Navy's Tenth Fleet, which he directed in Operation Teardrop, designed to thwart a U-boat attack on New York City.

Courtesy of McCann family (Edie Sims)

Lie Face Down
Office of Civil Defense, Albany, New York
8 January 1945

Col. Edward C. O. Thomas, director of the New York State Office of Civilian Protection, announced that there would be no blackout in the event of a submarine attack on New York City. "It would interfere with salvage and rescue," he told the Associated Press. Most of the casualties would come from falling glass and buildings, he said. In the eventuality of attack, he advised city residents to lie face down, out in the open, away from building walls, and to cover their heads with their arms.

The colonel's view added to that of New York City mayor Fiorello La Guardia. Responding to Admiral Ingram's forecast of a "probable" attack on the city, the mayor said earlier that day, "It's a warning to the public not to relax in war production. I hope it isn't so. But we've got to hustle and provide our forces with everything they need so that we can end the menace as soon as possible."

Hitler's Miracle Weapon
13th Submarine Flotilla, Dora Complex, Trondheim, Norway
23 February 1945

An Allied coast watcher was the first to report the departure of a Seewolf sub from the 13th Submarine Flotilla base, forty miles inland on a meandering, ice-free fjord. The Third Reich had intended the Dora Complex to be part of the largest German naval base in northern Europe. The bunker-like repair and refit center beneath the massive, flat, steel-reinforced, eleven-foot-thick concrete ceiling was designed to protect up to fourteen submarines from aerial attack. Hitler's dream was for an ocean-commanding presence sortied from Trondheim, a Norwegian stronghold dating back to Viking days. With the Third Reich teetering on collapse, German grossadmiral Karl Doenitz prepared one last gamble with the deployment of Seewolf subs from Dora and other Norwegian ports. The boats—U-518, U-546, U-805, U-808, U-853, U-880, and U-1235—were equipped with snorkels, a revolutionary means adapted from the Dutch of extending to the surface a retractable breathing pipe that allowed submerged U-boats to operate their air-breathing diesel engines while charging their batteries and sustaining propulsion without surfacing. Two other submarines— U-530 and U-548—were to follow the Seewolf pack and deploy to the Canadian east coast.

The Seewolf boats were war veterans, survivors of an Allied counter-offensive that by the end of 1944 had sunk an astonishing 646 U-boats, including their forty-four-member crews. Among the battle-tested was U-853. The previous June 1944, the boat had ventured to the mid-Atlantic to gather weather data for the German high command, then bracing for the D day invasion of the French coast by English and American troops. The Navy escort carrier *Croatan* (CVE-25) and six destroyer escorts in Division 13, part of Ingram's command, lay in wait. On 7 June the carrier located the sub, initiating a ten-day pursuit. U-boat skipper Helmut Sommer was so elusive that American sailors began to call his sub the "Moby Dick." Like the mythical white whale of Hermann Melville's classic, U-853 had survived so many narrow disasters during the war that even crew members referred to the boat as "der Seiltänzer"—"the tightrope walker." In *Croatan*, division captain John Vest, the Navy's preeminent U-boat hunter, was determined not to let the sub slip away this time. On 17 June a weather report radioed from U-853 revealed the sub's location thirty miles south of the carrier. Vest quickly scrambled two FM-1 Wildcat fighters, which caught the sub on the surface and strafed it with gunfire. Two crew members were killed, and a number of others, including the skipper, were critically injured before the sub could descend to safety. U-853 barely made it back to Norway for repairs.

Now, in late February 1945, U-853 and the eight other boats began the staged departure from Norway. Their orders were to rendezvous at sea and then proceed out of radio contact to the United States, where boat commanders were to open sealed orders and carry them out. Was the mission to bomb New York City?

No one at Tenth Fleet headquarters could tell for sure, although there were clues that an attack on New York was the plan. The previous September, a spy captured by the Navy after a U-boat landed him on the coast of Maine told the Federal Bureau of Investigation (FBI) that the Germans were preparing submarines equipped with missiles. Three months later, two more spies put ashore in Maine were tracked to New York City and captured. Under interrogation, they revealed the rough outlines of an attack on East Coast cities by a fleet of missile-equipped U-boats.

Although there still was no hard evidence, intelligence experts in Washington and London believed that the Germans were capable. Scientists at the top-secret Nazi rocket research center of Peenemünde on the island of Usedom in the Baltic Sea had equipped U-511 with a rocket launcher bolted to its upper deck and successfully launched Wurfkörper 42 Spreng missiles from a depth of forty feet. The lack of a dependable guidance system, however, plus the pressing need to develop the Vengeance Weapon 1, or V-1, put further progress on hold. In July 1943 the plan was resurrected after the deployment of the V-1. But again a submarine version was shelved as the development of the land-launched V-2, Hitler's "miracle weapon," proceeded. By late 1944, when V-1 and V-2 rockets were in mass production at underground factories, Peenemünde technicians again turned to the U-boat missile program, focusing on creating a modified V-2. Project Prüfstand XII would involve U-boats equipped with snorkels and slowly towing V-2s mounted in watertight cylinders. Within range of New York, the containers would be flooded to bring them to a vertical position; after that, the rockets would be launched by remote control from the U-boats. That specter kept lights burning under McCann's watch at Tenth Fleet headquarters in Washington as the nine submarines headed west across the Atlantic.

Ultra
Station X, Buckinghamshire, England
Early March 1945

Confirmation that Seewolf boats were on the way came from British cyphers at Station X, a highly secretive listening post near London. Seven U-boats—two groups of three with a lagging seventh boat following—were involved. In addition, two other subs had been deployed as well. The U-boats were to make a slow crossing without breaking radio silence in order to avoid detection and then execute orders once on station off the coast of the United States and Canada. The news created what one expert termed "a brief binge of chaos" in Washington. But for the English crypto-analysts, the revelation was just the latest in a long string of disclosures that continued to give the Allies a decided upper hand in the war.

Station X cryptologists were the epicenter of a spy network based at the Bletchley Park Estate, west of London. The mansion was a sprawling mishmash of Victorian Gothic, Tudor, and Dutch Baroque architecture located in the leafy suburb of Buckinghamshire. Intelligence gathered there was incredibly accurate and was collectively called Ultra. Few knew how the information was derived. That secret was jealously protected and would not be revealed until long after the war. Those with inside knowledge were a cadre of English experts who eventually would collaborate with Americans assigned to Station X in 1943.

The intelligence operation came about on 15 August 1939, when Britain's Government Code and Cypher School moved to Bletchley Park after Germany invaded Poland to launch World War II. The cypher school's purpose was to decrypt the Axis military code created by German Enigma mechanical cyphers. The Nazi high command used the Enigma-generated code to communicate with its armies, air forces, and navies throughout Europe, North Africa, and the Atlantic Ocean. Fortunately for Britain, Polish crypto-analysts had deciphered the code in 1932. They smuggled the information to the English in 1939, just before the Nazi invasion. Immediately, scientists went to work at Bletchley Park to use it to read thousands upon thousands of German radio transmissions recorded by a network of wireless "Y Service" listening posts in Britain. By mid-war, a workforce of twelve thousand mathematicians, crypto-analysts, linguists, engineers, and clerks bent to the task of translating the intercepts into English. In wooden outbuildings, scientists created a clattering, large mechanical computer called "the Bombe" and a later electronic version called "Colossus I" to quicken the process.

In the course of the war, the computers had churned out dazzlingly accurate information about enemy troop and ship movements. Ultra intelligence directly led to British naval victories in the Battles of North Cape and Cape Matapan and setbacks for German general Erwin Rommel's North African army. Ultra also revealed the position of fifty-eight of the sixty German divisions on the western front prior to the D day landings in June 1944. Decoded transmissions between the German and Japanese embassies led to the breaking of the Japanese military code as well. Japan's war plans, including all ship departures, routes, and destinations, were revealed—a decisive coupe for the Allies in prosecuting the Pacific war. Station X operatives also were the first to reveal the massacre of Jews at German prison camps and Germany's drive to develop guided missiles and possibly an atomic bomb.

Thanks to those at Bletchley Park, the deployment of the Seewolf pack and the two U-boats destined for Canada brought Admiral McCann and the Tenth Fleet into high alert in March and April 1945. Station X had provided not only the deployments but also the exact routes each submarine would take. McCann figured an attack on the East Coast could be expected by mid- to late April— unless the Tenth Fleet and warships under Ingram's command destroyed them.

Operation Teardrop
USS *Stanton* (DE-247), North Atlantic
15 April 1945

Fog, high wind, and tumultuous seas had prevented carrier-based aircraft from searching for the U-boats. Thus, the initial hunt for the Seewolf subs fell to the *Stanton* and several other warships plowing the surf south of Iceland. The destroyer escort had maintained her listening patrol for several days as forty- to fifty-knot winds churned the sea into a monstrous boil. Still, there was no sign of the enemy as night fell on the fourth day.

By McCann's earlier directive, the *Stanton* was one of forty-two destroyers and destroyer escorts, four escort carriers, and four air wings with seventy-six total planes deployed by Admiral Ingram as twin barrier forces of submarine "hunter-killers." The first, more northern group, the First Barrier Force, consisted of the carriers *Mission Bay* (CVE-59) and *Croatan*, each protected by a screen of four destroyer escorts, with another twelve destroyers strung out before them forty to fifty miles to the east in a 120-mile-long line in the mid-Atlantic. The forward destroyers were spaced from five to ten miles apart. The

Second Barrier Force included the carriers *Core* (CVE-13) and *Bogue* (CVE-9) and their escorts plus a similar line of fourteen destroyers, all deployed south of St. John's, Newfoundland, along the 14th meridian. If the U-boats got past the First Barrier Force, the second was in place "to bar off the entire eastern seaboard of Canada and the United States to a phalanx of snorkel boats," as Ingram put it.

Designated Operation Teardrop and finalized in early January, the warships were organized along lines already proven successful by Admiral Ingersoll in the South Atlantic. The port of Argentia, Newfoundland, was the forward operating base. There the two barrier forces were assembled and posted in the North Atlantic.

The wild early spring weather made it impossible for the U-boats to use their snorkels in their crossing, forcing them to surface to recharge their batteries. Fortunately for them, barrier aircraft were stranded on their carrier flight decks. Nevertheless, sonar and radar arrays on the destroyers remained formidable under all conditions—as U-1235 was to discover on the evening of 15 April.

The *Stanton* was the first to make radar contact at 3,500 yards at 2135 hours and headed for the sub, then knifing its way west through massive whitecaps and hiding in the dark. Alerted to the presence of the charging destroyer, the boat dived and disappeared. Using sonar, *Stanton* reestablished contact and set a course directly over the submarine while lobbing hedgehog antisubmarine mortar shells in its direction. U-1235 went deeper. Another attack began. The U-boat again escaped with *Stanton* in relentless electronic pursuit. The warship delivered a third salvo. Nearly three hours into the attack, the destroyer *Frost* (DE-144) joined *Stanton*, and the two blanketed the sub with hedgehog projectiles and depth-charge canisters until two massive explosions ripped the ocean, rattling barrier ships ten miles away.

At 0117 hours, Cdr. F. D. Giambattista on *Frost* announced over the radio, "That is the end of the attack and I think that's the end of the sub." U-1235 ceased to exist. One down, eight to go.

"Fire and Ram!"
USS *Frost*, North Atlantic
16 April 1945

Both the *Stanton* and *Frost* remained in the area, searching for U-1235's two sister boats known to be accompanying it. Within forty-five minutes, *Frost* discovered U-880 on radar making a desperate run for it at five hundred yards. "Close the target. Illuminate. Fire and ram!" Giambattista shouted.

Star shells from the destroyer failed to illuminate the sub because of fog pockets. The ship's searchlights, however, brought U-880 into full view; it had surfaced and was closing on the destroyer as if to attack. *Frost* opened fire with 3-inch deck guns, tattooing the boat's conning tower and forcing it to dive. Two other destroyers—the *Stanton* and USS *Hue* (DE-145)—rushed in. At 0406, the *Stanton* scattered hedgehogs over the sub, causing it to explode. The concussion was of such intensity that those on the destroyer thought she had been hit by a torpedo. Even *Croatan*, fifteen miles away, was rocked by the blast, which cracked crockery in the ship's galley. Diesel fuel from ruptured tanks on the U-boat spread across the ocean as sonar contact with the sub slowly faded and disappeared. U-880 was no more. Two down, seven to go.

"Unscathed"
Tenth Fleet Headquarters, Washington, D.C.
20 April 1945

Admiral McCann at the plotting table was haggard from loss of sleep over the past several days, which had started with the attacks on the first two U-boats. Incoming teletype accounts had delivered moment-by-moment accounts of the drama playing out at sea. The swift and accurate attacks by *Stanton*, *Frost*, and *Hue* were encouraging. But four days had passed without another sighting. The admiral had grown frustrated by the barrier planes' inability to tighten the net. Without the planes, the barriers were proving less effective. Even when carrier-based B-24 Liberator and Avenger aircraft could fly, the results were discouraging. They had yet to detect or attack a single U-boat. Without the aerial screen, there was grave risk that the U-boats might sneak past Ingram's forces. Where was the sister sub of the U-1235 and U-880? Had U-805, known from Ultra to be traveling with the two boats, slipped past unscathed? And what about those unusually powerful explosions that had destroyed the first two submarines? Were they proof that the boats were armed with the dreaded missiles and targeting New York City? Time was running out.

The gravity of the situation bore down on Admiral McCann, a man used to incredible challenges in his long career. He had retrofitted a decommissioned Navy submarine, renamed the *Nautilus*, that was the first to seek a route beneath the Arctic ice pack in 1931. He had pioneered a submarine rescue chamber that had saved for the first time in history submariners trapped on the ocean bottom in 1939. He had organized the rescue of wounded sailors during the Japanese attack on Pearl Harbor in 1941. He had helped resolve problems with faulty torpedoes that had hounded Navy submarines in the Pacific in the first two years of the war. And he had commanded USS *Iowa* (BB-61) in support of the Marine invasion of Peleliu, Gen. Douglas MacArthur's landing on Leyte in the Philippines, and air strikes on Formosa and the Ryukyu Islands off Okinawa.

Surmounting challenges always had been Admiral McCann's hallmark. He was quite aware of the power of tenacity and creativity in overcoming life's challenges. He was a child of the rugged mountains of western Massachusetts, where a tradition of Yankee ingenuity and military service set an early anchor. There, near his hometown of North Adams, a man-made wonder of the world—built against nearly impossible odds—provided a testament to boys like him of what perseverance and willpower could accomplish.

CHAPTER 2

PECULIAR PLACE

The Hoosic River
North Adams, Massachusetts
1896

North Adams, Massachusetts, a small city in a narrow valley between two mountain ranges, enjoyed extraordinary prosperity when Allan Rockwell McCann was born there on 20 September 1896. Tucked deep in the Berkshires near the border of Vermont and New York, the city of 24,000 had tapped gold from wildly rushing streams and rivers that powered mills and factories laid out along the confluence of both branches of the Hoosic River. The factories and the ingenuity of their owners made North Adams famous for the quality and variety of goods produced there. Shoes, hats, textiles, cabinetry, wagons and sleighs, bricks, marble works, and machine-shop products created full employment. North Adams, home to the largest textile plant in western Massachusetts, was a leader in printed fabrics modeled after the latest patterns from Paris. Daily, a hundred freight and twenty-eight passenger trains serviced the city during Allan McCann's youth. The resulting wealth endowed North Adams with fine mansions, well-appointed Victorian homes, a thriving retail business district, four major downtown hotels, as many theaters, a street-railway system, top-rated schools, and houses of worship with extraordinarily high steeples that define the city's skyline to the present day.

"Mack" was one of four children, three girls and a boy, born to James and Carolyn McCann, who had emigrated from Canada in the 1880s. In a city where businesses frequently were named for the initials of their owners, J. A. McCann was an esteemed tailor for the P. J. Boland Overcutting and Company, which had a block of stores in North Adams and another in New York City. J. A. fashioned clothing from English, Irish, and Scotch woolens that could "be had nowhere else in this city," according to a 1909 newspaper advertisement. He noted of his employer, "If you consider it worth while to appear somewhat differently dressed than is the great majority, you can find much to interest you at this house."

For kids like J. A.'s young son Allan, the lure of the outdoors in and around North Adams was addicting. Children spent endless days fishing, hunting, sledding in winter, going camping and swimming at the nearby Windsor Lake, watching parades, and attending concerts at Colgrove Park in town. North Adams also had become the nation's hot-air ballooning capital thanks to the availability of hydrogen at the North Adams Gas Works plant and launch grounds. Multiple ascents from the valley by world-famous aeronauts enthralled citizens. One of the largest balloons ever—the *Conqueror*—was christened in North Adams and later participated in an international race in Europe in 1908. But it was the simple joys close at hand—most of all the mountain trails once used by Mohawk and Mahican tribes to cross the steep Hossac and Greylock ranges en route to the Hudson River to the west or the New England coast to the east—that engaged the valley's kids.

It's the exceptional beauty of those ancient, forested mountains around North Adams that give them a niche in American literature. Henry David Thoreau, William Cullen Bryant, Henry Ward Beecher, and Nathaniel Hawthorne spent time there. The latter, author of *The Scarlet Letter*, stayed in North Adams for two months in the summer of 1838. From the wild heights of 3,000-foot-high Hoosac Mountain, Hawthorne looked down on the pocket settlement of North Adams, closely guarded to the southwest by 3,500-foot-high Mount Greylock, the highest peak in the state. Wrote Hawthorne of the town in the valley, "The village, viewed from the top of a hill to the westward at sunset, has a peculiarly happy and peaceful look . . . and seems as if it lay in the hollow of a large hand. These hills, surrounding the town on all sides, give it a snug and insulated air; and, viewed from certain points, it would be difficult to tell how to get out, without climbing the mountain ridges; but the roads wind away and accomplish the passage."

Hawthorne had come to vacation in North Adams and while there explored the city's nationally known natural wonder—a stone bridge of white marble that spans a five-foot-wide chasm into which a stream plunges three hundred feet through a dazzling maze of alabaster boulders, deep pools, and caves carved from pure white marble bedrock 550 million years old. One face of the bedrock away from the fissure was a quarry, the original source of North Adams' wealth. The marble dazzled in the sunlight, at times temporarily blinding workers blasting it loose. By the later nineteenth century, the marble works had become of secondary importance, replaced by the city's burgeoning industrial might made possible by an engineering marvel five miles east of town.

"Like Shoveling Eels"
Hoosac Tunnel, North Adams, Massachusetts
1906

Awe would be an apt description of the looks on the faces of North Adams schoolchildren visiting the Hoosac Tunnel, a mammoth hole carved into the western base of Hoosac Mountain. As was the tradition in the city, Allan McCann and other kids hiked alongside railroad tracks to the western portal to see for themselves one of the man-made wonders of the world. With the swift-flowing Deerfield River rushing past below, McCann and his pals peered into the twenty-six-foot-wide, horizontal abyss with twin rail lines that dwindled to a pinprick of light at the far end.

It had taken twenty-five years—from 1851 to 1876—for the Troy and Greenfield Railroad to build the Hoosac Tunnel. Progress had been difficult for more than a generation owing to unexpected geologic obstacles and off-and-

A locomotive rushes from the nearly five-mile-long Hoosac Tunnel circa 1910 en route to Allan McCann's nearby hometown of North Adams, Massachusetts. The tunnel was one of the wonders of the world that intrigued McCann as a young boy. North Adams, in a picturesque valley in the Berkshire Mountains, was known throughout the world for its industrial innovations.

Courtesy of Paul W. Marino/North Adams Historical Society

on political battles to secure public funding for a project critics deemed "the road to ruin." Through brute willpower, investors overcame the odds and slowly pierced the mountain of limestone, slate, mica, gneiss, and nearly impenetrable quartz. In the end, the tunnel stretched four and three-quarter miles from east to west, making the Hoosac the longest tunnel in the Western Hemisphere to that time. It gave North Adams a rapid transit link by train to Boston. Until then the Hoosac mountain range, known to Bostonians as "the Western Wall," blocked commercial access between the city and points west. The opening of side-by-side rail lines through the tunnel turned McCann's hometown into a commercial hub for the fastest trains in the world. They zipped beneath the mountain to supply city goods not only to the Boston seaport but to flourishing cities to the west, including Albany, Buffalo, Cleveland, Chicago, and St. Louis.

Stories of what it took to build that tunnel—courage, mechanical innovation, tragedy, setbacks, and triumph—transfixed young McCann and served as a guidepost for what was possible in his later naval career. The railroad employed Irish and Italian immigrants, French Canadians, and American citizens who used black powder to shatter the stone at the eastern face of the tunnel and haul the debris out. As historian Carl R. Byron described it, "After whacking a hole two or three feet deep, the crew tamped a powder charge into it and ignited a powder-trail or goose-quill fuse with a candle. If the blaster was not a sprinter, it would not be long before he was maimed—or dead." On the western face, workers discovered a wall of limestone holding back a watery, mud-like ooze that flowed into the space of any shovelful of spoils removed from the tunnel. Workers called the gook "porridge stone" and said working with it was like "shoveling eels." To compensate, they trenched down from the summit; drained it of the liquid; built a tube of bricks that were mortared together as a permanent, waterproof barrier where the tunnel would be; and then backfilled the trench and proceeded to the next section. Step by step, the tunnel builders repeated the process until they reached solid rock—a distance of 883 feet—and then continued the brick arch another 6,690 feet into the mountain for safety's sake. It took 20 million bricks to build the tube, and all were manufactured at a kiln factory on site.

This kind of engineering genius pushed the tunneling forward. To speed the work, rail employees dug the Central Shaft twenty-seven feet wide and more than a thousand feet deep from the mountaintop to intersect the calculated route of the tunnel so that miners could work in both directions toward the western and eastern egresses. The shaft was to provide ventilation for the tunnel when it was complete. Tunnel builders also bore a second pit, called the Western Shaft, to try to drain away water from the western portal. Boring both the shafts and the tunnel marked the first use in history of a new, more powerful explosive— nitroglycerine—which was manufactured at a large plant about a half mile from the western portal. The two-story factory produced 250 pounds per day. It was in the Hoosac Tunnel also that the first pneumatic-powered jackhammers were put to work by nine hundred diggers working in three shifts around the clock.

The so-called Great Bore was a more costly endeavor than anticipated. Accidents claimed the lives of 196 miners. In one incident, a work train just inside the eastern portal vanished when a spark ignited five hundred pounds of explosives on board, shattering windows in North Adams ten miles away and killing several tunnel workers. Heavy steel drill bits occasionally fell from buckets being lowered to workers in the shafts. In one case, a newly sharpened drill fell from the rim, impaling a worker from head to foot. In the worst accident, a lift house built over the Central Shaft accidentally burst into flame and toppled into the pit, killing thirteen diggers who were 538 feet down.

Financially, what was projected to be a $2 million project cost nearly nine times as much—$17.3 million. Despite all the travails, however, the railroad triumphed as the various portions of the tunnel came together with less than three-quarters of an inch error—a stunning achievement. The tunnel was electrified so that steam locomotives could bank their coal-burning boilers for the tow through the tunnel. For the mechanically inclined citizens of North Adams, the Hoosac Tunnel was a proud moment, memorialized in the town seal and proof that the "road to ruin" was actually the road to success. The technological marvel was a significant part of the town's history studied by students at Drury Academy, North Adams' preeminent private high school, which molded Allan McCann for the rigors of the U.S. Naval Academy in Annapolis.

"Powers of Oratory"
Drury Academy, North Adams, Massachusetts
1909

Drury Academy was built on a hill overlooking North Adams in 1840 in memory of local citizen Nathan Drury. In 1865 it was demolished and rebuilt as a monolithic brick edifice trimmed in white marble. The French Second Empire–style architecture was notable for its mansard roofline punctured by dormer windows and dominated by a four-sided clock-and-bell tower with observation deck. Students came to Drury from a system of feeder elementary schools throughout the Berkshires, making it one of the largest schools in Massachusetts, capable of accommodating eleven hundred students in eighteen classrooms. "Old Drury" was known throughout the nation for its academic credentials, leading school officials to boast, "A diploma from Drury will admit the holder to almost any college in the country without the requirement of an entrance examination."

The stern nature of scholarship at Drury was a fact impressed on McCann from the opening bell of his freshman year, as noted in the class yearbook:

> The regular school day at Drury opens with devotionals in the two main rooms, when the battered, brown, sliding door is thrown back and the Doctor takes his stand facing the rooms. Then at the ringing of signals a clattering is heard on the stairs, the balustrades creak as some freshman unceremoniously slides down the smooth railing, and then in march the two lower classes, to sit anywhere and everywhere there is half a seat vacant. Silence reigns supreme for ten or fifteen minutes, during which the principal reads or give us a few wise hints on "the manliness or womanliness that should be upheld to make our school a model one."

A day at Drury consisted of six periods, with five minutes between them except for a fifteen-minute intermission for snacks at the midpoint of the day. The airy Greek room in the fourth floor attic of the school had comfortable armchairs for studying classical literature, and on the first floor there was a large laboratory jammed with seats for science and biology lessons. The last week of each term included final tests that required each student to write, "I have neither given nor received aid on this examination, and have seen no dishonesty on the part of others."

A major focus of the curriculum was rhetorical speaking. The two upper classes were required to entertain the lower classes every fortnight during the autumn and winter by delivering orations. Said one student, "It is one of the compulsory things at Drury, and so we grin and bear it in the hope of some day startling the universe with our powers of oratory." McCann developed a booming voice that would soon command respect in the Navy. The discipline instilled in Drury students fit him well. He was a serious pupil with a tall build and handsome physique—auburn hair cut close above his ears and pushed back on his forehead to frame heavy brows and penetrating eyes. He was popular with his schoolmates and was attracted to his future wife during his high school years. Katheryne Frances Gallup, pretty and vivacious, was the daughter of Harvey Gallup, an insurance businessman and future city councilman, mayor, and state senator.

The Gallups were one of the oldest families in the United States. They traced their lineage back to Capt. John Gallup, a merchant mariner who came to New England in 1630 with the Dorset Company and was a member of a church that was given title by colonial governor John Winthrop. The Gallups prospered in the new country. Descendants fought in both the French and Indian Wars, and the American Revolution.

Drury students like McCann came of age with an appreciation of the region's military heritage. North Adams was once the site of Fort Massachusetts, built in 1745 to guard the western frontier from incursions by the French and their Indian allies and to protect against territorial seizures by the Colony of New Hampshire. In 1746 French forces laid waste to the fort after a thirty-six-hour siege in which one defender was killed. Thirty others, including three women and five children, were taken prisoner and marched to Lake Champlain. Massachusetts rebuilt the fort in 1747 in a much stronger way and successfully turned back another attempt by the French to destroy it that year. Later, during the Revolutionary War, a colonel from Fort Massachusetts commanded colonial troops at the Battle of Bennington, a pivotal victory that contributed to the defeat of the British at the subsequent Battle of Saratoga and the eventual outcome of the war.

To honor one of the foremost leaders of the American Revolution, Samuel Adams, local citizens named their settlement at the foot of Greylock Mountain after him. Eighty years later, North Adams made its most singular military contribution to the nation during the Civil War. Huge government contracts enabled the city to clothe the Union army. Likewise, pig iron produced there went into iron plating for USS *Monitor*, the first of many ironclad turret gunboats and the one that fought the Confederate navy's ironclad CSS *Virginia* to a draw in the famous Battle of Hamptons Road in the Chesapeake off Norfolk, the first clash of ironclad vessels in history.

North Adams not only contributed its industrial knowhow to help achieve the Union's ultimate triumph over the Confederacy, it sent its sons off to war and then memorialized them in a stone monument of a solitary union soldier on a pedestal overlooking the town square a few blocks from the McCann residence.

In addition to being aware of the struggles of nation building, Drury's students also were well versed in presidential politics. McCann was almost three years old when President William McKinley visited North Adams in June 1899. McKinley drew a massive crowd to Monument Square, where he reviewed a local parade and was serenaded with "The Battle Hymn of the Republic," "America the Beautiful," and a "Drury Yell" by local students. In 1903, when McCann was seven, President Theodore Roosevelt addressed eight thousand people in North Adams from the vestibule of a railroad car in a downpour. Roosevelt made a return appearance in 1912, when McCann was a Drury junior. This time Roosevelt was campaigning for president as a candidate from the fledgling Bull Moose Party. He had founded the progressive party after the Republican Party denied him its nomination in favor of incumbent president William Howard Taft, whom Roosevelt opposed.

Presidential politics and North Adams' position in world commerce encouraged city youths and their families to serve the community and the country. Thus, when warfare in Europe threatened the peace at home, young McCann contemplated a future in the U.S. Navy.

Academy Nomination
Office of Representative George Pelton Lawrence,
North Adams, Massachusetts
10 December 1912

For James and Carolyn McCann, the possibility of their only son attending the U.S. Naval Academy in Annapolis was exhilarating. If he could secure a nomination, it would not only alleviate the family of the financial burden of higher education, it would bring incalculable honor to the family in tight-knit North Adams. The city had in its past spawned two academy graduates, both from Drury.

Frank Julian Sprague secured an appointment in 1874. After graduating from the academy, he went to work as an assistant to Thomas Edison in 1883. He later developed a revolutionary new electric motor adaptable to industrial machinery. Also to his credit were the electric elevator and the nation's first electric street railway in Richmond, Virginia, a technology later adopted by North Adams. Burton Chippendale, two years ahead of McCann at Drury, entered Annapolis in 1911 and would become the commanding officer of the ammunition ship USS *Nitro* (AE-2) in the Pacific during World War II and later the commander of the U.S. Naval Training School.

As it turned out, Representative George Pelton Lawrence lived only a few doors down from the McCanns and was impressed with their son. Lawrence was considered a rising star in North Adams and was, as one historian described him, "incredibly popular." A native of the city, he was appointed in 1885 as the youngest judge ever to serve on the Massachusetts bench at age twenty-six. In 1897 he was elected to fill out the term of Representative Ashley B. Wright, who succumbed in office. Lawrence served as Massachusetts's First Legislative District representative for more than a decade. In 1910 he secured a large sum of federal money to build a palatial post office in North Adams, a testament to his growing influence in Congress. By December 1912, however, he had left office to care for his wife, whose health was failing.

One of Representative Lawrence's last acts was to nominate Allan McCann to the Naval Academy. He informed McCann and his parents at his office in downtown North Adams. A recommendation didn't necessarily guarantee that the academy would accept the sixteen-year-old Drury senior. McCann would have to qualify by passing an admissions examination—a notoriously difficult task that had stymied many others.

On 15 April McCann took the test in Pittsfield, Massachusetts, about ten miles south of North Adams. He flunked. Although his grades were passable in geometry, English, and geography, he failed to pass three key aptitude areas important to a midshipman's training—history, arithmetic, and algebra. Fortunately, he had another chance to take the test on 5 June. He dropped out of Drury without graduating in order to prep for the upcoming examination and this time qualified with much higher scores.

On 23 June 1913, Representative Allen Tower Treadway, who succeeded Lawrence in office, formally appointed Allan Rockwell McCann to the U.S. Naval Academy—just in time for World War I.

CHAPTER 3

LUCKIEST CLASS

U.S. Naval Academy
Annapolis, Maryland
28 March 1917

*E*ns. Allan Rockwell McCann graduated from the U.S. Naval Academy an unprecedented two months early. The United States needed a large Navy, plus sailors and officers to man new ships. The armada was forming quickly to wage war against Germany and its allies. It was a unique opportunity for McCann and other graduating midshipmen eyeing what was to be the most modern, well-equipped Navy in the world. In a letter to his father in North Adams before graduation, McCann expressed unbridled enthusiasm: "This is the luckiest class that ever graduated from Annapolis."

The march toward war had been inexorable in McCann's four years at Annapolis, although few in the United States believed that a European war would ever involve Americans. When hostilities erupted across the Atlantic in the summer of 1914, President Woodrow Wilson cautioned citizens to be impartial; this was a fight between the Central Powers of Europe—Germany, Austria-Hungary, Turkey, and Bulgaria—and the Allied Powers (the Triple Entente) of France, Russia, and Great Britain. The United States had no reason to get involved. The president made that clear in declaring the nation's neutrality: "This is a war with which we have nothing to do," he said. Still, signs that the country could easily be drawn into the fight were obvious to those in the military. The pace of naval preparations had increased dramatically beginning in 1914. Rear Adm. Bradley Fiske, an opponent of the pacifist policies of Secretary of the Navy Josephus Daniels and a man who was worried that a German victory could imperil American interests in the Caribbean and Philippines, wanted

Allan McCann as a midshipman
at the U.S. Naval Academy in
1917; he and his class graduated
early after Congress declared
war against Germany.

Courtesy of McCann family
(Edie Sims)

to put the Navy on a war footing following a period of fragmented and confusing naval administration. Fiske circumvented Secretary Daniels and persuaded
allies in Congress to create the office of chief of naval operations (CNO) to
be filled by a senior admiral. For the first time, the Navy had an all-powerful
individual to coordinate its planning, shipbuilding, operations, and personnel
policies. By 1915 the Office of Naval Intelligence and the General Board of the
Navy had concluded that Germany was winning the ground war against France
and Russia and beginning to strangle England's supply line through a submarine blockade. The board argued that it was critical for the United States to
begin building a navy the size of Great Britain's fleet in case England faltered.
It advanced a plan for forty-eight battleships to be built by 1922 at a cost of $1.2
billion. Prodded by the president, who worried that such a lusty goal unwit-
tingly could propel the United States into the war, the board reduced its request
to ten battleships to be built within five years. Still, presidential and congressional approval lagged.

That began to change in 1916, when Germany declared unrestricted submarine warfare and ship losses spiked at the rate of thirty-two British-allied
ships lost for every one German U-boat. At such a rate, England could not
hope to replace its fleet fast enough, and this fueled predictions that Great
Britain might capitulate to Germany in six months. This greatly worried the
Wilson administration because Germany had global aspirations and finally

convinced Congress to approve the shipbuilding program in August. The president signed the 1916 Big Navy Act on 29 August. It was a three-year plan to build 156 new warships, including 10 battleships, 6 battle cruisers, 10 cruisers, and 50 destroyers. Once these ships were added to its existing warships, the U.S. Navy would become the largest and mightiest fleet in history. The president, still trying to keep the nation out of war, ultimately concluded that conflict was unavoidable when Germany resumed unrestricted submarine warfare. The public disclosure of an intercepted cable written by German foreign secretary Arthur Zimmermann to his ambassador in Mexico also helped sway Wilson. The communication suggested a secret alliance between Germany, Mexico, and Japan by which Mexico would declare war on the United States in return for Germany's support in recovering the one-third of Mexico lost to the United States in 1848—an area that included California, Nevada, Arizona, Utah, New Mexico, and Texas.

For Midshipman McCann, the effect of these international developments was dramatic. In 1914, his first year at the academy, the Navy reorganized the brigade of midshipmen into a regiment of four battalions of three companies each. Two years later, Congress authorized expanding the regiment from 1,094 to 1,746 midshipmen. Thus, by the fall of the 1916–17 school year, McCann's last, 312 more midshipmen were enrolled than the year before, and more growth was coming. Still, that would not be enough officers to supply the expanded fleet. Congress responded by passing the 1916 Big Navy Act, which created a naval reserve force. Most of the officers for the new ships would come from the reserves' noncommissioned ranks, ordered to report to Annapolis in July 1917 for a ten-week crash course in becoming line officers. Meanwhile, classes in marine engineering, naval construction, weaponry, mathematics, and foreign languages taught by line officers were accelerated at Annapolis in order to turn out commissioned ensigns as quickly as possible. The first of the newly minted officers included McCann, who ranked in the middle of his class at graduation on 29 March 1917. The academy dispensed with traditional graduation ceremonies, and within a week President Wilson stood before Congress to demand action because of Germany's U-boat offensive, which had torpedoed passenger ships carrying Americans. "The present German submarine warfare against commerce is a warfare against mankind," the president told the lawmakers. The country's neutrality was no longer feasible, he said, appealing to the House of Representatives and the Senate to "lead this great peaceful people into war, into the most terrible and disastrous of all wars, civilization itself seeming to be in the balance." On 6 April 1917 Congress responded by declaring war on Germany, initiating what Wilson declared "the war to end all wars."

That war, however, would bypass young Allan McCann, who spent most of it on a battleship in the Chesapeake Bay. He served on USS *Kansas* (BB-21) until

September 1919, rising to the rank of lieutenant. For the duration of the war, the battlewagon served as an engineering training ship operating out of Hampton Roads, Virginia. The dreadnought, launched in 1905, ventured outside the bay occasionally on cruises to New York City. But that was it. Meanwhile, U.S. destroyers and other vessels shifted from American bases in the Pacific and Caribbean were deployed to guard convoys bearing nearly 2 million American troops plus supplies to Europe, where they reversed the course of the war. McCann served as watch and division officer on board *Kansas* and earned a Victory medal. By the summer of 1918, as the war wound down, he had reevaluated his career track and asked to be assigned to submarines.

"Iron Coffin"
New London, Connecticut
23 September 1918

Just seventeen months after graduation from the academy, Allan McCann reported to the Navy's new submarine base and school in New London, Connecticut, a hillside hamlet on the Thames River, three miles inland from Long Island Sound. Although his decision for undersea duty seemed at odds with the normal promotion track in the surface fleet, his reasoning at the time was sound. With his engineering acumen honed at the academy, the lieutenant found the undersea vessels uniquely different, interesting, and challenging—and likely to play a large role in future conflicts. The value of submarines had proven itself emphatically in the near defeat of England by German U-boats. They had shown themselves as more than capable of spanning oceans and being a decisive weapon. More than a half dozen were known to have patrolled the east coast of North America, laying mines outside harbors in the United States and Canada. One single sub, the U-151, sank six vessels totaling 15,000 tons off the Delaware coast in a six-day period, causing insurance rates for coastal shipping to soar by 1,500 percent.

Not only was the submarine a valuable weapon to any navy, there were inducements for young officers to join the submarine fleet. The subs represented the quickest route to command for a Navy combatant because they had small crews with fewer officers, many of whom would transfer to newly launched boats. The Navy, which at the start of World War I had only thirty submarines in service for coastal defense, demanded more and increased their numbers by building them in government yards in addition to acquiring them from private shipbuilders.

McCann also had personal reasons for becoming a submariner. For one, the Silent Service enabled enlisted submariners and officers to draw hazardous duty pay authorized by former president Theodore Roosevelt after he spent a

Portrait of Allan McCann's high
school sweetheart Katheryne
Gallup about the time the two
married in the fall of 1918.

*Courtesy of McCann family
(Edie Sims)*

harrowing two hours undersea in USS *Plunger* (SS-2) in 1905. Also of benefit to
McCann was relocating from Virginia to New London, a quaint and fabled whaling port that was closer to his fiancée in North Adams. Two weeks after arriving
at the base, McCann took leave to marry Katheryne Gallup on 7 October in
what their hometown newspaper described as a "very quiet wedding."

At the base, McCann began an intensive four-month study of submarines
while he was attached to USS *Fulton* (AS-1), a sub tender at the base distinguished for its foggy "British weather" and the coming and going of the black
boats on the Thames. McCann was among a handful of officers and enlisted
sailors who had volunteered for sub service. They trained together at the base's
two-year-old school, where enrollment rarely exceeded two hundred students
at any one time. The 587-acre campus and base grew out of an obsolete ship
coaling station on the opposite side of the Thames from the U.S. Coast Guard
Academy and just upstream from a private submarine construction yard, later
to be known as the Electric Boat Company. The school was named Submarine
Base New London because of its close proximity to the better-known city.

The training facility was born about the same time the Navy launched its
first government-built submarine, the *L-8*, in 1917, seventeen years after it purchased its first submarine, USS *Holland* (SS-1), in 1900. Development had been
rapid in an era of experimentation with this new form of naval warfare, driven
by the German threat. The Navy brought about the E-, H-, K-, L-, M-, N-, O-,

and R-class boats during the war. Most were engaged in patrols off the East Coast and in the Caribbean to safeguard the Panama Canal during the war. But K-, L-, O-, and E-class subs were deployed to Europe for offensive operations off Ireland and in the Azores. Unfortunately, they did not match the speed and durability of the German subs. The Navy's boats could barely make fourteen knots and were beset by design defects. At war's end, the new S-class boats emerging from private shipyards were faster and larger, designed to travel with the surface fleet as an escort-style torpedo craft. But they also were hampered by metallurgical problems and unreliable diesel engines.

As the pace of development increased to perfect the undersea boats, there was greater emphasis on preparing officers and crew members to operate the vessels and find solutions to obstacles in the ultraexpensive, complicated warships. The new sub school focused on screening enlisted volunteers drawn from the fleet while molding officers and crews into cohesive units that could work effectively in tight quarters at sea. Exhaustive psychological, physical, and aptitude tests weeded all but the most qualified. Those who failed any of the tests were returned to the surface fleet.

From the outset, Lieutenant McCann and all other submariners understood one thing: they had to accept the physical risks of an occupation that made it an all-volunteer service. A malfunction of equipment or a single mistake by any officer or crew member could be catastrophic and sudden. The short history of the submarine navies around the world was replete with disasters. From 1901 to 1917 more than fifty submarines from Australia, Britain, France, Denmark, Japan, Russia, Italy, and the United States experienced serious accidents while not engaged in enemy action. Gasoline explosions, collisions, flooding, fires, and other unknown disasters often doomed their crews. The submarine had become a symbol of revulsion to the public, partially owing to their stealth missions but also because of tragedies in peacetime. Many considered the undersea navy the "iron coffin" service. Within two weeks of McCann's arrival in New London, this epithet was dramatized just down the coast.

"Save Me"
Brooklyn Navy Yard, New York
5 October 1918

The disaster that befell USS *O-5* (SS-66) began in the midafternoon during tests of the boat's rebuilt diesel engines. The sub, under the command of Skipper George A. Trever, was tied up alongside Lt. Cdr. Robert H. English's *O-4* (SS-65), back from the European war zone for repairs to its conning tower. *O-4* had been holed by friendly fire from a British merchantman that had mistaken it for a

German U-boat off the Irish coast. With repairs completed, both boats were to cast off later that day for Newport, Rhode Island, to join a flotilla of twenty U.S. submarines destined for the Azores.

Lieutenant Commander Trever had reported to the yard commander's office to get his sailing orders and had returned to the boat to observe engine trials. The idea was to use the *O-5*'s diesels to recharge the sub's acid storage battery cells, dozens of which lined the keel of the 173-foot-long craft. Each was as tall as a human and weighed more than a thousand pounds. The boat's twin, air-breathing diesels, in a large compartment near the stern, were designed to provide propulsion during surface running while charging those batteries. Once submerged at sea, electric motors, powered by the batteries, would take over. The elements of this power system were linked together and capable of discharging enormous energy. The risk during charging operations was that volatile hydrogen gas would discharge and accumulate inside the sub if it was not carefully monitored and evacuated with electric blowers by the boat's electricians.

Initially, the starboard engine successfully completed a twenty-minute run while charging the batteries, evenly divided into two battery compartments, fore and aft of the central control room, the nerve center of the boat below the conning tower. With the first test complete, the port diesel commenced operation, pushing an additional charge into the cells. Four minutes into the test, the diesel shut down for fifty minutes so that repairs could be made to a faulty valve. The test resumed and all looked normal. As expected, the storage batteries were fully charged and began emitting hydrogen. Blower fans and exhaust ventilation lines were in place to siphon the gas and remove it from the boat. But unbeknownst to the crew, engine vibrations had caused a quick-closing, spring-loaded flapper valve over the main exhaust line to close. Within minutes, Ens. William J. Sharkey in the after battery became alarmed.

"Do you smell that gas? There is a lot of gas in here. You better get it out of here," he ordered Crewman J. I. Still, a second-class electrician laboring in the compartment with other crew members and yard workers.

"Blowers still running?" Sharkey asked Still.

"Yes."

"What notch?"

"They look to me to be at second notch."

"How about your forward ones?"

"They must be running same as these," Still replied.

"Speed them up!" demanded Sharkey.

Summoned from the control room by the ensign, Captain Trever stepped through the bulkhead door into the after battery. He too smelled hydrogen. Assured the blowers were functioning properly, the skipper inspected the gas intake lines and found them open. He moved on to the exhaust pipe that led through the overhead to discharge gas from the boat aft of the conning tower. With a start, the commander found the main flapper discharge valve inexplicably closed. "Here's your trouble!" he shouted, reaching up to open the valve to begin evacuating the gas.

It was too late. A fireball erupted over the batteries, thrusting steel decking on which the men were standing up against the overhead. Both the skipper and the ensign hit the decking violently; it crushed Sharkey's skull and left Trever bleeding from the scalp and with both legs broken below his knees. Like the skipper, Still suffered a gash to his scalp and multiple leg fractures. The men were buried in debris as flames burned in the keel, filling the compartment with smoke.

Captain English, who had been visiting a nearby destroyer, had just returned to O-4 when he and Lt. Benjamin S. Kilmaster, the boat's executive officer, heard the explosion and saw smoke rising from the open after-deck hatch of O-5. Reacting instinctively, English yelled for an ambulance to be summoned and for his crew to bring fire extinguishers and gas masks. Enlisted submariners and yard workers poured out of O-5, bringing with them the injured Still.

Ignoring his own safety, English climbed down the ladder into the engine room. Dense smoke drove him back topside. Told that Trever and perhaps others were below, English strapped on a gas mask from his boat and reentered at the risk of a secondary explosion. Making his way forward, he encountered blankets, mattresses, rubber molding, gaskets, clothing, and canvas from the battery deck burning and filling the compartment with acrid smoke. The skipper groped his way, shouting Trever's name.

English later recalled,

> I worked my way forward on the starboard side of the after battery compartment, and after getting probably half way I heard the commanding officer on the opposite side of the compartment calling my name and asking me to save him. The whole battery deck had been thrown up and fallen down in a general debris. I made my way along, feeling as I went. I made my way across and finally my hand touched him, and there was some debris on him, probably holding him down. It could not have been the battery deck itself, because I did not actually remove the debris; I pulled him out from under it, and picked my way back to the [engine room] door.

Undogging the bulkhead door, workers grabbed an exhausted English with Trever in his arms, pulled him to safety, and then closed the door. They passed Trever up the ladder to the dock to an ambulance that sped him to a hospital.

English, now revived, wondered about others trapped below:

> I tried to find out who else was in there and there was a ques-
> tion about Ensign Sharkey. Some stated he had gone ashore and
> others said they thought he was down there but had mistaken
> him for me, and as long as there was a doubt about him and not
> knowing whether there were other people because the place was
> steaming up, I put on the mask and went back to see if I could
> find anybody lying there. I didn't get further than half way into
> the compartment before it was too hot and I had to go out.

With further rescue useless, the submarine was towed a safe distance from English's *O-4* to a nearby coal docking pier as the fire continued to burn. In consultation with English, senior officers at the Navy yard decided to seal the submarine's hatches in hopes of putting out the fire by depriving it of oxygen. That effort failed, however, because of air leaks in the after battery. Meanwhile, the hull became increasingly hot and threatened to rupture and sink the sub.

The officers went to Plan B: unseal the hatches and send New York fire-fighters below to snuff the blaze. Entering the engine room, the firefighters first used fire extinguishers to try to cool red-hot electrical wires still drawing current from the storage batteries. The effort failed. They then turned fire hoses on the blown-up batteries, being careful to keep the water away from an electrical switchboard in the compartment. A short circuit there could cause disaster.

Meanwhile, English and crew members reentered the sub in an attempt to reach the switchboard. If they could get to it, they could break the circuits to the batteries. "As soon as it was definitely decided that it was an electrical fire, we knew that we had to get the switches thrown on the switchboard in order to stop it," recalled the skipper. "Every effort was made by four or five different men to reach those switches, including myself, but due to the fire around the switchboard and the electrical short circuit encountered, we could not reach the board. We then made an effort [from the forward battery room] to discon-nect the forward battery and the after battery and its terminals and we finally accomplished it, after which the after battery quickly discharged itself and the fire was put under control."

Crew members reentered the after battery and found Sharkey's badly burned body under a pile of metal lockers. A Navy board of inquiry interviewed witnesses the following week. In its findings, it praised Captain English's com-mand of the situation, citing him for his "clear-headed, prompt, courageous action." He was a "tower of strength" throughout the ordeal. The board ordered heavier spring-loaded clips installed in flapper values and a small pin inserted in the lower end of the valves in *O-5* and other submarines to make sure that they could not close on their own.

The Navy awarded Ensign Sharkey its highest honor, a posthumous Navy Cross, for alerting the skipper to gas emanating from *O-5*'s battery. The submarine had not suffered irreparable damage. A $44,000 refit of the after battery put her back in seaworthy condition. As for Skipper Trever, his condition worsened, and he succumbed to his injuries nine days after the accident.

"Men of Submarines"
Submarine Base New London, Connecticut
Late October 1918

Lieutenant McCann and others at Submarine Base New London studied the *O-5* disaster while engaged in their own training. They could find solace in the fact that a defect in the operation of the flapper valve spring mechanism led to the explosion and that the Navy had ordered corrections. There was additional comfort knowing that on the scale of things, the risk of sub duty against the backdrop of the tragedy was still rather small given the large number of boats being launched in navies around the world.

For the next few months at the base, the officers and enlisted submariners mastered every conceivable aspect of the undersea navy and passed tests that made the Navy reasonably confident they would be competent submariners. Adm. Charles L. Lockwood, a pioneering World War I submarine skipper, reflected on what the Navy was looking for. "The tasks of diving, attack and surfacing take scores of interlocking motions by dozens of crewmen with split-second timing," he said.

> But more is demanded than mere mechanical ability. The men of submarines—from captains to cooks—must have certain well-defined characteristics. They must be alert without being brittle; they must be interested in their shipmates without being nosy; they must appreciate food without being gluttons; they must respect privacy without being seclusive; they must be talkers without being gabby; and they must be friendly without being tail-waggers. They must, in short, be round pegs for very closely machined round holes. The wrong kind of a man aboard a sub, on a long cruise, can become an insufferable thorn in the sides of shipmates. He can, emotionally, cause almost as much damage as an enemy depth bomb. . . . In no other branch of military service are men required to remain away from normal human contacts as long as submariners assigned to lengthy patrols that

demand long hours—sometimes days—at depths far below the least glimmer of sunlight and far away from the natural feel and smell of natural air. Moreover, these conditions must be endured with good cheer in overcrowded, sometimes ill-smelling, dew-dripping, steel compartments. Those whose tempers or temperaments cannot stand the strain are soon eliminated.

At the submarine school, adaptability and proficiency were relentlessly emphasized in classrooms and subs based at the school. The students set about to master complex machinery and weaponry, plus pneumatic, hydraulic, and electrical systems that enabled a submarine to patrol the oceans and attack enemy targets. Instructors coaxed and grilled them to perfect their abilities and knowledge of the intricate undersea vessels while burning axioms from submarine veterans into memory: "There is room for anything on a submarine—except a mistake" and "Without teamwork, a submarine is no more than a bastard cousin to a foundering whale."

The submariners committed to memory thousands of valves, gears, pipes, and switches inside the warships, veritable spaceships of the seas. They tore down torpedoes and put them back together to better understand how they operated and how to maintain them. Each student drew from memory accurate diagrams of more than thirty electrical, mechanical, and pneumatic systems in the boats and learned to perform the specialty of all other crew members. Even the person chosen to be the boat's cook had to be able to fire a torpedo, operate the diesels, and dive or surface the boat when called on in an emergency. From officers to enlisted submariners, each worked in timed precision with the others, like a well-drilled football team, to maneuver the school's practice subs in the Thames and nearby Long Island Sound six miles downstream.

After completing his initial training, McCann remained attached to the *Fulton* until 11 December 1919, when he became the executive officer of USS *K-6* (SS-37), one of the older boats in the Navy's fleet. Six months later, in May 1920, he moved up to command. It was the beginning of a rotation into various classes of subs—*K-6*, newly launched USS *S-19* (SS-124), USS *N-4* (SS-56), and *L-3* (SS-42). On 6 April 1922 he became division commander and skipper of USS *R-21* (SS-98), flagship of Submarine Division 1, which departed New London for Panama. En route, *R-24*'s engines broke down and McCann's boat, later assisted by Cuba-bound steamship SS *Bethore*, towed the sub to the Navy base at Guantánamo, Cuba. With repairs made, the division set out again for the Navy's burgeoning submarine base on the east coast of Panama.

CHAPTER 4

AWFUL MESS

Coco Solo Naval Reservation
Panama
27 October 1922

The R-boats under the command of Lieutenant McCann arrived at Panama's Coco Solo Naval Reservation, which had been under construction since 1919, to fortify the strategically important Panama Canal, whose Caribbean terminus was nearby. The base's name translated as "lone coconut palm," and its structure was built on the site of a swampy mangrove forest at the head of the half-mile-wide, channel-like Manzanillo Bay, which empties into the Caribbean Sea. Several piers jutted into the bay from shore installations intended to service a growing collection of coastal defense submarines, their large mother ships, and a variety of other vessels. Alongside the tenders, the boats were mere slivers, like black toothpicks moored to each other in as many as six to a side, hugging the bulk of the mother ships, veritable floating machine shops that could service submarines anywhere in the world.

Coco Solo was directly opposite the city of Colón, built on the swampy islet of Manzanillo. The city was encircled by broad Limón Bay to the north, Manzanillo Bay to the south, and Folks River to the west, where it empties into Manzanillo Bay. Limón Bay, the much larger of the two bodies of water, had long served ships ferrying supplies to and from Central America through Colón's port of Cristobal on the southern fringe of Limón Bay.

Americans founded Colón in 1850 as the Atlantic terminus of the Panama Railroad, a rail line connected to the mainland by a causeway and spanning the fifty-one-mile-wide Isthmus of Panama. The railroad—linking Colón to Panama City on the Pacific coast—was built to serve passengers seeking a quicker route to California's gold fields. It was a shortcut that saved them from a hazardous 7,800-mile voyage around Cape Horn in South America to reach San Francisco. Both Panama City and Colón developed rapidly, the latter becoming a wealthy port of entry. By the time of McCann's arrival, Colón featured an ornate municipal palace; beautiful homes along wide, palm-lined boulevards; and a thriving business district with scores of nightclubs, cabarets, and movie theaters, a top attraction for sailors on leave.

The accelerating prosperity of Colón and Panama City was primarily attributable to construction of the Panama Canal, a project begun by a French company in 1881. After nine years and the loss of 22,000 workers from disease and accidents, the company went bankrupt and eventually was taken over by the United States after Panama secured its independence from Colombia with American help. Theodore Roosevelt, who became president in 1902, campaigned for the canal and persuaded Congress that it was in the strategic interest of the United States. The canal's value had become clear to Roosevelt four years earlier, when the battleship USS *Maine* (ACR-1) was destroyed in Cuba at the outbreak of the Spanish-American War. The Navy deployed USS *Oregon* (BB-3), stationed in San Francisco, to replace the *Maine*. What could have been a three-week journey had the canal been in existence was a voyage of more than two months around Cape Horn to reach Cuba, where the ship participated in the Battle of Santiago Bay. In 1904 the Roosevelt administration began the gargantuan, ten-year task of bisecting the mountainous Continental Divide with an interconnected system of locks, two man-made lakes, and spillways to create a shipping channel that, like the Hoosac Tunnel in North Adams, was one of the engineering wonders of the world.

Early on, the United States was bent on securing the Panama Canal from foreign threats, particularly those generated by the great military powers of Europe and the surging power of Japan. The waterway was too intrinsic in uniting the economic and strategic interests of the United States to be left unguarded. Theodore Roosevelt, eight years before young Allan McCann braved a rainstorm to see him on his campaign whistle-stop in North Adams, made the canal's security a priority. The first line of defense would be small patrol craft, destroyers, and submarine squadrons that patrolled the Caribbean and made their presence known at islands throughout the region. The *R-21*, which McCann commanded, was one of twenty-seven such boats, faster and slightly smaller than other submarines and seemingly ideal for patrol duty in the Caribbean and both the Atlantic and Pacific entrances to the canal. But duty was never easy in the R-boats. Future admiral Thomas C. Hart demonstrated that in 1921, when he led a flotilla of ten from New London to Manila in the U.S. territory of the Philippine Islands. Every one of the boats broke down, overtaxing the sub tender traveling with them and forcing a layover in Hawaii for repairs.

The story was the same for McCann's division: breakdowns of the diesel engines required the boats to be taken under tow back to base. In that era, none of the submarines had air conditioning, and this left the compartments hot and dripping with humidity in the tropical heat. For division commander McCann, a routine patrol of the Canal Zone sent the *R-21* and sister subs negotiating the canal east to west and back again from their base at Coco Solo. Like the rail tunnel in North Adams, the canal never ceased to impress the lieutenant on the twenty-hour passage through it. The enormity of the canal—the massive locks with cement walls fifty-five feet thick, the lock gates eighty-two feet high, the electric locomotives that guided the boats through the lock chambers, and the deep cut through the Continental Divide—inspired a sense of wonder at what humanity could accomplish. Transiting the canal from Coco Solo began in the breakwater at the foot of Limón Bay, which led to the first set of locks and man-made Gatun Lake, spanning nearly half the isthmus. The main canal extended from the western side of the lake through a deep, eight-mile-long ravine carved through the rocky spine of Central America. It took 6,000 workers using dynamite and heavy equipment to blast away rock, which was loaded onto 160 trains daily for removal from the site. The Gaillard Cut enabled the canal proper to be built at a maximum elevation of eighty-five feet above sea level. Nearing the Pacific at the western end of the canal, two sets of paired locks lowered the boats onto man-made Miraflores Lake, which they crossed to a final set of locks that eased them down an inlet and into the deep waters of the Pacific.

To protect American investment in the canal, the Navy had stationed an arsenal of submarines at Coco Solo. The boats regularly transited the canal to the Navy base at Balboa on the Pacific side of the waterway. The squadrons included O-class subs of which the *O-5* inevitably drew interest at Coco Solo. Submariners knew well what happened to her at the Brooklyn Navy Yard and the loss of her skipper and executive officer. In an era of rapid submarine development in the early 1920s, she was a reminder of a legacy of mishaps that continued to plague submarines around the world. Fifteen had suffered a grim fate since the tragedy on board *O-5*. Lost or damaged were British subs *G-11* (grounding), *H-11* (collision), *K-5* (foundered), *K-15* (flooding), *H-42* (collision), and *L-9* (typhoon). The Russian boat *Fieldmarshal Graf Sheremetev* also was lost to flooding. For the United States, the toll included the *O-12* (SS-73) in a diving accident; the *H-1* (SS-28) from grounding; the *S-5* (SS-110), which foundered; the *R-6* (SS-83) from flooding; the *S-48* (SS-159), which foundered; the *S-38* (SS-143) from flooding; and the *S-37* (SS-142) from an explosion. In all, eighty-six officers and enlisted submariners from various nations had lost their lives on seven boats. Yet it was a second tragedy involving the *O-5* that would rivet world attention and leave McCann aghast and determined to eventually do something about it.

The Gatun Locks of the Panama Canal dwarf American C-class submarines, circa 1918. Lieutenant McCann was in charge of a division of R-boats in 1922 and helped organize the rescue of trapped submariners at the bottom of Limón Bay near these locks. The incident inspired McCann to draw up plans for a submarine rescue chamber.

Naval History and Heritage Command, Washington Navy Yard, Washington, D.C.

"Feeling of Hopelessness"
Limón Bay, Panama
28 October 1923

It was Sunday and the submariners in the *O-5* were roused before dawn to prepare the boat to get under way. Lt. Harrison Avery, the skipper, had routine orders to escort a line of submarines of Submarine Division 8—the *O-3* (SS-64), *O-6* (SS-67), and *O-8* (SS-69)—across Limón Bay to the entrance of the Panama Canal and then proceed through it to begin a deepwater patrol off Panama City. Avery's sub was in normal operating condition except for a faulty latch on the watertight door between the central control room and forward battery compartment, one of the vessel's six compartments. For two months, the door had been secured in an open position with a lash to keep it from swinging erratically when the sub was on the surface.

The *O-5* got under way at 0550 hours from Coco Solo and had rounded Colón to a marker buoy off Cristobal, Colón's port facility on Limón Bay, to pick up Panama Canal pilot G. O. Kolle at 0615. Kolle knew the currents in the bay, the destinations of ships arriving and departing from Cristobal, and the hazards of the Panama Canal, including mudslides caused by recent heavy rains. As he boarded the *O-5*, a banana freighter from Havana left its overnight anchorage in the bay to make its way to Dock No. 6 in Cristobal. Swinging eastward toward the port, the captain of SS *Abangarez*, W. A. Card, had the submarine in view. "When nearly abreast of No. 4 channel buoy I saw submarine *O-5* apparently stopped off the Mole Buoy and taking on the pilot," he later said. "At this time she was on the *Abangarez*' port bow and started to move ahead slowly as if to clear the stern of SS *Arawa* backing out from Pier 6. When the submarine was clear of the SS *Arawa* I noticed an increase in her speed as if trying to cross our bow. As soon as I decided that was her intention, I blew the danger signal, put our engines at full speed astern and let go our starboard anchor with fifteen fathoms of chain."

Three blasts of the ship's warning whistle echoed across the bay. The 380-foot, 5,000-ton cargo carrier shuddered as its engines tried to reverse course. The ship's anchor clawed at the soft mud of the ocean bottom to try to stop the forward momentum.

On the bridge atop the conning tower of the *O-5*, Avery assumed the ship was making for the Gatun Locks at the foot of the bay to begin a transit of the canal. He ordered engines stopped to let the big ship pass. Kolle knew otherwise; the ship was coming into port at Cristobal and was on a collision course with the submarine, now lying motionless in the bay. The pilot shouted the alarm as Avery ordered "go ahead" at full throttle to the engine room below. Word never got that far. It was too late.

At 0624, a wall of steel—the bow of the towering *Abangarez*—rammed the starboard side of the *O-5* in a screeching, jolting knife thrust, peeling a ten-foot-high, three-foot-wide gash through the hull and main ballast tank and into the control room. The sub rolled to port fifteen degrees and then righted herself beneath the prow of the freighter, which backed off. Seawater cascaded from the control room into after compartments. Avery gave the order to abandon ship. Crew members scrambled through deck hatches without closing the hatches or the numerous ventilation ports, including the main induction, a three-foot-wide pipe that fed air to the diesels during surface propulsion. With seawater pouring into the sub, the *O-5* sank bow first into the depths in less than a minute, leaving a whirlpool of foam and bubbles.

Abangarez crew members threw life preservers to survivors and picked up eight, including Lieutenant Avery. Other ships in the area rescued nine others. Eight minutes into the disaster, CMM C. R. Butler broke surface in an air bubble. In all, seventeen were pulled to safety. Five others were missing. The question lingered: Did they drown trying to get out? Or were they able to save themselves behind watertight doors in one or more of the sub's six compartments?

When word arrived in Coco Solo that the *O-5* was down, Navy deep-sea divers mustered on board a salvage tug and headed for the scene. Three hours into the sinking, the ship anchored over the submarine, and hard-hat divers, tethered to air hoses, descended thirty-six feet to the floor of the bay, landing near the stern. The boat sat upright, mired in the mud. The divers worked their way forward, hammering on the hull to determine whether survivors were inside. When they reached the forward section, they heard hammer strikes from one or more crew members inside the torpedo room, the largest compartment in the sub. How many were trapped was unknown because none inside understood Morse code. The concern was how to rescue them. The only known method was to somehow hoist the submarine to the surface using cranes or pressurized pontoons. Pontoons big enough to do the job were no closer than two thousand miles away. However, the world's two largest crane barges, designed to handle lock gates in the Panama Canal, were available. Capt. Amon Bronson Jr., commander of the Coco Solo sub base who took charge of the rescue, requested their assistance. Unfortunately, a rock slide loosened by the rain in the canal's steep Galliard Cut had blocked the waterway. Both barges—the *Ajax* and *Hercules*—were on the far side. Excavation of the slide by shore-based drag lines intensified. By 1400—ten hours after the *O-5* disappeared—men and equipment had dredged enough of the blockage to enable the *Ajax* to squeeze past and make for the submarine. The giant crane arrived over the submarine at 2230. By then, photographer R. G. Lewis of Fox Movietone News also was on hand to document the unfolding rescue operation.

Sixteen hours had passed. Down below CEM Lawrence Brown and TORP2 Henry Breault prayed for salvation. They were the only survivors inside the sub. Breault had been working in the torpedo room and had climbed the ladder through a deck hatch to escape when he heard the skipper's order to abandon ship. Realizing the off-duty Brown was asleep in a bunk below, Breault darted back through the hatch, closing it with the turn of a wheel to set its watertight seal as the bow started its descent. Brown was awake but had not heard the order to exit the boat. With no time to spare, the two men groped through the flooding forward battery and control rooms in an attempt to escape through the conning tower. The fast-rising seawater blocked their way and forced them to turn back. Because they had no time to unlash the bulkhead door between the control room and forward battery, they retreated to the torpedo room. They made it just in time, muscling the watertight door into position to stop the water flow. Momentarily, the two men heard an explosion in the after battery as the boat's storage batteries short-circuited and ignited chlorine gas. Fortunately, the torpedo room door protecting the two men held.

Brown and Breault were safe but trapped. The only possible exit was the overhead hatch. However, both realized that opening it would unleash a torrent of seawater into the compartment, making it impossible for them to get out without drowning. They chose to wait and hope for salvation. In fact, a plan to save the men was in the works. With the O-5's sister boats moored along-side the *Ajax*, sub commanders, including Lieutenant McCann, dressed in his service dress white uniform after leaving his office in Coco Solo to rush to the scene, huddled with salvage workers to discuss how the stranded vessel could be hoisted high enough to free the trapped men. Sheppard Shreaves stepped forward to facilitate the plan.

Shreaves was a thirty-eight-year-old Virginia native who was a dockmaster and foreman shipwright for the Panama Canal's mechanical division. He was a soft-spoken though tough, barrel-chested, experienced hard-hat diver, one of the best stationed in Panama. He volunteered for the perilous mission that would require him to get down to the sub to assess damage and then tunnel under the bow and loop a hoist cable around it. The idea was for the *Ajax* to hoist the bow high enough to break the surface and enable those inside to free themselves from the forward hatch.

Navy divers gave Shreaves a detailed briefing on the position of the O-5 and the location of the two trapped men. "Shep," wearing a canvas bodice, weighted shoes and belt, plus a watertight, heavy-metal helmet with a glass viewing port, was lowered over the side of the barge shortly before midnight. Powerful floodlights illuminated the shadowy deck of the submarine below as he descended. "I could spot the O-5 on the bottom by the air bubbles exhausted from the compartment where Breault and Brown were trapped," Shreaves later explained. "To survive, they were bleeding air from 3,000-pound compressed air reserves in the torpedo room."

With his air supply hose trailing behind him from his helmet, Shreaves lowered himself through the hole in the control room. "The light of my lamp was feeble against the pitch black," he recounted. "The inside was in an awful mess, and it was tight and slippery going. I was constantly pushing away floating debris. When I reached the forward bulkhead of the engine room I hit it with my diving hammer. Faint raps were returned. Breault and Brown were alive. I acknowledged their taps, but almost with a feeling of hopelessness because I couldn't do anything for them at the time."

Inside the torpedo room, Breault and Brown separated to both sides of the darkened compartment, illuminated only by a single flashlight. They began pounding on the hull, ecstatic to make contact with a diver. Breault resorted to tapping out the rhythm of a popular tune to try to indicate to the diver that he and Brown were unharmed and cheerful. High atmospheric pressure, no food or water, and mounting headaches from accumulating carbon dioxide forced them to conserve energy with little movement and conversation.

Shreaves worked his way back out and then signaled for a fire hose to be lowered so that he could begin the strenuous process of tunneling under the submarine. He recalled, "I began water jetting a trench under the bow. Sluicing through the ooze was easy: too easy, for it could cave in and bury me. Swirling black mud engulfed me. I worked solely by feel and instinct. I had to be careful that I didn't dredge too much from under the bow for fear the O-5 would crush down on me. Once in a while, I'd rap the hull with the nozzle to let the boys know someone was working to bring them out. Their raps were returned, weaker each time."

It took hours but finally the tunnel reached the far side. Shreaves pushed a thin guideline under the keel. Men on the surface then pulled a four-inch steel cable under the hull and attached it to a hook lowered from the *Ajax*. Shreaves returned to the surface to report to Captain Bronson. There he was examined by doctors concerned about the length of his dive and his extreme exertion. With the diver catching his breath, the *Ajax* pulled the cable through Shreaves' trench and then tried to raise the O-5. The weight of the vessel and seawater in its compartments plus the suction of mud against her hull was too much to overcome. The cable snapped. Brown and Breault felt the sub tilt upward slowly and then were tossed roughly to the floor when the cable sling broke.

Without hesitation, Shreaves went back down and pushed a replacement cable under the boat. Again it broke, sending the bow back to the floor of the bay while tossing the two survivors about. By midmorning of the second day, the twenty-four-hour operation to save the men had made little progress. Time was running out as the air supply keeping Breault and Brown alive dwindled.

The rescuers decided on a new plan to send Shreaves down one more time to loop a third cable under the bow. As directed, he also would link up high pressure air hoses from the barge to the engine room and return to the surface.

"I came up from what I hoped would be my last dive. I was near exhaustion," explained the diver. "The job below was done and we were ready for a third lift. At 12:30 p.m. on the 29th, from topside, I released compressed air into the engine room of the O-5 to unflood that compartment and lighten the boat. Water and mud bubbled to the surface as in a boiling cauldron. I signaled the *Ajax* to slowly lift the O-5. God, how we prayed the cable would take it this time. The intense silence of the rescue force and spectators was electrifying— almost unbelievable."

Slowly the bow rose and then cut through the surface. The *Ajax* held it steady as compressors furiously pumped air down into the sub. The boat sloped upward twenty degrees from its stern pivoting on the mud below. The barge nudged under the bow, bringing it to rest on the bulkhead with seawater draining off the forward deck. All eyes fixed on the torpedo room hatch as it came into view. It seemed like an eternity. Suddenly it flipped open, and both Breault and Brown, wasted but alive, crawled out as spectators roared their jubilation. Many wept openly. Said Brown of the third lift, "We felt we would escape this time, but it seemed like forever. The last 20 minutes were unbearable. We heard our comrades walking on deck. Breault opened the hatch and we could see daylight. We were saved!!"

Rescuers helped the two men into a waiting launch, which sped them and Shreaves away to Coco Solo for decompression in a chamber on the base to keep them from getting decompression sickness, known as the bends. Afterward, they transferred to Colón Hospital for a thorough medical examination. All three were in good health and released. Outside the hospital, Shreaves was the man of the moment: "I was a big hero for a while. The boys carried me around on their shoulders. Everybody rushed down to the Stranger's Club in Colón for a big celebration. But me, I went to sleep at the party."

A Navy inquest found fault mostly with the skipper of the O-5 for not keeping his sub under motive power prior to the accident and not being aware that the freighter was coming into port when that information was readily available. Lieutenant Avery also was blamed for not ordering repairs of previous damage to the bulkhead door between the control room and forward battery compartment, which contributed to the flooding. The verdict holding Avery responsible for the collision was later overturned. The sub, built at a cost of $638,000, was a total loss and scrapped for a paltry $3,125 on 12 December 1924.

Accounts of the dramatic rescue impressed President Calvin A. Coolidge. In a ceremony on the White House lawn on 24 April 1924, he presented Breault with the Medal of Honor on behalf of the U.S. Congress for his selflessness and bravery in going back into the doomed submarine to rescue his friend. Shreaves, who established a world record for the longest-duration dives in recorded history during the O-5 rescue, received a Congressional Lifesaving Medal for his role in saving Breault and Brown. Of the three men who died in the accident, the bodies of two were recovered but a third was never found.

The O-5 disaster gnawed at Allan McCann. He would ponder the inability of anyone to get to the stranded men, who were only thirty feet below the surface in their steel trap. He was detached from command of the R-21 within six months to become a diesel mechanics instructor on USS *Chewink* (AM-39) at the sub base in New London. He also served as the base's chief engineer and repair officer and provided technical advice to the Peruvian Naval Commission at Electric Boat. On 24 November 1926 McCann returned to the Canal Zone as skipper of the submarine USS *S-46* (SS-157). The boat participated in fleet exercises and training cruises in the Caribbean and Pacific.

In his off hours, McCann ruminated on the *O-5* sinking and other sub tragedies. He believed some way had to be found to give future submariners a chance to survive when trapped in their iron vessels in coastal waters. He started to envision an enclosed rescue chamber that could be lowered to a stranded sub in order to bring survivors up. Even though he thought of his concept as "crazy" by Navy norms, he submitted it in a letter to his division commander. The response and the possible realization of McCann's dream would have to wait, however. The skipper had received orders to take the *S-46* to Pearl Harbor to join the Pacific Battle Fleet and participate in tactical exercises with other submarines. There McCann would play a role in another life-and-death drama that would draw worldwide attention.

CHAPTER 5

WORLDS TO CONQUER

Market Street
San Francisco, California
23 May 1927

*T*he morning newspapers created quite a buzz amid the thunderous clanging of streetcars spilling over with passengers en route from the Ferry Building at the foot of San Francisco Bay to the tall buildings of the business district a mile away. Hawkers screamed the news, holding up front-page headlines from extra editions of the *San Francisco Chronicle* and the *San Francisco Examiner*: "Lindbergh Does It . . . To Paris in 33½ Hours . . . Crowd Roars Thunderous Welcome . . . Breaks Through Lines of Soldiers and Police and Surging to Plane Lifts Weary Flier from His Cockpit."

James D. "Jim" Dole, forty-nine, who had just arrived by steamship from Honolulu, and his business associate Harry McConaughty sat side by side inside one of the streetcars as it trundled up Market Street. McConaughty had tucked one of the broadsheet extras into his coat pocket. The two men discussed the great courage it took for Charles Lindbergh to fly solo across the Atlantic in his *Spirit of St. Louis* single-winged aircraft and the resulting frenzy that gripped the United States and Europe about the possibility of swift intercontinental air travel. Dole, a member of the National Aeronautic Association and the owner of a 200,000-acre pineapple plantation on the island of Lanai in Hawaii, suggested to McConaughty the possibility of flying nonstop the other way—from San Francisco to Hawaii over the Pacific. The San Francisco manager of the pineapple king's import business at first dismissed the idea as wishful thinking. "It's not as far-fetched as you think, Harry," Dole replied. "New York to Paris is 3,600 miles even though some of it is overland. Makes an interesting

James Dole, founder of the Dole pineapple plantation in Hawaii, conceived an airplane race from San Francisco to Honolulu to demonstrate the feasibility of nonstop airline travel to the islands.

Hawaii Aviation Preservation Society

comparison with the 2,400 miles from here to Honolulu. Think what it would mean to us out there."

Dole grew wistful, his eyes tracing the tops of Market Street's mercantile edifices set against a cobalt blue sky: "Harry, Honolulu will be as great a city as this one, in time. And it will be great because men like this flier Lindbergh believe in it. That's where I would like to meet him. I'd like to shake his hand as he lands his Ryan monoplane at our John Rodgers Airport when it's finished. Say in a month or two, when he's back from Europe and looking for new worlds to conquer."

McConaughty considered his employer's ambition to make Hawaii more accessible to the masses. Various pilots had already attempted to link the islands with California. In 1925 a two-engine Navy seaplane, the PN-9, was the first to succeed—sort of. After a flight of 1,992 miles from San Pablo, California, the plane ran out of fuel 470 miles short of its destination. Cdr. John Rodgers and his crew landed on the ocean and floated for nine days to within twenty miles of Kauai, where the submarine *R-4* rescued them. Given such risks, McConaughty thought fliers would have to be enticed to take on the challenge. "You might get Lindbergh over here the same way Raymond Orteig got him to Paris," he suggested to Dole. "Offer him a reward."

Orteig, a Frenchman who owned two New York City hotels, put up a $25,000 cash prize in 1919 to the first aviator in a heavier-than-air plane to complete a nonstop crossing of the Atlantic in its full width in either direction. The year was significant because in 1919 the lighter-than-air German dirigible R-34 made a round-trip from England to New York without incident. But the journey was slow and didn't garner public interest as much as fixed-wing aircraft that could fly much, much faster did. Orteig's proposition was a dangerous one, however. Over the next seven years, nineteen aviators perished while trying. A biplane piloted by two Frenchmen flying west over the Atlantic had apparently made it in 1927 but disappeared over New England, never to be found. Lindbergh took off on his historic quest only a few days later and ultimately collected Orteig's reward. Given the way the hotel magnate's challenge galvanized the nation and world, would the same kind of offer provide traction for Dole?

"An excellent idea . . . post a reward," he said to McConaughty, envisioning Lindbergh entering the contest. "The others will follow later, and we'd have regular commercial service before you knew it. Think of it, Harry! Think of how many times during the canning season I've cabled you to rush spare parts for one of our machines. And a ship takes five to six days. And think of the tourists; how many more would come over to see the islands if they could get there in one day."

Dole returned to Hawaii and began lining up sponsors for a contest that would be open for one year with the prize set at $25,000. Before plans could jell, however, two planes made the crossing in July 1927. U.S. Army lieutenants Albert Hegenberger and Lester Maitland were the first to succeed in a trimotor Fokker; they landed at the Army's Wheeler Field on Oahu in twenty-five hours and fifty minutes. Just ten days later, a Travelair aircraft named the *City of Oakland* and piloted by two civilians crash-landed in a thorn tree on the Hawaiian island of Molokai when the plane ran out of gas sixty miles short of its destination after a twenty-six-hour thirty-six-minute flight from Oakland, California.

Both achievements were disappointments to Dole, who hadn't gotten his contest organized before the planes made the crossing. In a discussion of his dilemma with *Honolulu-Star* newspaper editors Riley Allen and Joseph Farrington, the two journalists suggested an alternative—stage a *race* to Hawaii. All planes entered in the "Dole Air Race to Honolulu" would take off at the same time from an island airfield in the bay between San Francisco and Oakland. The first one to Honolulu would win the cash. The editors thought a race would generate an aerial circus for daredevils, an international sensation with or without "Lucky Lindy." Dole was enthusiastic and set a start date of 12 August 1927. A prize of $25,000 would go to the first flier to reach Honolulu, $10,000 to the runner-up. Dole asked the Honolulu chapter of the National Aeronautic Association to establish the rules and safety criteria for the race so that "it may cost no brave man either his life or limb," as Dole put it.

The announcement that Jim Dole was seeking qualified fliers for a race across the Pacific electrified the nation. Sid Grauman, a Hollywood theater mogul, promptly tapped into that passion by offering a $30,000 purse to the first aviator to fly from Los Angeles to Tokyo. And the San Francisco Citizen's Flight Committee suggested increasing Dole's prize money to $50,000 if he would extend the race to Australia. These were far-fetched goals for the times. Fliers thought of the San Francisco-to-Honolulu challenge as more feasible and began flocking to the city by the bay as July came to an end.

The Dole Derby
Pearl Harbor, Honolulu, Hawaii
31 July 1927

As the *S-46* tied up at the harbor's sub base, Lt. Allan McCann had no way of anticipating that he would play an ancillary role in a flight of exotic planes racing with each other for $35,000 in prize money in what journalists soon dubbed the "Dole Derby." Rather, he and his crew were contemplating battle-readiness exercises with American destroyers, cruisers, battleships, and other S- and R-class submarines operating out of Pearl Harbor.

The submarines were an intrinsic part of the Navy's Orange War Plan for dealing with potential hostilities with Japan. For two decades, the United States had viewed with concern the threat posed by the growing Japanese navy, which in a single day in 1905 sank the entire Russian Baltic fleet in the Strait of Tsushima, between Japan and Korea. Tokyo subsequently posed a strategic danger to American trade interests in China and in the Philippines, territory won from Spain after the Spanish-American War of 1898. Complicating matters in 1907 was Japanese immigration to California, which had provoked racial conflict and resulted in government-ordered segregation in San Francisco. To deal with the possibility that Japan might retaliate by seizing Hawaii or the Philippines, the Navy had developed its Orange War Plan. Initially, it projected the U.S. fleet, steaming from harbors on the East Coast, through the Panama Canal and into the Pacific to combat enemy forces. After World War I, Japan was awarded a string of South Pacific atolls owned by Germany as a thank-you from Britain for Tokyo's help in thwarting U-boats in the Mediterranean during the war. The new Pacific holdings included the Mariana, Caroline, and Marshall island chains, all of which intersected American sea-lanes to the Philippines. The U.S. Navy adjusted to the new reality by modifying the Orange War Plan to include a new Pacific command that could quickly deploy battleships, heavy cruisers, and support ships from bases in San Diego and Long Beach. In addition, squadrons of submarines were to be deployed to Navy bases in Pearl Harbor, in Dutch Harbor in Alaska's Aleutian island chain, and at various U.S. territories in the

South Pacific, including the Philippines, Midway, and Guam. Their primary mission would be to scout the movements of Japanese warships and radio back intelligence to the U.S. battle fleet commander. The subs would prowl Japanese shipping lanes and patrol the coasts of China and Japan if needed.

McCann's *S-46* and her sister S-boats were not the ideal vessels to do what the Navy needed done, that is, stay at sea for seventy-five days at a time and voyage 12,000 miles without refueling across vast reaches of the Pacific. A new kind of submarine was necessary, especially in the wake of the 1922 Washington Naval Arms Limitation Treaty, which began a process of cancelling the Navy's ship construction programs. Submarine development declined significantly. Yet the Navy secured enough funds from a tightfisted Congress to begin development of a large, new V-class boat capable of spanning the Pacific and fast enough to accompany the fleet anywhere in the world. The V-boats did not live up to their potential, however. They proved to be too slow and were equipped with Navy-built diesel engines based on the MAN design that often broke down. In addition, the ungainly boats could not dive beneath the surface within a minute, the standard for avoiding detection and bombardment from enemy aircraft. For the time being, as the Navy went back to the drawing board, S- and R-boats would have to do in the Pacific.

The Navy had one trump card, however. In development was an ultra-secret magnetic exploder for submarine torpedoes. The triggering mechanism ensured detonation whenever a torpedo passed through the magnetic field known to extend beneath iron-hulled ships. Laboratory tests at the Navy's Bureau of Ordinance at the Newport Naval Station in Rhode Island proved that the exploders worked as designed. A test-range trial also succeeded. No longer would torpedoes have to make physical contact with enemy targets to destroy them. Navy captain Thomas Hart, a submarine pioneer, was so enamored that he wrote a congratulatory letter to the bureau, noting that the test on 8 May 1926 was "the opening of a new phase of torpedo warfare which gives the United States a tremendous advantage over any prospective enemy."

The existence of the weapon was jealously guarded. Not even the captains of Navy submarines knew how it worked, although they knew its potential. Thus, as August 1927 arrived, Lieutenant McCann and the other S-boat skippers in Hawaii were confident of success if war came to the Pacific. For the moment, however, their attention was directed at events not to the west of Hawaii but rather to the east: Lifeguard duty for a group of aviators about to take off from California for Honolulu. The federal government had endorsed the "Dole Derby," hopeful that it would enhance the country's growing aeronautical achievements in the wake of Lindbergh's incredible flight to Paris. The entire Pacific Feet would be placed in readiness. Adm. Richard H. Jackson, Pacific Battle Fleet commander, stationed a division of destroyers between

San Francisco and Hawaii as a safety net for the aviators. Likewise, the carrier *Langley* (CV-1) and the aircraft tender *Arrostook* (CM-3), with their planes, stood off the California coast to offer assistance. Near the islands, R- and S-class submarines, including McCann's *S-46*, took position around Hawaii to provide the bulk of assistance to any downed flier; there were three off Hilo, three others with the minesweeper *Ortolan* (AM-45) between the big island of Hawaii and Maui, three between Molokai and Maui, two with the sub tender *Holland* (AS-3) between Molokai and Oahu, five with the minesweeper *Widgeon* (AM-22) between Oahu and Kauai, and five boats north of Kauai. Scores of commercial freighters and passenger liners plying the ocean between California and Hawaii also were alerted to be on the lookout for the planes. They included *Wilhelmina*, calculated to be 1,400 miles from Honolulu; *Los Angeles*, 800 miles from Los Angeles; SS *Manukai*, 950 miles from San Francisco; SS *President Harrison*, 800 miles from the city; SS *Manulani*, 1,160 miles from Maui; SS *Inora*, 800 miles from Honolulu; and SS *Manoa*, 1,320 miles from San Francisco.

Mystery Monoplane
Matson Building, San Francisco, California
8 August 1927

Capt. C. W. Saunders, director of the California chapter of the National Aeronautic Association and the chairman of the Dole flight committee, had the honor of drawing starting positions for the pilots of fifteen planes officially entered into the race, which would begin at the grass airfield on an island in San Francisco Bay near Oakland. The race committee had received thirty-three entries from all over the country, but Charles Lindbergh wasn't one of them. Too busy and unable to prepare a proper aircraft on such short notice, he had bowed out. Navy commander Richard Byrd, famed for his Arctic explorations by air, declined for the same reason. No matter. Many illustrious fliers had accepted the challenge. They included America's first World War I flying ace, William P. "Lonestar Bill" Erwin, who had shot down nine German planes; Maj. Livingston G. Irving, another war ace; Arthur Goebel, a movie stunt pilot notable for his ability to fly upside down; and Capt. Arthur V. Rogers, a British pilot who brought down thirty-two German planes in the war. There also were many civilian and military fliers with varying degrees of experience. Colorful emblems of corporate sponsors adorned their planes. Pilot/attorney James Giffin's two-engine, triple-winged international triplane, *Spirit of Los Angeles*, for example, entered on behalf of movie cowboy star Hoot Gibson, displayed the actor's smiling face on its fuselage. Observers compared the wings of the ungainly aircraft to a stack of wheat sheaves. Two other planes stood out: *El Encanto*, with its silver, all-metal single wing, and *Oklahoma*, with its fuselage covered with metal. All other planes registered for the race were of traditional construction with steel tubing and spruce skeletons covered by fabric.

To a man, the pilots believed the race was feasible because it was 1,200 miles shorter than the entire route flown by Lindbergh. However, "Lucky Lindy" had flown over landmasses a portion of the time and could have easily landed in case of trouble. Plus, his destination was the entire coast of France, not an island in the middle of the Pacific. The ocean was the real threat for the Dole fliers. The route to Honolulu passed entirely over the Pacific, a stretch six hundred miles longer than Lindbergh's Atlantic transit.

Signs of how difficult the race would be began to pile up soon after Captain Saunders, from his office, selected the order in which the fliers would become airborne from numbered pieces of paper shuffled in his ceremonial "hat," a metal wastebasket covered in papier-mâché. First pulled was the proverbially unlucky number 13 going to young Navy lieutenants George D. Covell and R. S. Waggener. The name of their Tremaine aircraft was unknown other than it was a "mystery monoplane" believed to be one of the best of the competition. Two days after their selection, the men took off from San Diego for Oakland and fifteen minutes later slammed into a cliff shrouded in fog. The plane plummeted in flames seventy-five feet to a beach, killing both men. The next day another qualified pilot perished outside Los Angeles. Capt. Arthur V. Rogers, twenty-nine, a decorated veteran of World War I's Lafayette Escadrille, was making a test flight in his single-winged aircraft *Angel of Los Angeles* while his wife and infant daughter looked on. As he was coming in for a landing, the plane suddenly nose-dived into the ground from a height of 125 feet. Rogers died in his wife's arms. The *Spirit of Los Angeles* also became a casualty when it spiraled into the bay on approach to the airfield in Oakland. Pilot Giffin, a Long Beach attorney, and his navigator escaped unhurt.

A lesser mishap involved a biplane flying in from Michigan and sponsored by William "Bill" Malloska, head of the Lincoln Petroleum Company in Flint. *Miss Doran* was named for fifth-grade teacher Mildred Doran from Caro, Michigan. She was on board and had grabbed national attention all the way across the country. Although she had no aviation experience, she was a fan of air travel. A graduate of Michigan State College, she was twenty-two, single, and the only female among the two dozen aviators invited to compete. It didn't hurt that she was attractive with large hazel eyes, dark curly hair, and a vivacious personality. En route, she wore an olive-drab flying suit to which were pinned five college fraternity pins. Her enthusiasm for flying and her friendship with pilot John "Augie" Peddlar, twenty-four, made her the airship's mascot. She took her place in a rear cabin of the huge plane, from which she communicated with Peddlar, the youngest of all the pilots in the race, via megaphones to overcome the noise of the engine. Having hopscotched across the country, the plane

Illinois schoolteacher Mildred Doran, pilot John "Augie" Peddlar (right), and Navy lieutenant Vilas "Cy" Knobe, the navigator, pose prior to their ill-fated flight from Oakland, California, to Honolulu in Peddlar's experimental aircraft, *Miss Doran*. Lieutenant McCann's *S-46* and other subs searched for the downed plane with the teacher on board.

Hawaii Aviation Preservation Society

was approaching Oakland from the south when it suffered a spark plug failure. Peddlar made an emergency landing in a wheat field in the San Joaquin Valley to replace the plug with much difficulty. Mildred Doran later shrugged off the incident, telling reporters in Oakland that the repair had taken longer than anticipated because the crew didn't have the right tools. "We threw them off at Long Beach because they were in the way and cluttering things up," she smiled.

Now at the landing strip in Oakland, *Miss Doran* passed a final government inspection. Six other airships, however, were disqualified, mostly for having inexperienced navigators or fuel tanks that were too small for the grueling crossing to Hawaii. To give the crews and their planes a chance to make modifications and requalify, the race was postponed for four days to Dole's great disappointment. He had hoped for a Sunday arrival in Honolulu when the 3,500 employees of his pineapple plantation could attend on their day off.

It's Time
Bay Farm Island, Oakland, California
16 August 1927

The early morning fog over San Francisco Bay had grudgingly dissipated as it normally did in midsummer. At 1100, the number of planes lined up wing to wing alongside the seven-thousand-foot grass runway had been reduced to eight qualifiers. A crowd of 100,000 spectators had gathered, jostling to get a view of the colorful planes, the pilots, the navigators, and the school teacher preparing for the greatest aeronautical challenge of their lives. Throughout the morning, people congregated, creating a festive scene with vendors serving up sandwiches amid the sound of ukuleles. Marines, national guardsmen, and local police had cordoned off the flight line. Motorcycle police escorted each of the flight crews to their planes on the east end of the field, where mechanics finished final preparations. Spectators with binoculars stood on nearby buildings while others watched from ships and pleasure craft just offshore. Newsreel cameramen for Pathe and Paramount prowled the crowd and photographed the aviators and their planes. KPO (National Broadcasting), KYA (the *Examiner*'s radio station), and KLX (representing the Oakland *Tribune*) set up to narrate the event. Scores of writers had arrived from the Associated Press, United Press, the *Berkeley Gazette*, the Oakland *Tribune*, and San Francisco's five dailies, the *Post Enquirer*, *Chronicle*, *Examiner*, *News*, and *Call*. Tractors towing a roller smoothed out the sandy west end of the flight line, which jutted toward San Francisco's Golden Gate entrance to the bay. Likewise a water wagon moved back and forth to wet down the dust stirred up by arriving autos and motorcycles and the milling of the crowd.

The aircraft *Oklahoma*, a blue and yellow Travelair monoplane from Bartelesville, Oklahoma, piloted by Bennett Griffin with navigator Al Henley, would be first to attempt liftoff at noon. *Oklahoma* was to be swiftly followed by

- *El Encanto*, the sleek Goddard monoplane piloted by Norman A. Goddard and Kenneth C. Hawkins, the favorites to win the race;
- *Pabco Pacific Flier*, an orange Breese monoplane from nearby Berkeley, with Army major Irving flying solo;
- *Golden Eagle*, the cigar-shaped, bright yellow Lockheed-built Vega monoplane piloted by Jack Frost and navigator Gordon Scott;
- *Miss Doran*, a red, white, and blue Buhl air sedan biplane—the only biplane—flown by Peddlar with navigator Navy lieutenant Vilas "Cy" Knobe and Mildred Doran on board;
- *Aloha*, a lemon-yellow Breese monoplane with a Hawaiian flower lei painted around its nose and flown by Martin Jensen with navigator Paul Schluter;

- *Woolaroc*, a yellow and blue Travelair monoplane and sister plane to *Oklahoma* with Hollywood movie stunt flier Art Goebel at the controls and active-duty Navy lieutenant William V. Davis Jr., a former Annapolis swimming star, navigating;
- *Dallas Spirit*, a Swallow monoplane piloted by William P. Erwin with navigator Alvin Eichwaldt.

All planes were to be airborne within a couple of minutes of each other. The exact time of departure would be noted.

Oklahoma was the first to taxi to the end of the runway and await the starter's flag. All other planes were lined up nose to tail just off the runway, their motors throbbing on idle. At exactly noon, a ceremonial pistol fired and a starter whipped his pennant swiftly downward toward the far end of the runway. The race clock had started. The excited crowd pushed toward the fence along the landing strip. At 1201 the sleek *Oklahoma* rumbled past, slowly gaining speed and soaring away smoothly. Gaining altitude, the plane headed west through the Golden Gate to the Pacific. Reporters near the awaiting *Miss Doran* overheard Mildred Doran shout encouragement to Peddlar, dressed in knickerbockers and his customary straw hat. "Now it's time, old friend," she enthused. "We're about to become 'somebody.'"

The streamlined *El Encanto* with its metallic wings was next up. Engine throttling at a fever pitch, the plane shot down the runway. Midway in its run, the plane's right wing hit the ground, broke free, and whirled skyward to the end of the airstrip 2,300 feet away. The fuselage crumpled over its left wing and abruptly came to rest off the runway. Lieutenant Goddard and Hawkins climbed from the wreckage unhurt, their plane a total loss.

Pabco Pacific Flier, the local favorite from Berkeley, was next to attempt takeoff. Halfway down the runway, pilot Irving was unable to nudge the plane into the air and aborted. The aircraft slid to a shuddering halt in marshland seven thousand feet from the start line. There Irving climbed out, cursing and signaling for a tow back to the start line to make another attempt.

At 1231, the *Golden Eagle*, sponsored by the Hearst Newspaper chain, thrummed away out over the bay, all systems go. Next, *Miss Doran*, its engine throttling at full bore, taxied to the start line and sped down the runway past the shouting, waving mob. The airship soared out over the bay toward the Golden Gate. Two minutes later, *Aloha* followed; then *Woolaroc* and *Dallas Spirit* in quick order to surging applause. *Woolaroc* traced a course 1,500 feet above Market Street in San Francisco so that planes carrying news photographers could film it as it passed to the west.

The flight didn't go as expected for *Miss Doran*. Spectators were startled to see the aircraft circling back to a landing on the island. Appearing anxious, Peddlar sifted through the fuel lines, looking for some sort of blockage. Aviator

Ernie Smith shepherded Mildred Doran to a nearby tent, where she waited on a cot, trembling uncontrollably. Reporters traipsed after her, trying to get a response. "Leave her alone, fellows," Smith barked. The journalists were concerned her plane might not make it to Hawaii. First the spark plug problem over the San Joaquin Valley, now this. "They ought to tell her not to go in that thing!" shouted one reporter gesturing toward the biplane. "Can't she be disqualified?" asked another. "Somebody talk some sense into Augie Peddlar!"

As Peddlar worked on *Miss Doran* for more than an hour, *Dallas Spirit* returned to the airfield, the fabric of its left wing torn because the aircraft's navigator hadn't fastened the door shut and it had swung open in flight against a hundred mile per hour slip wind. Berkeley's *Pabco Pacific Flier* made another try to get airborne. Again, it failed, belly flopping back onto the runway. Pilot Irving climbed free and stomped the ground while flailing his arms in disgust. Soon, *Oklahoma* returned to the airstrip with its engine coughing black smoke less than an hour after it departed. Major repairs would be necessary.

It took two hours for repairs to be made to *Miss Doran*. Finally, the plane's big engine roared to life. Navigator Knobe walked through a storm of dust thrown up by the plane to the tent where the teacher waited. "It's time, Mildred. We've fixed 'er," he announced. Moved by how nervous she had seemed, he suggested she reconsider: "Look, Mildred, Augie and I think it would be a good idea if you didn't go." Summoning her courage, she stood up and brushed by him. "That's ridiculous, Cy. Of course I'm going." Observers noticed tears on her cheeks, maybe owing to the dust. But maybe not. She had been the focal point of so much attention as the only woman among the fifteen fliers. Perhaps she believed it would be too humiliating to drop out. She didn't say as she made for the plane and climbed in.

Miss Doran lifted off to tumultuous applause and zoomed away over San Francisco, Hawaii-bound with pilot Peddlar determined to make up time. Only four competitors continued on toward Honolulu—*Golden Eagle*, *Aloha*, *Woolaroc*, and *Miss Doran*. Unfortunately, only one of the planes—*Woolaroc*—was equipped with a two-way radio to help navigate and seek assistance in an emergency. *Golden Eagle* had a receiver, enabling it to track the direction of radio transmissions to aid navigation. But *Miss Doran* and *Aloha* would have to depend entirely on compasses and sextants to find their way.

"Two Goals"
Over the Pacific Ocean
17 August 1927

Pilot Martin Jensen believed his *Aloha* had taken a good lead over the other fliers by remaining fifty to a hundred feet above the ocean to make better use of his fuel. Jensen was a veteran flier of commercial routes between the Hawaiian Islands. This was much different than interisland flying, however. With gray Pacific waves rolling by below and fog just above, the trip was monotonous and taxing. As night descended, dense fog prevented star sightings to verify that the plane was on course. Jensen took the plane up to four thousand feet. It was not high enough. He tried three times to get higher but each time the plane went into a tailspin. Luckily, his skill as a stunt flier who had made his mark in the movie *Thirteen Black Cats of Hollywood* enabled him to overcome vertigo and save the plane each time.

Aloha flew on at low altitude for many hours, depending entirely on instruments and an altimeter that registered a hundred feet above a gray sea that faded into blackness. The air density over the Pacific had given a false altimeter reading, however. "I was five or 10 feet above the water for an hour or more," Jensen later estimated. "I hit the top of a wave and the spray from this ripped a long slit in the stabilizer fabric. The fact that I never took my hands from the throttle or stick gave me instant control, after which I raised to about 500 feet to continue the long flight."

Far above *Aloha* was *Woolaroc*, well equipped with four compasses and a bubble sextant for precise sun and star observations. Pilot Goebel maintained a steady course on a previously plotted great circle route from San Francisco to Hawaii. He had boasted before the flight that the crew had stowed every conceivable means of navigation to ensure their ability to stay on course, day and night. "There are two goals," he said. "The Hawaiian Islands or the bottom of the Pacific Ocean."

Woolaroc, named for the vast hunting preserve of woods, lakes, and rocks owned by the sponsoring Phillips Petroleum Company, flew high—six thousand feet—to stay above low-hanging clouds that could obscure the crew's vision. A Navy destroyer and various other ships tried to exchange radio signals with the aircraft as it passed. Because of the overcast below, the crew never saw any of the vessels, however.

"Great to Be Here"
Wheeler Airfield, Honolulu, Hawaii
17 August 1927

Jim Dole had counted the hours as the race progressed. He told the *Honolulu Star Bulletin*, "Hawaii is on the lips of the world today, in the minds of countless millions of people." *Woolaroc* was the first airplane to be sighted 450 miles from Oahu. The SS *City of Los Angeles* had exchanged messages with the aircraft. When the plane closed within two hundred miles of Honolulu, the Wahiawa Radio Station adjacent to Wheeler Field picked up a signal from *Woolaroc*. Pilot

Goebel estimated that they would arrive in two and a half hours. The station flashed word to the city. The weather was perfect for landing. Hawaii governor Wallace R. Farrington, Dole, and other community leaders made for the airfield to greet the planes as they came in. Upward of 25,000 spectators also swarmed the airport. Police estimated nearly 10,000 cars parked around the air base and a line of vehicles two miles long waiting to get in. While all waited, Army planes performed aerial stunts, bands played, and young Hawaiian women in native costumes sang and danced.

In *Woolaroc*, Goebel and Davis soon picked out the misty coast of Maui and changed course for their destination on Oahu seventy miles away. Davis couldn't contain his excitement and started dropping smoke bombs to trace the plane's passage across the channel and past Diamond Head as it made its approach to Wheeler. A small pursuit plane flew alongside, its pilot grinning broadly and signaling that *Woolaroc* would win the race. Army and Navy planes raced up to meet the aircraft as Goebel made an aerial victory lap around the Army base. He then brought the plane in for a landing past the cheering throng. The wheels touched down after a flight from the mainland of twenty-six hours, seventeen minutes, and thirty-three seconds. *Woolaroc* taxied to the bunting-draped reviewing stand, coming to a halt nose first before the governor and Jim Dole at exactly twenty minutes after noon. They and other well-wishers greeted the pilot and navigator as they stepped from the aircraft. Hawaiian hula girls placed heaps of floral leis around their necks in a traditional island greeting. Other garlands were draped over the engine, which had sputtered to a stop. Goebel and Davis, in his blue Navy uniform, beamed. "Say folks, it's great to be here," said the pilot scanning the field for any other Dole aircraft. "Well, honest to gosh . . . I'm the first one here?" he asked rhetorically. "I thought surely some were ahead of us." Goebel raised his hands over his head and broke into a victory dance. Afterward, Jim Dole presented him and Davis a check for $25,000.

The crowd remained at the airport to await the other three planes, hoping *Aloha* would grab second prize. Marguerite Jensen, wife of the pilot, asked Goebel if he had seen *Aloha*. When he replied that he hadn't, she began to cry and was helped back to the reviewing stand by two Army officers.

In fact, the plane was within two hundred miles of Oahu, and Jensen was using a hand pump to keep his fuel tank full; the aircraft did not have a gas gauge, and he didn't want to risk a stall. Each time the pump was used, however, large amounts of precious fuel leaked overboard. As the plane neared landfall, the crew members prepared the life raft just in case they had to ditch in the ocean. The engine kept going all the way to a bumpy landing on the grass turf at Wheeler. *Aloha* clocked in at one hour and fifty-eight minutes behind *Woolaroc*. That was good enough for $10,000. Jensen and navigator Schluter

The *Aloha* barely avoided ditching into the Pacific but landed safely in Honolulu to claim second place cash winnings of $10,000 in the Dole race.

Hawaii Aviation Preservation Society

looked exhausted and wind-blasted from their ordeal. A measurement of *Aloha*'s remaining fuel revealed only five gallons left, enough for no more than thirty minutes of flying. Jensen climbed down from the cockpit, smiling broadly and holding up a bag of mail from the mainland. Mrs. Jensen ran to him, delirious with joy and demanding, "Martin, where the hell have you been?"

What about the other two planes? As evening set, the dispirited crowd retired from the airfield certain that the airships had crashed somewhere.

"Gas Gone . . . Floating on Wings"
S-46, Pacific Ocean
20 August 1927

Allan McCann had been deployed to the area where the aviators approaching Hawaii from the east would most likely come down. The lieutenant commanded a group of three submarines—the *S-46*, *R-8*, and *S-42*. Lookouts on the conning towers had neither seen nor heard any approaching aircraft. The subs continued sweeping the ocean, looking for telltale signs of *Miss Doran* and *Golden Eagle*. Both aircraft had stowed necessary means for the crews to survive if their planes made a soft landing on the ocean. On board each were flotation life belts, life rafts, emergency rations, and hacksaws to cut away the fixed wheels to keep the planes afloat as long as possible.

Back in Honolulu, a celebration scheduled for all the fliers had been called off. A distraught Jim Dole posted $10,000 for anyone who rescued the crews of either plane. Bill Malloska in Flint, Michigan, pledged $10,000 for the recovery of those on board *Miss Doran*, either dead or alive. And George Hearst offered $10,000 for those on board *Golden Eagle*. Jensen took his *Aloha* for a five-hour search over Oahu after mystery flares were seen on Mauna Loa the night after the race. Jensen found nothing. The Navy's battle fleet of fifty-four vessels executed a carefully plotted search pattern that covered 350,000 square miles of ocean between California and Hawaii over the next few weeks. Army pilots also joined in the search, looking for wreckage on the Hawaiian Islands and the straits between them. One of the search planes crashed into the sea, killing its two-man crew.

A correspondent for the San Francisco *Examiner* in Honolulu heard a rumor that Mildred Doran was safe on remote Maui and filed a story. It was picked up by the Associated Press. In Flint, newspapers rushed special editions to press. Movies being shown at city theaters were halted so that the announcement of Doran's rescue could be made. Jubilation reigned but it was short lived. The report proved to be false.

In Oakland, Captain Erwin and his navigator Eichwaldt had repaired the damaged wing of *Dallas Spirit*. The two took off three days after the race to help in the search while continuing on to Hawaii. Their plan was to island hop all the way to Hong Kong to claim a $25,000 prize offered by a Texas millionaire. The plane had enough fuel to keep it airborne for forty hours at a time. En route, the crew sent messages in Morse code that told a tale of misfortune far at sea:

0310: the ceiling is increasing and the sun is breaking through.

0440: Visibility is very good. We are able to cover eighty mile patch.

0510: We just passed the SS *Mana* at 5:10 and dipped in salute. They answered us on their whistle. Of course we could not hear it but we could see the steam. We might pick up the squadron of destroyers before dark but that depends on the speed. All o.k.

0548: We just passed a destroyer.

0712: We have thirty miles visibility and are flying at 900 feet. Have seen nothing.

0851: S-o-S . . . Belay that. We were in a spin but came out of it o.k. we sure were scared. It was a close call. The lights on the instrument panel went out and it was so dark Bill could not see the wings.

0902: We are in anr . . .

There were no further transmissions. The thirty planes on the *Langley* plus the three on the *Arrostook* converged at the last-known position of the plane. They found no trace of *Dallas Spirit* nor its occupants.

The search for the missing planes would continue until 5 September. Nothing was ever found save a bottle washed up on Westport Beach in Aberdeen, Washington, two weeks after the race. A message inside purported to read, "Gas gone . . . Water running low . . . been floating on wings . . . days. Miss . . . oran."

It was a sad final epitaph. The toll of aviators killed before, during, and after what had become the "infamous" Dole Air Race stood at eleven. But that would not dissuade aviators from pushing the envelope in an attempt to conquer the Pacific. By year's end, twenty-five men and three women had perished trying. For Jim Dole, his dream of passenger and freight air service between the mainland and Hawaii would have to wait. It would be a matter of a few years before larger and more powerful aircraft came of age to make that dream come true.

McCann and the submarine force recovered no evidence, no flotsam whatsoever, in the days and nights searching for Mildred Doran and the other fliers. For the lieutenant, time marched on. At the end of August, he took the *S-46* back to San Diego and then to the Mare Island Naval Shipyard in San Francisco Bay for overhaul. The sub was to return to Pearl Harbor and resume operations with the battle fleet.

The following year, the Navy finally responded to the sketch plan McCann had submitted for a submarine rescue chamber. He would be detached from command and ordered to the Navy's Bureau of Construction and Repair. There he would be joined by a legendary sub skipper named Charles B. Momsen, who, like McCann, dreamed of a means to bring trapped submarines up from the depths. Together they would make that dream a reality.

CHAPTER 6

Utterly Helpless

Cape Cod Bay
Provincetown, Massachusetts
17 December 1927

In the gathering dusk on 17 December 1927, the U.S. Navy's *S-4* (SS-109) was making a submerged trial run over a measured mile offshore from Provincetown, Massachusetts, at the tip of Cape Cod. She and the *S-8* (SS-113) had arrived from the Portsmouth Naval Shipyard in Portsmouth, New Hampshire, after modifications to their forward torpedo tubes. The boats had entered Cape Cod Bay while en route to the sub base at New London. The *S-8* had finished the course ahead of her sister sub and had set out for the base. In *S-4* Lt. Cdr. Roy K. Jones had just raised the periscope on his run. Two coast guardsmen assigned to Provincetown's Wood End Lighthouse couldn't believe their eyes as the scope broke surface under the prow of a Coast Guard cutter. The *Paulding* (CG-17) was speeding to intercept suspicious craft, possibly a Prohibition rumrunner loaded with illegal booze for delivery to Boston bootleggers. Before the alarm could be raised, the cutter rammed the sub, slicing deeply into her starboard hull just forward of the boat's deck gun. In less than a minute, the *S-4* and her forty-person crew plummeted to the bottom, 110 feet down. Thirty-four officers and submariners drowned in a crush of seawater flooding five of the boat's six compartments. In the torpedo room, however, Lt. Graham N. Fitch and five crew members closed off a watertight door just in time. They were safe but trapped. Under an ocean pressure of fifteen tons per square inch, it would be impossible to push open the compartment's deck hatch to attempt an escape. Even if the trapped men could pry the hatch, swimming to the surface on a single breath was virtually impossible. They would have to wait and hope the sub somehow could be raised to free them.

Overhead the *Paulding*'s captain issued a distress call and lowered lifeboats to seek survivors. With darkness descending over the murky bay, illuminated by floodlights from the cutter, nothing emerged from the vessel below except air bubbles and a widening oil slick. The cutter passed back and forth, dragging a grappling hook in hopes of snagging the hull to fix the boat's location for Navy divers who were on the way from New London. After six hours, *Paulding* finally caught the submarine. However, gale-force winds caused the ship to heave and snap the heavy manila rope.

The *S-8* reversed course and at midnight arrived alongside the cutter. Locating the sunken boat with sonar, the sub anchored above *S-4* and determined that people were alive down below. Ens. Robert Dennison, an officer on the *S-8*, recalled the moment: "We heard pounding from her hull. The water was rather shallow, but the weather was terrible."

Deep-sea divers arrived at daybreak. By then, newspaper and radio reporters had congregated in Provincetown, joining throngs of spectators hoping that the men would be rescued. The divers in metal helmets were lowered one by one to the submarine, where they inspected damage and attached an oscillator to the hull to communicate with those inside using Morse code. It was quickly established that six were alive and that their air would last only about forty-eight hours. The radioman in the *S-8* tapped out a series of questions that could be answered with one hammer blow for yes, two for no. Is the engine room flooded? Yes. Is the control room flooded? Yes. Are there any survivors in compartments aft of the torpedo room. No. As bits of news arrived, gloom prevailed. The survivors were too deep. No cranes big enough to hoist the sub out of the ocean were available. Another way would have to be found to rescue the men, but success was doubtful. "Two of my classmates were in the *S-4*," said Dennison. "It was heart-breaking."

In succeeding hours, the *S-8* relayed messages from the men's families and status reports on the rescue effort. As the hours wound on with little action to save them, the trapped men pleaded, "Please hurry."

Navy officers had debated what to do. The only likely option was to drop air hoses to the sub to blow her ballast tanks in an attempt to refloat the vessel or at least bring her bow to the surface so that the men could get out through the forward deck hatch. The tanks, however, had suffered extensive damage and couldn't contain compressed air that bubbled up ferociously to the surface as fast as it was pumped below. Then the weather worsened. One diver was entangled in the wreckage and was narrowly rescued by another. The Navy had no choice but to wait. Sixty-two hours into the disaster, a diver lowered to the sub in a risky maneuver placed his helmet against the hull and listened to fading last messages hammered out by the survivors: "Is . . . there . . . any . . . hope?" The storm complicated matters, the trapped men were told. They pounded out a final message: "We understand."

The six men soon died of suffocation. When the weather cleared after four days, divers entered the *S-4* to recover the bodies. By then, a tidal wave of criticism had washed over the Navy for its inability to reach the men. It was a public relations disaster. Something had to be done.

The Momsen Lung
Potomac River, Morgantown, Maryland
Summer 1928

A young submarine captain, concerned about mounting deaths in submarines around the world, had conceived a unique rescue apparatus that he believed would enable crews to escape their sunken vessels. He was now preparing to unveil it to the world in the middle of the Potomac off Morgantown, Maryland, a hamlet forty miles downriver from the Washington Navy Yard. Lt. Charles B. "Swede" Momsen had arranged for the crew of a Navy dive boat to take him to a 110-foot-deep cavity in the river floor. For the lieutenant, the dramatic ascent without Navy authorization would bring a fitting end to his two-year campaign to avenge the deaths of submariners he had known in peacetime accidents.

Momsen, square-jawed, tall, and muscular with an affable personality, was familiar with deep-sea diving. He had graduated from the Naval Academy in 1919 and joined the sub service in 1921. Just as McCann had witnessed the sinking of the *O-5* in Panama in 1923, Momsen had witnessed a similar, horrifying sub disaster in September 1925 off Block Island in Rhode Island. On the evening of 25 September, the *S-51* (SS-162), commanded by Lt. Rodney Dobson, was making ten knots on the surface while patrolling the Atlantic when the passenger steamer SS *City of Rome* erred in its navigation and rammed the submarine, crushing her. Several crew members, including the captain, escaped the doomed vessel before it disappeared with its remaining crew of twenty-seven. In less than a minute, the boat came to rest on the sea bottom 131 feet down. Some of the survivors, including the captain, drowned while struggling to shed their clothes on the ocean's surface. Three enlisted men survived when a lifeboat from the *City of Rome* picked them up after an hour-long swim and steamed away for Boston.

The Navy ordered the nearby *S-1*, commanded by Momsen, to the last-known position of the *S-51* to try to locate the sub. When she arrived, the only telltale sign of the tragedy was an oil slick. Momsen sent out electronic pulses in hopes that a signal would be returned from the boat below. "We tried to contact her but there was only silence. Those of us on the bridge of the *S-1* simply stared

USS *V-5* crewman A. L. Rosen-Kotter demonstrates in 1930 the use of the Momsen lung, designed by Lt. Charles B. Momsen to enable submariners to swim to the surface from a stricken vessel. Lieutenant McCann joined Momsen in the development of rescue equipment in Washington, D.C., and Key West, Florida.

Naval History and Heritage Command, Washington Navy Yard, Washington, D.C.

at the water and said nothing at first," Momsen recounted years later. "At least it was fast. They probably never realized what happened. No one at that time knew anything about the principles of escape and rescue. We were utterly helpless." One seaman muttered in despair, "Oh my God! Oh my God!" Momsen sent him below.

The captain, who was well acquainted with those in the *S-51*, would learn later of the contorted face and shredded fingers on the body of his friend and academy classmate James Dudley Haselden, one of the four lieutenants on board. Before he blacked out, Haselden tried to claw his way out of the steel tomb by undogging a deck hatch that would not open.

The mental images of Haselden's last moments haunted Momsen. After the tragedy, he went to work personally designing and constructing a prototype of a breathing device that could help save submariners. On 25 February 1928 he tested it in a model boat basin at the Washington Navy Yard. Wearing a woolen diving suit, he strapped to his chest the implement's rubber rebreathing bag inflated with pure oxygen, secured a clothespin to his nose and inserted a breathing tube from the sack into his mouth. Then he walked down the incline of the basin until submerged and remained there for three minutes. He took several breaths through a mechanical valve that clicked open and closed. Each exhale passed through a canister of soda lime to chemically cleanse it of poisonous carbon dioxide and revitalize the air. Momsen later repeated the test at ten feet while weighted down with a piece of scrap iron and breathing freely from his rescue apparatus. Without the Navy's knowledge, the lieutenant made several additional tests in the yard's pressurized tank to simulate submarines at depths of 100, 150, 200, 250, and finally 300 feet. The rebreather seemed to work well.

The next step was to make a real ascent, and this brought him to the middle of the Potomac off Morgantown. Momsen had arrived with a large, inverted pickle barrel made of steel. Cross boards had been fastened inside its open end for Momsen to stand on so that he could look down to view the river bottom. The test began in full daylight before onlookers on the shore and in pleasure boats. As Momsen ducked under the lip of the barrel and stepped up onto the cross boards, the container was lowered into the river. An air pocket trapped in the barrel was enough to sustain Momsen on the way down. Approaching the bottom, heavy silt swirled up around his legs. The container hovered above the muck, giving Momsen enough room to duck under the lip of the barrel for his ascent. He deployed a line with a buoy from the barrel. The rope was marked off in segments by "stop" corks. It would be necessary in a real sub accident for survivors who had been breathing compressed air to stop at the corks and take several breaths before surfacing in order to avoid the crippling effects of decompression sickness, known as the bends. On the river bottom, Momsen inflated his rebreather, ducked under the lower lip of the barrel, and began his ascent. He used his hands and legs to control his speed up the rope. It took ten minutes before he emerged in blinding sunshine, a rock from the Potomac floor clenched tightly in his fist. He held it high for all to see before tossing it back. No one missed the poignancy. Had Momsen's device been available to the men of the S-4 or S-51 trapped at the same depth, they might very well have survived.

The lieutenant's achievement made national headlines after a young reporter for the *Washington Star* filed a story from the scene. The news quickly popularized the "Momsen lung" to the lieutenant's great dismay. Navy brass learned of Momsen's fete by reading the newspapers like everyone else. Chief of Naval Operations Adm. Charles Hughes was among the first to greet the sub captain on his return to the Navy yard. "Young man, what the hell have you been up to?" demanded an agitated Hughes, who nevertheless gave credit to the lieutenant for risking his life to demonstrate that trapped submariners could be saved. The Navy ordered more tests, which proved that the device officially known as the "submarine escape appliance" was dependable.

"Impractical"
Washington, D.C.
July 1928

The presidential Board on Submarine Safety and Salvage had convened to hear testimony from Momsen. The lieutenant was the talk of Washington for what he had done in the Potomac. What the panel did not know was that he and another sub skipper, Allan McCann, had independently conceived of designs for a rescue chamber that could be lowered to a stranded sub to take off survivors. Although the designs had gotten as high as the Navy's Bureau of Construction and Repair, no action had been taken for many months. In concluding his testimony about his rebreather, Momsen made a plea for one other device the Navy ought to pursue—a submarine rescue bell. The lieutenant proceeded to describe in detail how such a machine would work and how he had conceived of the idea after the *S-51* disaster in 1925. A civilian on the panel was shocked. Why, he asked Momsen, had the proposal not been submitted to the Navy? "It was," he replied.

Like McCann's similar sketch plan, Momsen's had been ignored by the bureau. For him, the bureaucratic silence was particularly irritating. Within a few weeks of the *S-51* tragedy, Momsen had conceptualized a large steel chamber in the shape of a bell with an open bottom that could ride up and down steel cables taken down to a sunken sub by divers who would attach them near an escape hatch. The general plan was for a large steel plate, like a bolt washer, to be welded in place around a sub's deck hatch. A rubber gasket would be attached to the bottom of the rescue bell, ensuring a watertight seal between the chamber and the steel plate once the two made contact. Afterward, the hatch would be opened to free those inside and take them back to the surface.

Several sub skippers who reviewed Momsen's plan were impressed. Likewise, Capt. Ernest J. King Jr., commander of the New London sub base, forwarded the plan to the bureau with his endorsement: "the most practical . . . [idea] for the rescue of entrapped submarine crews available." When months passed with no response, Momsen thought a fundamental flaw had been discovered, something he hadn't thought of. So he turned to developing the submarine escape appliance instead.

Still, the rescue bell never left Momsen's mind. He learned the truth of what happened in June 1927, when shore duty placed him in the bureau. On his first day, he sifted through a stack of papers a predecessor had left behind in an "awaiting action" basket. In the bottom, having lingered there for twelve months, was his proposal with Captain King's endorsement. Stifling anger, Momsen approached his superiors the next morning to persuade them to give his idea consideration. They grudgingly gave it a brief overview and returned it stamped "impractical from the standpoint of seamanship." Momsen was appalled; seamanship was not the bureau's purview. Nevertheless, the matter remained closed. A Navy friend cautioned Momsen not to waste time fuming over the matter. He should wait; something was bound to happen. It didn't take long. The suffocation of those on board the S-4 ignited a national brouhaha aimed squarely at the Navy for having no means to save the trapped men.

Now standing before the presidential panel, Momsen's rescue bell finally received a sympathetic hearing. The board demanded that the Navy not only deploy Momsen's lung device but also develop the kind of rescue chamber the lieutenant had conceived. The panel's encouragement made all the difference.

"Wetter and Wiser"
Brooklyn Navy Yard, New York
Fall 1928

Work began, under Momsen's guidance, to create two chambers for the bureau from an experimental seaplane hangar once attached to the deck of Momsen's former command, the S-1. The hangar had proven unwieldy for housing a spotter float plane. Scheduled to be sold off as scrap, Momsen had it instead shipped to the Navy yard, where it was cut in two. Workers turned each half into a workable prototype five feet in diameter and seven feet tall. Lt. Morgan Watt of the Construction Corps transformed Momsen's sketch plan into detailed drawings for two prototypes, each open on the bottom and tapering to a peak where cables and hoses could be anchored to provide power and air to rescuers inside. From a distance, the two units looked like large church bells, hence their public moniker.

As work continued at the Brooklyn yard, the bureau directed engineers at Electric Boat to come up with a third design for a rescue chamber. In one of the two bureau-built "bells," a diver would descend with two steel cables unrolled from reels inside the bell. The diver would attach the cables to the bolts inside the deck hatch collar of a stranded sub and clear any debris from around the opening so that the bell could make a watertight seal. Operators would control the chamber's descent and ascent by winding and unwinding the reels. Other design features included compressed air rather than electricity to operate machinery inside the bell in order to avoid accidental short circuits in case of flooding. The second bureau bell had a different method of reaching a submarine: three cables with anchors that operators would lower from winches onto the hull around the hatch to bring the bell down over it.

Maintaining neutral buoyancy during the descent was the greatest hurdle to overcome. Momsen's team solved it by simply painting a green stripe around the interior of the bells near the open bottoms. If sea level remained below the green line, then enough compressed air existed in the bell to create neutral buoyancy. If the sea rose above the stripe, the bell was too heavy. A blast of compressed air from valves in the bell would return the bell to neutral or positive buoyancy. In his enthusiasm for the work in progress, Watt decided to test one of the units in a flooded dry dock in the Navy yard. With manual controls, he lowered the bell to the bottom and began an ascent with compressed air. Without cables to anchor the bell to an object below, the chamber became unstable, making it nearly impossible to control. Venting air during the ascent, the chamber became heavy and started to drop quickly. When Watt recompressed the bell to bring it to neutral buoyancy, he overcompensated. The bell shot to the surface, turned on its side, took on water and sank. Luck was with the officer, however: the chamber landed upright with enough air underneath the bell to spare Watt from drowning. A crane was required to lift the rescue chamber back to safety. When Watt told Momsen of his near-death experience, he took it with good humor. "You're wetter and I'm wiser," the inventor quipped.

With the bells in development, Momsen commuted back and forth to Key West, where he prepared for a deep ascent with his rebreather from the ill-fated *S-4*, the sub rammed and sunk off Provincetown. The boat had been salvaged and turned over to Momsen for service as a test platform to perfect rescue techniques. The sub's conversion included refitting the control room and battery for the test crew. Three remaining compartments—motor room, engine room, and torpedo room—were stripped so that they could be flooded for practice escapes. The deck hatch over the motor room was fitted with a steel skirt extending down into the compartment four feet. Other types of extensions were built around the torpedo room and engine room hatches. The idea behind them was that in a real emergency crew members would flood the compartment until it reached the bottom of the trunk skirt leading to the escape hatch. The remaining air bubble collected at the top of the chamber would keep survivors alive long enough for them to put on their rebreathers. Meanwhile, the increase in atmospheric pressure inside the compartment would theoretically overcome the weight of sea pressure on the hatch, enabling those "trapped" to open it with relative ease. With their rebreather bags engaged, the submariners would dip under the lip of the skirt, push open the hatch, and exit the boat. At least that was the theory. But would it work in reality?

Edward Kalinoski, a rail-thin chief torpedoman from Jersey City, New Jersey, volunteered to accompany Momsen in the first escape from the *S-4*, which had been towed to a practice site in the Caribbean. With the sub resting on the ocean floor forty feet down and a flotilla overhead, the two men flooded the motor room, slipped on their lungs, and swam up through the hatch to the surface with no difficulty. They repeated ascents from as deep as a hundred feet, the maximum the Navy would go. Momsen insisted on going for two hundred feet. The Navy, worried that something might go wrong, balked. That did not dissuade Momsen. He had the *S-4* repositioned much deeper and then made a successful 207-foot ascent. It was astounding—the first time in history that a human being had survived coming up from such depth without a diving helmet.

Ultimately the Navy embraced the submarine escape appliance and acknowledged Momsen's perseverance, risks, and achievements by awarding him the Distinguished Service Medal. He subsequently reported to New London to train submariners in how to use the devices to swim to the surface from the bottom of the base's new water-filled, 138-foot-tall submarine escape training tower.

While Momsen was engaged, work on the rescue bells neared an end by mid-1929. With sea trials of all three chambers about to begin, Lieutenant McCann's concept for a closed rescue chamber caught the Navy's attention in Washington. "The next thing I knew I received orders to the Bureau of Construction and Repair. I hated to lose my command for I was still a little skeptical about my idea," McCann said of his sudden detachment from the *S-46*. "On arrival in the bureau I was briefed on the problem and the developments to date. As the two bureau bells and the one by Electric Boat were almost ready to test we decided to organize an experimental [Submarine Safety Test] unit for the purpose. As Momsen was familiar with everything up to date, he was ordered to the unit which was to be commanded by Commander Palmer Dunbar."

The Momsen Submarine Rescue Bell
Key West, Florida
Winter 1930

The strange spectacle of the three prototype bells arriving by train from Brooklyn and New London provoked wonder in those outside the Navy. Each of the creations was loaded onto the fantail of the sub tender *Falcon* and taken out to the *S-4*, which was submerged at seventy-five feet. On hand was McCann, who struck a close bond with Momsen, a relationship that would persist for years to come. As submarine skippers, both had extensive engineering backgrounds, understood the unforgiving risks of undersea operations, and got along well during the test period. The same age, they could have graduated in the same class at the Naval Academy, but Momsen washed out as a plebe during a cheating scandal. By force of will, he secured another appointment and graduated two years behind McCann in 1919. Momsen served under McCann in the USS *Kansas* (BB-21) during World War I and was executive officer of the *O-13*

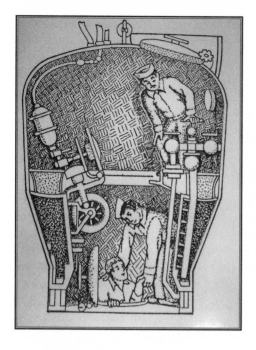

Artist's illustration of the McCann rescue chamber developed in 1929 in Key West, Florida. As designed by Allan McCann, it could be lowered to a stranded submarine at depths greater than two hundred feet. McCann's version overcame problems in earlier rescue bells pioneered by Momsen. Both men collaborated in the effort.

Naval History and Heritage Command, Washington Navy Yard, Washington, D.C.

in Panama at the time of the *O-5* sinking, when McCann was assigned to the rescue efforts. Now the men were once again united on the threshold of history.

As the tests began, the first of the two bureau bells—the one with multiple anchors—proved unsatisfactory. Explained McCann,

> It had three anchors which were supposed to be dropping more or less equally spaced around the submarine hatch. Each had a winch handle inside the bell. The air hose from the tender supplied air for breathing purposes and to keep the water from rising in the bell as the depth, and of course the water pressure, increased. This sounded good on paper but practically it kept us on the qui vine continually for if we maintained enough pressure in the bell to keep the water level at the lower edge of the unit we had difficulty hauling it down with the anchors because of the excess buoyancy. If we let the water level rise too much we would take on negative buoyancy and drop to the bottom out of control.

There was another problem. Bell operators could seldom find the sub or the hatch that they were striving to seat the unit on. "So, the bell went into the discard," said McCann.

Electric Boat's design of an enclosed, pressurized bell also was a failure. Explained McCann, "It was eliminated almost immediately mainly because it had to be hauled down to the submarine by the trapped crew and required a great deal of physical exertion. This had the effect of burning up much needed oxygen and increasing the carbon dioxide content of the boat's atmosphere."

The final design favored by Momsen showed promise for its more direct link to the submarine via cables taken down to the hatch by a diver. "This entirely solved the orientation problem," said McCann. "The man who had to be properly oriented was the diver."

Momsen and ChTorp Charles Hagner of the S-4 test crew made the first descent, landing with a thud. Hagner opened a valve to vent air pressure inside the bell, increasing sea pressure on the enclosure to make a watertight seal. As a precaution, Hagner turned down four bolts between the chamber and the sub to make sure the seal would hold. The two men then stepped down onto the deck directly over the hatch, still buried under a foot of residual sea-water. Momsen alerted Lt. Norman Ives, commander of the S-4, to prepare for twenty gallons of water to drain into the sub through the trunk once the hatch cracked open. Seawater swirled into the boat's hold. After it cleared, Lieutenant Ives looked up with a smile. Momsen momentarily was speech-less. After so many trials and so much conflict with superiors, he could hardly believe this was really happening. Gathering himself, he asked Ives, "Request permission to come aboard."

After a round of welcoming handshakes, two of the S-4's crew to be "res-cued" climbed up into the bell with Momsen. Hagner closed the hatch, removed the restraining bolts, and increased the air pressure to break the seal with the S-4. The bell started its ascent and soon broke surface next to the Falcon to make history. The long quest had proven out; trapped submariners could be saved.

The chamber made additional trips down with McCann along for the ride: "Momsen and I made several connections with the S-4 on the bottom and we were able to enter and leave the submarine as we wished—but—there was the decompression problem, that nasty little necessity. Also the two cables some-times had a tendency to twist and fail to untwist as we approached the hatch."

After the tests, McCann left Key West by train to return to the bureau. He admitted to being unimpressed with any of the three designs, although the latter was more to his liking. "I felt first that the operating crew should not be subject to sea pressure at any time if it could be avoided," he said. "Secondly, I was convinced that my original scheme of a single cable attached to the center of the submarine hatch would work. At least, if the chamber rotated during the descent it would not prevent seating the unit and sealing it there." A single-cable chamber also would be less affected by the overhead tender's heaving in the sea, a problem that made the bell dangerously unstable near the surface.

During the train ride, McCann sketched out what he thought a remodeled rescue chamber should look like along the lines of his original plan: "The tests convinced me that a single cylinder would not work—too unstable, particularly during that period when the unit floated free. I decided we needed a pear shaped unit to put the major part of the buoyancy at the top and the weight at the bottom."

Back at the bureau, engineers drew up working blueprints for the McCann version, a ten-foot-high, pear-shaped chamber of steel with a large, airtight upper chamber and a narrow lower compartment open to the sea and designed to connect with a submarine. From a distance, the unit looked like a large, inverted tumbler painted white. A crew of two would operate it from the upper compartment entered through an off-center overhead hatch. Electrical and pneumatic cables would provide air, light, and telephone connections from the surface. An elongated combing extending down from the lower chamber was designed to create drag, stopping any rotation during the descent. A diver would descend with the end of the chamber's single cable and fasten it through an eye bolt on the rescue hatch of a submarine. This eliminated the problem of twin cables twisting under Momsen's plan. The single cable also simplified docking the chamber, whether upright or on a list. Self-contained motors in the rescue chamber's upper chamber enabled operators to wind the chamber down the cable to dock with a sub. There they would pump seawater accumulated in the lower chamber overboard to create a powerful vacuum in the lower compartment. Sea pressure would squeeze down on the rubber gasket around the chamber's combing and secure the craft tightly to the submarine's hull. Operators then would descend to the submarine's hull, undog the hatch, and free survivors. As many as eighteen could be seated in the upper compartment. McCann incorporated water cans, large enough to sit on, around the periphery. The cans would be filled with water before the descent and then drained accordingly to compensate for the weight of each person taken on board, thereby preserving the chamber's neutral buoyancy. After flooding the lower compartment, the seal would be broken, setting the chamber free for the ascent.

The redesigned chamber cost $10,000 and resolved all remaining issues in McCann's mind. He believed it could be used to save submariners as deep as six hundred feet, the design limits of a whole new class of submarines being developed by the Navy. Next step: Test it.

The McCann Submarine Rescue Chamber
Block Island, Rhode Island
29 July 1931

McCann, Momsen, and others involved in the project had assembled off Block Island, Rhode Island, for the first trial of McCann's rescue chamber. The circumstances of the test couldn't have been more propitious. Two months earlier, on 9 June, the British submarine HMS *Poseidon* (P-99) had plummeted 130 feet to the seafloor after colliding with a merchant steamer off the coast of China. The sub's officers and enlisted men, thirty in all, were trapped. Eight used a British design of the Momsen lung to make an escape, although two drowned. The rest remained trapped and slowly suffocated. Had McCann's chamber or Momsen's bell been available, the submariners might have been rescued.

For those assembled over the hull of the *S-4*, located sixty feet down on the seabed off Block Island, now was the time to prove McCann's advanced design was seaworthy. Again, two *S-4* crew members stood ready to be "rescued." Momsen and McCann had already successfully tested the chamber during development in the flooded dry dock in the Brooklyn Navy Yard. The chamber had even performed docking with hatches that were tilted as much as 30 degrees. In New London, the *Falcon* had taken it offshore, where it was lowered to four hundred feet for an hour to ensure that it was watertight. Now, for the first simulated rescue, the *Falcon* anchored in shallower waters off Block Island, where Momsen and McCann manned a descent to rescue the two volunteers in the *S-4*. The chamber performed as expected. In subsequent tests, it performed just as flawlessly at deeper depths. By late August, Momsen had made a descent to take off twenty-six officers and men from the *S-4*, the ultimate proof of the chamber's durability in an emergency.

It had taken years, but Momsen, McCann, and their tight-knit codevelopers had overcome all challenges to make rescue of trapped submariners not only possible but probable. McCann and Momsen also developed decompression tables for deep-sea divers that would be used henceforth throughout the world. By the fall of 1931 the Momsen lung had become standard equipment on all Navy submarines. It was now mandatory for every officer and enlisted sailor passing through the sub school to use the rebreather bag to make hundred-foot ascents in the escape training tower designed by Momsen. A similar tower was under construction at the sub base at Pearl Harbor. Meanwhile, five other McCann rescue chambers were in production for deployment to sub bases across the globe—New London, Key West, Balboa, San Diego, Pearl Harbor, and Cavite Naval Base in the Philippines. It remained to be seen, however, whether they actually would be put to use in a real emergency. Time would tell.

In the meantime, an entirely new challenge was about to take shape for Allan McCann at the Philadelphia Navy Yard in Pennsylvania. The bureau detached him to work with a famed Australian explorer to modify an antique Navy submarine with one aim: to sail the boat under the Arctic ice cap in hopes of reaching the North Pole.

CHAPTER 7

MAD SCHEME

Schloss Lenzburg
Lenzburg, Switzerland
Summer 1930

Schloss Lenzburg, an ancient castle covering the crest of a three-hundred-foot-high knob twenty miles due west of Zurich, seemed an unlikely place from which to launch one of the most incredible voyages in human history. But that's exactly what Sir George Hubert Wilkins had in mind when he visited this Swiss fortress, owned by his friend and colleague Lincoln Ellsworth, for his honeymoon.

Schloss Lenzburg, the oldest castle in Switzerland, dated back to 1036 and came into Ellsworth's family when his father, James, purchased it in 1911. The wealthy Chicago banker and medieval art collector had intended to buy only a twelfth-century table known to be inside the fortress. But there was a catch: Ellsworth had to buy the castle to get the table. He made the purchase for 500,000 francs and moved in. In 1925 his son inherited the fortress plus his father's fortune. Now, five years later, Lincoln Ellsworth welcomed Wilkins and Australian actress Suzanne Bennett to a setting ideal not only for their honeymoon but for discussions of worlds yet unknown.

Both men were renowned adventurers. Wilkins, who grew up on an Australian sheep station, had been knighted by the queen of England after he made a pioneering 2,100-mile flight over the top of the world from Point Barrow, Alaska, to Spitzbergen, Norway, in 1928. He also was second in command of J. L. Cope's expedition to Antarctica in 1920 and was a naturalist the following year on Ernest Shackleton's voyage to the continent in his ship *Quest*. Chicago-born Ellsworth had earned celebrity status for his flight to the North Pole in a dirigible in 1926.

Famed Arctic explorer Sir George Hubert Wilkins of Australia overlooks Schloss Lenzburg, the oldest castle in Switzerland, owned by Lincoln Ellsworth, heir to his father's fortune as a Chicago banker. Wilkins convinced Ellsworth in 1930 to finance the leasing of an American submarine and underwrite a subsequent voyage to the North Pole. Lieutenant McCann was involved in modifying that submarine, the *O-12*, into Wilkins' *Nautilus*.

Used with permission, courtesy of the Ohio State University Library, http://library.osu.edu/ sites/exhibits/nautilus

Wilkins, forty-one, lean and tall, with a receding hairline and favoring the fashion of an English gentleman with a mustache and a prominent goatee, had a proposal for Ellsworth, fifty, a clean-shaven man with a sunny disposition who favored tweeds and bow ties. Wilkins came to the point. He needed Ellsworth's financial backing for an unprecedented expedition: sail a submarine under the Arctic ice cap from the Atlantic to the Pacific via the North Pole, where the sub would surface to rendezvous with the great German airship *Graf Zeppelin*. The idea of a submarine voyage under the pole had been bobbing around in Wilkins' thoughts since he had joined his first polar exploration in 1913. The 1913 expedition had been commanded by the hard-driving Canadian ethnologist Viljalmur

Stefannson, of whom Wilkins would later note, "He taught me to work like a dog—and then eat the dog." Stefannson believed submarines would be the best means for circumnavigating the ice cap; they could bring to fruition the science-fiction fantasy popularized by French author Jules Verne in his submarine novel, *20,000 Leagues under the Sea*. Stefansson realized that most—if not all—of the ice floated over a deep sea. Navy captain Robert Edwin Peary, who had reached the North Pole by dogsled in 1909, could find no evidence of land. He and his small party lowered a metal weight on a piano wire through a hole drilled in the ice and plumbed the depths to nine thousand feet, yet reached no bottom.

In his pitch to Ellsworth, Wilkins envisioned an epic adventure that would cement both men's legacies and yield untold scientific breakthroughs. Both knew from their Arctic exploits that there were many openings in the ice cap called "leads," also known as "polynyas." During the summer melt seasons, they could be found about every three miles. A submarine could use them to duck in and out of the ice floes between the Atlantic and the Pacific, replenishing the boat's air supplies and recharging batteries en route. Along the way, scientists could make observations and take air, ice, and seabed samples.

At Schloss Lenzburg, the deal was struck. Ellsworth put up $70,000 and a loan of $20,000. If he was able to join the expedition, he promised another $80,000. More money would have to be raised from additional sponsors, but at this stage the expedition was a go, especially because Wilkins had already lined up a submarine. He was able to do that through an acquaintance, Connecticut submarine architect Simon Lake, who had long been enamored by the possibility of an under-ice voyage to the North Pole.

Lake, who grew up in New Jersey, drew inspiration as a child from Verne's tale of the futuristic *Nautilus*. In 1893 at age twenty-seven, Lake entered a competition sponsored by the U.S. government to design a practical submarine. Although the contract was won by naval architect John Holland, Lake went ahead and built *Argonaut I*, launched the same month in 1897 as Holland's *Plunger*, the first U.S. Navy submarine. Lake sailed his submersible along the New Jersey coast in the open ocean and at various other locales. The 36-foot-long boat had wheels for tracking across the ocean floor in search of shipwrecks and a compartment in the bow to allow divers to leave the boat while submerged, similar to the fictional *Nautilus*. Lake's sub also was powered by a gasoline engine that, when submerged, trailed an air hose attached to a float to draw combustible air. Jules Verne was so impressed on reading about the *Argonaut I* that he sent Lake a congratulatory telegram and noted, "While my book 'Twenty Thousand Leagues Under the Sea' is entirely a work of the imagination, my conviction is that all I said in it will come to pass."

In 1898 Lake conceived plans for an Arctic submarine with sled rails fastened to the topside superstructure with a retractable wheel that would allow

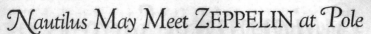

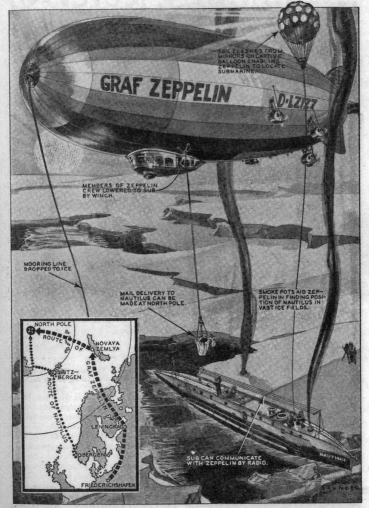

Details of the methods by which the Graf Zeppelin and the Nautilus, Sir Hubert Wilkins' polar submarine, hope to complete at the North Pole the most amazing rendezvous in all history, are pictured in the above drawing. The map shows the route these craft will follow. The Nautilus, described in detail in last month's issue of Modern Mechanics and Inventions, is now on its way to the North Pole.

Cover illustration of Sir George Hubert Wilkins' dream of a rendezvous between his *Nautilus*, the Navy's converted *O-12*, and the German dirigible *Graf Zeppelin* at the North Pole to exchange passengers and mail.

Modern Mechanics and Inventions, *1931*

the sub, with a slightly positive buoyancy, to ride along the underside of the ice. The submarine would also carry a drill to bore holes in the ice to draw air into the vessel. The idea, publicized in an article in the *New York Journal*, drew much criticism. The inventor, stymied in attempts to line up investors and unable to sell *Argonaut I*, didn't give up. He founded the Lake Torpedo Boat Company in 1900 and was able to sell one of his conventional submarines to Russia. Eventually, he obtained contracts from the U.S. Navy for his designs, although he never abandoned his interest in an Artic sub.

Wilkins, hungering after the same goal, had talked up the idea in August 1929 while making an around-the-world flight in the *Graf Zeppelin* with Dr. Hugo Echener, head of Germany's Zeppelin Airship Company. Wilkins suggested that his submarine deliver mail to the *Zeppelin* at the North Pole. Echener agreed that it was possible, but only if Wilkins could get financial backing for such a daring expedition. The explorer thought the necessary finances might come from William Randolph Hearst, the extremely wealthy newspaper magnate who might cash in on rights to the story. But before he worked on the funding, the Aussie had to find some way to secure a submarine. He approached U.S. Navy Secretary Charles F. Adams in hopes of obtaining one of the Navy's mothballed World War I–era vessels. When Adams turned him down, he turned to Lake.

The inventor was eager and offered the explorer a submarine he had built in 1907, the *Defender*. Wilkins considered the boat, but she was too small at only ninety-two feet in length with room for a ten-person crew. He needed a boat double the size to accommodate twenty crew members and scientists plus their instruments. The obvious solution was again to approach the U.S. Navy, which was preparing to scrap O-class submarines under terms of the five-nation London Naval Treaty, signed in April 1930. With Lake's intercession on behalf of Wilkins, the Navy latched onto the idea. However, because Wilkins wasn't a U.S. citizen, it could not directly lease a sub to him. Rather, it deferred to Lake's company to negotiate a lease through the U.S. Shipping Board for one dollar; this enabled Lake to charter one of the O-boats to Wilkins.

The Navy offered the *O-13* (SS-74). When Wilkins balked over the boat's unlucky number, the Navy offered the *O-12* (SS-73), a much less seaworthy boat laid up on the Delaware River in Pennsylvania. With a five-year lease and an understanding that the sub would be returned to be scrapped, Wilkins took charge. The Navy, intrigued by the mission and what could be learned about operations below the ice, attached one of its best hands-on structural engineers to oversee modifications to the boat. Lt. Cdr. Allan McCann was that liaison officer and would be the ship's superintendent during the conversion. Overall authority to decide what changes would be made, however, fell to the man who leased the boat, Simon Lake. He knew her well; he had built her in 1916.

"Lost in Snow Storm"
Philadelphia Navy Yard, Pennsylvania
15 July 1930

Work on the *O-12* began in a dry dock at the Philadelphia Navy Yard in July. Reclassified by the Navy as *OV-16*, the sub seemed ideal for the mission. At 175 feet in length and with a displacement of 560 tons, she could travel up to 7,000 miles without refueling. She was powered by Exide batteries when submerged and twin diesel engines on the surface. She could dive safely to two hundred feet and carried enough air to sustain a crew of twenty for five days.

The extreme environment of the Arctic and the expedition's scientific goals required novel alterations as conceived by Lake with McCann's help. Thirty-two changes would dramatically alter the boat's appearance. The bow torpedo tubes were removed to make room for a pressurized diving chamber that would allow scientists to lower instruments from a hatch to the ocean floor. Heavy quartz view ports were installed the length of the hull, and five-thousand-watt headlamps were mounted on the bow to light up the underside of the ice. A twelve-foot, collapsible bowsprit would serve as an ice bumper. A hollow, two-foot-wide ice drill would unfold and enable the sub to bore through the mantle to a height of thirteen feet above the superstructure to draw air into the boat while submerged and enable crew members to escape if necessary. Enough nine-inch-diameter extensions would be stowed to give the crew the ability to extend the drill more than sixty feet above the vessel if necessary.

Because modifications were progressing slowly and at great expense at the government yard, Lake moved the sub across the Delaware to the Mathis Shipyard in Camden, New Jersey. A retractable conning tower with a periscope was added. A new superstructure was also installed—a wooden enclosure four feet wide and six feet tall that covered additional buoyancy chambers to improve stability when the sub surfaced. Long metal rails with cleats at each end, termed "sledge runners," were anchored to the superstructure to allow the sub to skid along the underside of Arctic ice—an idea from Lake's original vision of an arctic sub that he had been unable to sell in 1898. An eighteen-foot-long outboard motorboat would be stowed under the superstructure. Among creature comforts, Lake incorporated Victrolas for playing music, an organ, a library, and a projector for motion pictures.

Wilkins wasn't happy with some of Lake's changes, especially the sledge runners, the ice drill, and the bowsprit, which he thought might cause the boat to hang up under the ice with no means to get free. The explorer wanted a photosensitive electrical cell that could measure the thickness of ice overhead to determine where best to surface installed beneath one of the quartz view ports. But Lake resisted. Wilkins threatened to withdraw funding but relented after Lake reminded him of their oral agreement that he—not Wilkins—had ultimate authority over the submarine.

Wilkins fretted over the spiraling cost of getting the *O-12* ready, which was coming in three times over budget. "I was appalled at the amount of work which would have to be done to put the boat in shape for the seas," he anguished to associates.

Work continued. Wilkins' job was to line up sponsors. Hearst Enterprises, through its *New York American* newspaper, paid $61,000 for exclusive rights to publish stories and photographs from the expedition. The publisher also agreed to pay Wilkins $150,000 if the airship and the submarine met at the North Pole to exchange mail and passengers. The Texas Company donated $10,000 and agreed to provide all necessary fuel and lubricating oils. Wilkins also published a prequel to his adventure—*Under the North Pole: The Wilkins-Ellsworth Submarine Expedition*—that raised an additional $3,200. Further, the explorer contributed $22,000 in lecture fees to the undertaking.

To add scientific legitimacy, Wilkins obtained endorsements from the American Geographic Society, the Carnegie Institute, the Norwegian Geographic Institute, and the Wood's Hole Oceanographic Institution, based on Cape Cod, Massachusetts. The latter contributed $35,000. Among the scientific goals of the mission would be to find a suitable place for a permanent weather station on the ice cap between the North Pole and Point Barrow, Alaska; sound the depths of the Arctic Ocean; analyze seawater for minerals and life forms; chart magnetic and seismic anomalies in the Arctic; determine the influence low temperatures have on submarines beneath the ice; and demonstrate how undersea vessels could open up the Hudson Bay area of Canada to commerce with the United States and Europe.

With work on the submarine nearing an end in the early spring of 1931, an experienced crew had assembled, chosen from twelve hundred male and female applicants from all over the world. The new skipper would be retired Navy lieutenant commander Sloan Danenhower, who had partnered with Lake to secure the *O-12*. Also hired was Navy chief petty officer Frank Arthur O. Blumberg, a veteran of fifteen years who was granted a year's leave to serve as the boat's chief electrician. Others included QM Edward Clark, Master Diver Frank Crilley (one of two experienced divers on board), CE Ralph D. Shaw, and Radio Operator Ray E. Meyers. Wilkins would be joined by a cadre of scientists who would come on board in Norway. They included Chief Scientist Dr. Harald U. Sverdrup of the Geophysical Institute in Bergen and an observer from the Carnegie Institute.

By mid-March 1931 the submarine was ready to go. McCann, who would monitor the expedition from Washington, was detached and command was turned over to Danenhower. On 16 March the sub cast off for the Navy yard in Philadelphia for a battery charge. Because of a snow storm, it took the skipper two hours to cross the river, a trip normally made in fifteen minutes. The *Philadelphia Call-Bulletin* ruefully ran the headline "Arctic Submarine Nautilus Lost in Snow Storm on Delaware River." Taking on fuel farther downriver, the boat finally set sail and cruised up the New Jersey coast with all systems go. As the boat entered New York Harbor, however, a harbinger of things to come stunned the crew. Assistant Radio Engineer Willard I. Grimmer, twenty-seven and newly wed, was swept overboard by a rogue wave and drowned.

"The Suicide Club"
Brooklyn Navy Yard, New York
23 March 1931

Despite Grimmer's death, a rechristening of the *O-12* went on as scheduled amid international fanfare. A crowd of eight hundred spectators gathered to gawk at the strange vessel, which looked like an enormous, elongated seedpod, tied up at the Navy yard. Dignitaries included Jean Jules Verne, the grandson of the author. The boat's sponsor, Lady Suzanne Bennett Wilkins, used a ceremonial bucket of cracked ice to officially rechristen the scarlet red hull of the *O-12* as the *Nautilus*. Lake chose the name in hopes of capitalizing on the association with author Verne's *20,000 Leagues under the Sea*. Wilkins, who was purely interested in the scientific aspects of the voyage, was skeptical, especially amid public criticism that the voyage was unrealistic. He also hadn't read *20,000 Leagues under the Sea*. Nevertheless, in a letter to donors headed "Wilkins-Ellsworth Trans-Arctic Submarine Expedition," Wilkins noted that he planned to "probe the silent places" and achieve "the prophetic vision of Jules Verne." The visionary Lake viewed the mission as a personal dream come true. He had long championed nonmilitary submarines unfettered by heavy armament and the need to dive and maneuver rapidly. The *Nautilus* was modified to patrol the depths at a casual four knots and had plenty of view ports for close observations. As Lake put it, "I'd like to make that trip over the bottom . . . drift the boat through the streets of Atlantis and peer in through the windows of the drowned palaces. Who knows?"

The *Nautilus* moved up the coast to the New London sub base and from there engaged in trial dives. One was intended to be a deep submergence off Block Island. Although the boat was designed for a test depth of two hundred feet, Danenhower would only risk taking her down to ninety feet. On his command to dive, however, the submarine plunged to the bottom; crew members were unable to stop her until she came to rest on the seabed 240 feet down, where the keel got stuck in the mud. Frantic efforts finally freed the *Nautilus*, and she floated back to the surface. Persistent mechanical and electrical problems beset the boat, delaying the expedition for two months while repairs were made. Wilkins and Captain Danenhower were anxious to get under way in the face of critics who branded those going on the voyage "the suicide club." The skipper offered up to the *Syracuse American* newspaper a worst-case scenario: "Should we fail over an extended period to get air, even by using our emergency drills and dynamite, our batteries would lie dead and useless, we could not move, we could not breathe, we should die," Danenhower theorized. "In that event we might float for years derelict against the underside of the Arctic pack." Such a grim prediction motivated one letter writer to plead with Wilkins to call off his "mad scheme to win notoriety. . . . I fear that when you submerge this summer within the Arctic Circle, we will never hear from you again." Wilkins shrugged off the concerns. He and his sponsors had gone too far to turn back.

On 4 June the *Nautilus* finally headed east. Breakdowns mounted, exacerbated by a severe storm that rattled the crew. By 13 June the engines had given out in the mid-Atlantic. Soon the batteries died, leaving the boat adrift. To Wilkins' chagrin, Danenhower issued a distress call. Two days later USS *Wyoming* (BB-32), which was making a training cruise to Denmark with hundreds of midshipmen from Annapolis, arrived and took the submarine under tow to Queenstown, Ireland, for temporary repairs. From there, a tug hauled the *Nautilus* to Devonport, England, for dry docking and additional repairs, which were delayed until parts could be flown in from the United States.

Back in Connecticut, Lake, who had begun distancing himself from the expedition, expressed doubt that the voyage could or should continue: "An engine cylinder was cracked, two of the pumps were not in condition, the ice drill and conning tower were not functioning properly, and I have been told that one of the large yokes of the generator motor was loose in the rack. In marine engineering, and especially in submarine engineering, there is almost no such thing as a minor defect. A little trouble is apt to multiply into many big troubles."

Wilkins was not dissuaded. Engine repairs were completed. The *Nautilus* would continue on. However, Wilkins' dream of getting to the North Pole to meet with the *Graf Zeppelin* had passed; he had been informed earlier that the boat had to leave Bergen no later than 10 July for there to be any chance of reaching the pole during the summer thaw. That date had passed. Hearst's offer of $150,000 had been dashed. Also lost was a chance to meet up with Wilkins' main benefactor, Lincoln Ellsworth, who had chosen to take the safer course of flying with the airship to the North Pole.

Before the sub departed from England, one crew member lost confidence and left the *Nautilus*. Another, John R. Janson, confided to a reporter, "I am not ashamed to say that from the time we met the storm in the Atlantic every man on the vessel was scared."

The journey resumed on 28 July, bound for Norway, passing without incident and giving Wilkins a boost.

"Most Vulnerable Craft"
Bergen, Norway
1 August 1931

Nautilus arrived in Bergen, a port city on the west coast of Norway, fifty-eight days after leaving the States and two months behind schedule. The five-day layover was just long enough to refuel and take on board a new cook, a photographer, and the party of Arctic scientists who, along with Wilkins, had given up their goal of reaching the North Pole. Still, there was enough scientific interest in venturing at least part way beneath the ice pack beyond Spitsbergen to justify making the voyage. But two more crew members were spooked and dropped out.

The boat departed on 5 August for a 590-mile transit north up the coast to Spitsbergen, Norway's "Land of Pointed Mountains" archipelago, from which the submarine would head across the Norwegian Sea in search of the ice pack. Mechanical difficulties and wild storms that nearly flipped the submarine impeded progress. Chief Electrician Blumberg battled electrical problems the whole way and became disillusioned. Engine problems, a ventilation system that failed, and fears that a collision with the smallest object might send the sub to the bottom haunted him.

The problem-plagued *Nautilus* on the edge of the polar ice cap, where suspected sabotage scuttled Wilkins' further attempts to reach the North Pole.

Used with permission, courtesy of the Ohio State University Library, http://library.osu.edu/sites/exhibits/nautilus

On 19 August the submarine finally encountered her first ice floe and paused long enough for the crew to celebrate by going ashore on an ice cake. For the next three days, the sub followed a polynya. Wilkins still held out hope that the boat could find a way to navigate under the ice as far as the pole. As he noted in his diary, "we will proceed cautiously northward beneath the ice, coming up in the leads and stopping beneath the floes to charge our batteries [by drilling holes to the surface for an air supply to the diesel engines]." On 22 August, Danenhower found an appropriate place to dive. But as the skipper made a last inspection topside, he discovered that the boat's horizontal diving rudders seemed to be missing. Diver Frank Crilley went down for a look and confirmed that the rudders were missing. It appeared that they were deliberately broken off. Without them, there was no steering mechanism for a normal dive.

To Wilkins and Danenhower, there was little doubt that sabotage had occurred to prevent the dive. Wilkins was furious. But what could he do? *Nautilus* had sailed five thousand miles to within six hundred miles of the North Pole but now was unable to dive. Everyone denied culpability. Despite the lateness of the season, Wilkins had clung to the idea of sailing at least some distance beneath the ice pack. Now even that goal seemed lost. Directed by Wilkins, the scientists carried out as many experiments as they could as August passed. Scientists went ashore to conduct ice studies and spent many hours in the diving compartment, lowering instruments to the seafloor to retrieve core samples and plankton.

On 31 August Wilkins and the skipper decided to try diving under ice three feet thick by flooding all of the sub's ballast tanks and setting the trim to two degrees down by the bow—in other words, they would make a shallow dive under the floe on a steady heading that brought the boat up on the other side. "The noise of the ice scraping along the top of the vessel was terrifying," Wilkins noted in his diary. "It sounded as though the whole superstructure was being demolished." But no damage was done. Through the view ports, the explorer witnessed an extraordinary scene. "While submerged, we had for the first time in history gained a seal's eye view of the Arctic ice pack," he reported in a dispatch to Hearst. "We knew what it felt like to be entirely surrounded by water two degrees below the freezing point of fresh water and capped by many tons of amethyst-tinted icicles. . . . With our depth gauge reading 33 feet, we were able to look out through *Nautilus's* quartz portholes to view the steel-like fangs of ice moving steadily through the water as it changed from the influence of light and thickness, ranging throughout the entire range of blues."

For Wilkins, it was a minor but nonetheless invigorating triumph. At least *Nautilus* could claim to be the first vessel to navigate beneath polar ice. Additional semidives were made in early September. Using the sub's floodlights, the crew photographed the underside of ice floes for the first time. However, the Lake-patented ice drill was a failure. Lake's folding periscope also suffered from consistent fogging.

With the storms of fall approaching, Danenhower persuaded Wilkins that it would be risky to stay any longer. It was almost too late. Crossing back to Norway, the boat was battered by a fierce storm that forced the crew to seek refuge in the port of Longyearbyen in Svalbard. After the sub departed Longyearbyen, a worse storm caused massive hull damage and engine failure. The *Nautilus* limped into Bergen but could go no farther. The boat was no longer seaworthy. Wilkins contacted the Shipping Board, which ordered the sub to be turned over to the Bergen Shipping Company, which would scuttle it. The *Nautilus* was to be towed to international waters off Norway and sunk on 29 September. When foul weather forced the sinking's cancellation, Wilkins returned to the United States. Finally, on 20 November 1931 a small flotilla accompanied the *Nautilus* to her final resting place in a deep fjord near Bergen. There crew members opened a valve in the forward ballast tank to begin the sub's descent. At exactly noon, without fanfare, she slid beneath the ocean, a scene akin to the closing chapter of Jules Verne's novel.

Back in the United States after the expedition, the Naval Examining Board concluded that many of Lake's innovations and the mechanical condition of the *Nautilus* made her inappropriate for Arctic conditions. Further, it found no fault with the crew members, who "were justified in their attitude and lack of enthusiasm." The disastrous end to the expedition continued to rankle at Wilkins. In the months to come, he tried to line up financing for a follow-up polar circumnavigation but was unsuccessful. Reluctantly, he turned his attention to Antarctica, where he would join his friend Ellsworth on four successful explorations.

"Great Personal Risk"
Long Beach, California
December 1931

McCann never lost interest in using submarines to cross under the North Pole. But his naval career moved on. He assumed command of one of the Navy's huge, experimental V-class boats, USS *Bonita* (SS-165), to help evaluate her in operations from the sub base at Long Beach. In mid-December 1931 a belated honor arrived. The Bureau of Construction and Repair had awarded McCann a commendation for developing the submarine rescue chamber. "It is noted," the citation read, "that through your intelligent application of an intimate knowledge of submarine materiel and submarine operation, and the various problems involved in deep sea diving, and through great personal risk in subjecting yourself to the dangers of underwater submarine abandonment while in the experimental stage, you have contributed directly and in large measure to the successful development of means for rescuing entrapped personnel from sunken submarines."

McCann was to remain attached to the *Bonita* for five years. The assignment was interspersed with additional duty on the Board of Inspection and Survey. On 18 April 1936 McCann joined USS *Indianapolis* (CA-35) as first lieutenant and damage control officer, and the following year he was assigned to the Damage Control Office on the staff of Commander Cruisers, Scouting Force, USS *Chicago* (CA-29). On 18 June 1938 he reported to the Bureau of Navigation in Washington. There he remained until the spring of 1939, when a submarine disaster off the coast of New England brought him and "Swede" Momsen together again to achieve what had never been done before.

CHAPTER 8

DESPERATE HOURS

One Mile off White Island
Atlantic Ocean
0840, 23 May 1939

*U*SS *Squalus* (SS-192) cut a frothy wake as she roared outbound on an ocean seething with whitecaps. The ink-black submarine, the most expensive ever built by the U.S. Navy, was twenty miles off the coast of New Hampshire and bearing southeast off the White Island lighthouse at the southernmost fringe of the desolate Isles of Shoals. From the bridge, Capt. Oliver Naquin surveyed his $4.3 million wonder speeding along at sixteen knots with no vessels in sight. Named for a snub-nosed, cold-water shark, *Squalus* was the first in a new class of submersibles named after fighting fish and designed to travel with the U.S. fleet anywhere in the world. As the forerunner of hundreds of "fleet submarines" to follow, she was unlike any other boat in Naquin's experience. Only the teakwood slats covering her deck and the 30-foot-high conning tower betrayed the 310-foot-long, 1,450-ton behemoth hidden beneath the waves. It took eleven months and 2 million work hours to build her, one of two sister ships launched in 1938 at the Portsmouth Naval Shipyard on the Piscataqua River between Maine and New Hampshire. Both she and USS *Sculpin* (SS-191) were revolutionary. They could dive deeper than their predecessors, stay down longer, and carry more offensive weaponry, including six torpedo-firing tubes in the ships' bow and four in the stern. The boats' watertight compartments were roomy and brightly lit with satin-finish stainless steel paneling to give them a sleek, futuristic look. The subs also had flush toilets, cold storage for food, and air conditioning to make them more habitable. Veterans of older subs disparaged these "hotel accommodations" but nonetheless were envious. Naquin, a native of New Orleans, appreciated being in command of such a vessel and how that contrasted with his service on the Navy's earlier "pig boats" less than half as large. "Diesel exhaust would be sucked below decks and we'd all reek of it," he recalled of earlier days. "My wife wouldn't let me in the house unless I'd head straight for the shower."

With the new *Squalus*, spirits soared. She had performed flawlessly through eighteen trial dives. Rear Adm. Cyrus W. Cole, commander at the Portsmouth shipyard, was so impressed by the precision of the previous day's three dives that he radioed congratulations, which were posted on bulletin boards throughout the sub. The crucial nineteenth submergence, one of the last hurdles, was now at hand. On Naquin's signal, the sub would dive while making flank speed, simulating the kind of emergency to be expected in a war zone—as if an enemy plane had spotted the boat on the surface and was making a bombing run. Under the

The USS *Squalus* (SS-192) heading out to sea from the Portsmouth Naval Shipyard in Portsmouth, New Hampshire, for a certification dive shortly before she sank in an accidental flooding while submerged in May 1939. Twenty-six officers and crew members drowned and 33 others remained trapped 240 feet down off the New England coast. Their only hope of rescue was the McCann rescue chamber en route from New London, Connecticut.

Naval History and Heritage Command, Washington Navy Yard, Washington, D.C.

watchful eyes of three civilian inspectors, including Don Smith from General Motors in the engine room and naval architect Harold C. Preble in the control room, the boat was to go from diving trim on the surface to being entirely submerged at periscope depth in about sixty seconds, staying below one hour, and then resurfacing to radio results to Portsmouth. It was to be an exact rehearsal of what the *Squalus* would do before the Naval Board of Inspection in June in order to qualify for the operational fleet.

Naquin directed the boat four miles farther out from the White Island lighthouse near the edge of the continental shelf. "Stand be to dive!" he barked at 0840. His command was relayed below. "All ahead emergency!" The boat's Klaxon diving alarm sounded a relentless "ah-ooo-gah" in all compartments. Naquin, his four officers, fifty-one enlisted men, and the civilian observers assumed their stations and knew exactly what to do. Deck hatches were sealed and dogged with hand-cranked wheels. Four diesel engines propelling the boat shut down. Twin overhead induction pipes, each twenty-seven inches wide, from which the engines gulped air through a roaring wind tunnel that opened to the surface aft of the conning tower grew silent. A mushroom-shaped main induction valve—the largest in the boat—slid over the opening to produce a watertight seal. Simultaneously, battery-operated motors assumed submerged propulsion. Enlisted men at large wheels in the control room amidships set the sub's bow and stern diving planes to drive the sub under. Hydraulic valves to ballast tanks girdling the boat's inner shell opened to flood them and give the vessel extra weight by the bow to take her down quickly. Geysers of air spewed skyward like a great leviathan. Naquin took one last breath and then jumped through the conning tower hatch, riding the rails of a short ladder to hit the control room deck as the boat's quartermaster dogged the last of the hatches, the one to the bridge.

As the big sub plunged nose down toward the Atlantic floor, Naquin held onto the periscope sheers alongside Preble, clutching a stopwatch in each hand to mark the beginning of the dive. He and the skipper studied the control room's electrical board, known as the "Christmas tree," as it blinked from red to green, assuring them that all the boat's myriad valves were closed off to the sea. The sub was watertight. Thirty seconds into the dive, Preble enthused to the skipper, "You are going to make it. This is going to be a beauty." At fifty feet, the boat was completely submerged. Preble and Naquin simultaneously shouted, "Mark!" Both stopwatches read sixty-two seconds. "Extra good," noted Preble.

As the boat passed sixty-five feet, the captain noticed a strange fluttering of air pressure in his ears. Yeoman Charles Kuney, listening on headphones to other compartments, repeated what he heard to the captain: "After engine room flooding! Forward engine room flooding!"

Then a shout on the line: "Take 'er up! The inductions are open!"

Naquin, Preble, and Lt. William Doyle, the boat's executive officer, blanched, staring at the Christmas tree in disbelief. This couldn't be. The board showed all green. How could the main induction be open? Yet, the unthinkable had happened. Massive columns of seawater gushed with enormous velocity into the boat's engine rooms, swamping everything in their paths.

In one reflex Naquin and Doyle shouted the alarm: "Blow main ballast! Blow safety tanks! Blow bow buoyancy!"

"For God's sake, close off bulkhead ventilation valves and doors!" demanded Preble.

The *Squalus* rose by the bow, struggling against the weight of seawater pouring into the boat. For a brief moment, it seemed she might make it as her bow broke the surface. Yet there was no stemming the thunderous tide filling the engine rooms. The weight was too much to overcome. The *Squalus* slid backward toward the seabed. Lights flickered as seawater began shorting the batteries.

From forward to aft, crew members tried to stave off disaster. In the engine rooms, they reached for the handwheels of hull stop valves under the inductions to close them off but were blasted aside by the power of the seawater. Most retreated to the after torpedo room, their only hope if only they could close the bulkhead's watertight door in time. But as the angle of the sub's descent increased, the flood overwhelmed them. In the control room, powerful jets of water erupted from a dozen ventilation pipes, knocking Preble flat as others struggled to keep their footing. EM Lloyd Maness struggled to close a three-hundred-pound steel door opening to the after battery. He heard frantic cries: "Keep it open! Keep it open! We're coming!" Seven men crawled and swam uphill. The water had reached waist high by the time the last of them—ship's cook William Isaacs—groped toward the safety of the control room. He collided with a submerged mess table and grappled with underwater objects to pull himself forward. Maness, straining against the flood, kept the door slide ajar so that Isaacs could sneak through. Then he pulled with all his might, his muscles quivering at the exertion, until the door closed with a metallic click.

CE Lawrence Gainor, in the passageway in the forward battery and preparing to close another bulkhead door, saw the commotion in the control room. He recalled,

> The lights were still on with water pouring in from the overhead. It looked like it was following the round contour of the hull, forming a huge water suction hole, a dark green color. I grabbed the watertight door and was nearly swept off my feet by water hitting me in the chest. As I got the door closed, I noted water hitting the glass eyeport at the top of the door. Others

were closing off the ventilation valves at the bulkhead. I felt the control room was flooded full. Knowing we were in deep water, I expected the end.

Gainor noticed the voltmeters monitoring battery cells below him going wild. Seawater had leaked in. A fire or explosion was imminent. Grabbing a flashlight, he dropped down a ladder into the narrow crawl space to locate one of two large disconnect switches. Disengaging it, he unleashed a miniature lightning storm of 70,000 amps sizzling blue-white and melting hull insulation. Half-blinded and sure he would be electrocuted, Gainor reached for the other switch and broke the circuit just in time. "Got it!" he exulted. The entire sub went dark.

Although survivors feared a plunge off the continental shelf and certain doom, the tail of the *Squalus* struck the bottom 240 feet down. The boat pivoted down on her keel, coming to rest in soft green mud with an eleven-degree up angle toward the bow. Inside, the bodies of one officer, twenty-three enlisted men, and two civilians, including Don Smith, were adrift in the water-filled after compartments. Thirty-three others were alive but trapped in the control room, forward battery, and torpedo room. From such depths, no one had ever returned alive.

"Shove Off Immediately"
Portsmouth Naval Shipyard, New Hampshire
1100, 23 May 1939, Two Hours after the Sinking

Admiral Cole was worried. The *Squalus* had not reported surfacing as scheduled at 0940. He contacted the White Island lighthouse. No one there could see any sign of the submarine. The admiral, a slip of paper in his hand, headed briskly for the dock, where he took Lt. Cdr. Warren Wilkin by surprise. He and the *Sculpin* were preparing to cast off later that morning. "I want you to shove off immediately," Cole said. "The *Squalus* may be in trouble. We're not sure. Here's her diving point. I want you to pass over it and let me know what you find without delay."

As *Sculpin* embarked, Cole returned to his office. He called the sub base in New London. The McCann rescue chamber might be needed for the first time in its history. The chamber, one of five spread across the fleet, was on the fantail of USS *Falcon* (ASR-2), a former World War I minesweeper converted to a naval tug and stationed at the base. Cole also phoned the chief of naval operations in Washington to get him to round up the Navy's best deep-sea diving experts and have them stand by.

Sculpin arrived over the last reported position of the *Squalus* at 1300. The coordinates on the slip of paper handed Wilkin, however, were off by five miles owing to a transcription error in Portsmouth. *Sculpin* lookouts could find no evidence of an oil slick or debris of any sort. But one lookout reported the red smudge of a distress rocket on the horizon. *Sculpin* turned in that direction and soon anchored next to a large yellow buoy enclosing a telephone, which was pulled on board. It had been deployed on a long cable from the *Squalus'* torpedo room moments after the tragedy in hopes of attracting a passing vessel. Captain Wilkin opened the buoy and retrieved the phone.

"Hello, *Squalus*. This is *Sculpin*. What's your trouble?"

Lt. (jg) John C. Nichols, repressing excitement, got on the line. He described conditions as Naquin had directed, noting that those in the forward torpedo chamber were in good condition. Nichols reported that the high induction valve was open and the engine rooms and after battery were flooded. He asked Wilkin to hold on while he got the skipper. Thirty seconds later, Naquin spoke with a calm, steady voice.

"Hello, Wilkin."

"Hello, Oliver. How are things?"

"I consider the best method to employ is to send a diver down as soon as possible to close the high induction and then hook on salvage lines to the flooded compartments and free them of water in an attempt to bring her up; for the present, I consider that preferable to sending personnel up with [Momsen] lungs."

At that moment, the ocean heaved in stiffening winds, snapping the cable. The phone went dead. Helplessly, the *Sculpin* stood by while radioing what was known to Portsmouth.

Cole went into high gear. He contacted New London, where the slow-going *Falcon* began the two-hundred-mile voyage north with the McCann rescue chamber. He alerted naval and Coast Guard bases up and down the coast to be on alert in case additional vessels were needed. He phoned Washington to request that the Experimental Diving Unit from the Washington Navy Yard be flown to Portsmouth. Time was of the essence. Among those requested: Cdr. Allan McCann and Lt. Cdr. Charles "Swede" Momsen.

Within hours, news of the disaster quickly spread on radio airwaves. Reporters and photographers massed in Portsmouth. The *New York Times* rushed a street edition into print, "59 Await Rescue on Sunken Submarine."

"Are They Too Deep?"
Airborne over Massachusetts
1900, 23 May 1939, Ten Hours after the Sinking

Momsen was the first to get airborne on a Marine Reserve amphibious plane from the Anacostia Naval Air Station in Washington. With him were two

Navy physicians and CM James H. McDonald, master diver and coholder of the world's deep-diving record—five hundred feet on a breathing mixture of helium and oxygen that the diving unit had been pioneering. McCann had been reached at the Bureau of Navigation in Washington, where he was planning officer in the Personnel Division. He followed Momsen in one of two planes bringing a dozen divers and their equipment.

As Momsen's plane prepared to land on the Piscataqua near the Portsmouth shipyard, he pondered how much depended on what he and McCann had accomplished:

> My memory went back to the first lung experiments, thrills of
> 10 years ago, to the long and tedious years spent in training sub-
> marine officers and enlisted men of the submarine service to use
> the lung; to the first diving bell, the cranky open bell that would
> dump and fall and half drown us if we were not careful, of the
> final design produced by Commander Allen R. McCann and the
> comfort that it was to operate. I recalled the hundreds of thrills
> encountered in training and developing this device. Now the
> dreaded hour was here! Would the dreams of the experimenter
> come true or would some quirk of fate cross up the plans and
> thus destroy all of this work? How many shipmates were waiting
> for the answer? What were they thinking? Were they too deep?

The plane cruised to a soft landing on the river after a three-hour flight. Momsen's party boarded an awaiting barge with their equipment and were ferried to the base for a briefing. Afterward, a Coast Guard patrol boat sped them out to the *Sculpin* and a growing flotilla of private and U.S. Navy rescue vessels. Searchlights lit up the choppy Atlantic in a circle three hundred yards across in case *Squalus* survivors came up using Momsen lungs. Admiral Cole, in the *Sculpin*, warmly greeted Momsen and put him in charge of diving operations that would commence once the *Falcon* arrived.

Far to the south, fog forced McCann and the rest of the divers in the last two planes to land in Narragansett Bay off Naval Station Newport in Rhode Island—125 miles short of Portsmouth. A launch met the divers, offloaded their equipment, and then darted for shore two miles away. There, the base commander placed his personal limousine at the group's disposal, plus a station wagon and a sedan driven by his chauffeur and two civilians. State and local police in Rhode Island, Massachusetts, and New Hampshire blocked intersections and flagged drivers off the road to clear highways for the rescuers who were jammed into the three vehicles. Led by motorcycles with screaming sirens and cars blaring their horns, the procession roared north. The pace was furious. On arriving in Portsmouth, Master Diver Walter H. Squire wiped his brow. "After that trip," he told reporters, "the terrors of deep sea diving are nothing." He, McCann, and the other divers boarded a Coast Guard vessel and left at once for the *Sculpin*.

"Try to Sleep"
USS *Squalus*, Atlantic Ocean
0040, 24 May 1939, Fifteen Hours after the Sinking

Conditions had steadily worsened in the submarine. There had been no word from those aft of the control room. The view from a glass porthole in the door Maness had closed was of a water-filled after battery. Taps on metal tubing running to the stern were not returned; it was clear that no one was alive. Captain Naquin took a head count. Thirty-three survivors. He ordered flashlights extinguished to save the batteries. There was nothing anyone could do but lie still in the dark to conserve air. Some, like F1 Carl Bryson, were strong swimmers and confident of survival. "Nobody had given much thought to dying," Bryson recalled. "We had Momsen lungs. We knew we had a chance. The escape was planned by lung. In fact, we had decided to grease down to protect from the cold of the water." Although he was distributing the lungs and demonstrating their use, Naquin ruled them out for the time being. He'd rather wait for the McCann chamber. He believed frigid ocean temperatures and the great depth, which would require a staged, twenty-five-minute ascent to prevent the bends, would make the chances of survival using only the lungs remote. Preble had never practiced such an escape following McCann and Momsen's decompression tables. Furthermore, he and Isaacs were cold from their dunking and were suffering from scrapes and bruises.

The big enemy at the moment was dwindling supplies of oxygen. Naquin had the men form up in two groups, one in the control room and the other in the torpedo room. The compartment between them—the forward battery— was vacated and closed off owing to the threat of chlorine gas emanating from the seawater-doused battery cells. Blankets, canned fruit, mattresses, and other supplies were retrieved from the compartment before it was sealed. Naquin, who remained in the control room, forbid any discussion of shipmates aft. He ordered survivors to remain calm, to nap, and to conserve air, which he calculated might last forty-eight hours. The control room and the torpedo room contained five bottles of oxygen with bleeder valves that Naquin controlled. He used the oxygen sparingly to slightly refresh the progressively stale, increasingly toxic atmosphere that had already caused three men to vomit and others to endure headaches. He had the men spread lime powder on the decks to help absorb the buildup of carbon dioxide. As the hours passed, temperatures dropped and an icy sheen formed on bulkheads in the compartments. Crew members huddled together under blankets and oil-skin rain gear. In the darkness, the skipper heard the chattering of teeth. Flipping on his flashlight, he took off his coat and draped it around the cold sailor. Using a Momsen lung to cross the forward battery, he went into the bow compartment occasionally to encourage others, telling them, "We should be getting help soon. You must stay quiet. Don't talk. Try to sleep." He whispered encouragement to Nichols, telling the young lieutenant he was "doing just fine."

With telephone contact to the *Sculpin* severed, the skipper sent three survivors into the conning tower to clear insulation from a portion of the steel wall and pound out Morse code with a hammer. The men thought they heard faint replies from the *Sculpin* but couldn't be sure. It wasn't until the harbor tug USS *Wandank* (AT-26) arrived that the penetrating power of her oscillator jolted the survivors and allowed messages to be exchanged. There was encouraging news that the *Falcon* was on the way. Hopefully, the weather would not deteriorate. The world waited.

"I Wanted to Holler Up"

USS *Falcon*, Atlantic Ocean

0430, 24 May 1939, Nineteen Hours after the Sinking

The best hope of rescue—the McCann rescue chamber—arrived in the predawn. The *Falcon* had steamed north at an agonizingly slow speed all through the night with the light gray, pear-shaped chamber strapped to her fantail. As if to emphasize how plodding the tug was moving, the destroyer *Semmes* (DD-189) sped by, as did the 10,000-ton cruiser *Brooklyn* (CL-40), up from the New York Navy Yard and loaded with thousands of feet of high-pressure diving hose that might be needed if an attempt were made to close the induction and refloat the submarine. Up ahead, at the scene of the sinking, the tug USS *Penacook* (YT-6) and *Wandank* spent hours dragging grappling hooks over the likely position of the submarine, trying to snag it. With the use of the heavier anchor from the *Sculpin*, *Penacook* finally latched hold of something. Divers would use that heavy manila line to descend to the submarine. But was it the *Squalus*? Said one rate, "God help us, and them, too, if it isn't the *Squalus* we've hooked."

The *Falcon*'s captain sent a precautionary warning by oscillator to the *Squalus*—"Fire no smoke rockets. I am mooring over you." Easing in close to the drag line from *Penacook*, the *Falcon* lowered four mooring lines in a spread-eagle fashion from the four corners of the ship. McCann, Momsen, Cole, and the divers transferred to the ship to take charge. As the sun came up, the ocean smoothed out and the sky cleared—a blessing.

The McCann rescue chamber arrives at the site of the *Squalus* sinking, strapped to the fantail of the Navy tug USS *Falcon* (ASR-2) on 24 May 1939. The world knew little about the existence of the chamber. The *Squalus* disaster was the first time it was used in a real emergency. McCann flew up from Washington to direct operations.

Naval History and Heritage Command, Washington Navy Yard, Washington, D.C.

Thirty-year-old BM Martin C. Sibitzky, the Navy's tallest diver at six feet four inches and a regular member of the *Falcon* crew, was selected to make the first descent. Earlier he had made a careful study of rescue chamber fittings on the *Sculpin*, which were identical to those on the *Squalus*. After lying prone on the *Falcon*'s deck in his heavy breastplate and eighteen-pound shoes while smoking a cigarette to relax, Sibitzky climbed onto a small diving platform rigged to a hoist. He wore two hundred pounds of rubber diving gear, including his weighted shoes, forty pounds of extra lead ballast on a belt around his waist, and a large metal helmet with thick glass view plates. Standing more than a foot taller than crew members working around him, Sibitzky, in his bulbous suit with air hoses leading to his helmet, looked monstrously alien. Electric underwear, newly developed in Washington, would protect him from the cold of the Atlantic.

By midmorning, a boon hoisted Sibitzky from the deck of the *Falcon* and lowered him into the sea, where it set him free. He guided his descent with the rope from the *Penacook*. Three minutes into the dive, he landed with a thud on the forward deck of the *Squalus* exactly where the anchor from the *Sculpin* had snagged her sister ship. It was only six feet aft of the forward escape hatch. Sibitzky could see the severed buoy cable lying across the hatch. As he made his way to the hatch to clear it, he could hear the hammer taps of those inside the sub. The diver's metal shoes clunking along the deck were exhilarating. "I was up in the escape trunk (just below the forward hatch) when he landed," said Si Donato Persico. "I could hear every word that he was communicating to the surface. Every other word was a cuss word as he grappled with the line. I was so elated I wanted to holler up to him. The only thing that separated us was the thickness of the hull."

Sibitzky cut the buoy cable free, and it slithered down the side to the seabed. He then asked that the four-hundred-foot-long, half-inch-thick steel downhaul cable from a reel inside the rescue chamber be lowered to him. It slid down the rope from *Penacook* to Sibitzky, who lost his grip on the end. Pulled back up, the cable was lowered again. This time he seized it firmly and shackled it to the center of the hatch. Pausing momentarily to catch his breath, he looked out across the ocean floor. He sensed the loneliness of his situation. The sun was barely visible high above, a dim star twinkling through a gulf of blackness that stretched endlessly away.

Sibitzky called for *Falcon* crew members to lift him back to the surface. He was drawn off the deck and floated away, dangling like a puppet in the vault of the ocean. By noon his handlers had him back on board. All was now in readiness to attempt what most in the world believed was impossible.

Inside the *Squalus*, euphoria swept the survivors. Skipper Naquin had drawn up plans after an oscillated message from the *Falcon* indicated that no more than seven men could come up at a time. That meant five trips. For the first, the skipper chose those suffering most, including Preble and Isaacs. Naquin designated Nichols, the sub's communications officer, to accompany them so that he could inform rescuers topside of the status below. As the men waited, the air was heavy with moisture and carbon dioxide making it painful to move about. Many suffered from severe headaches and looked bedraggled. But, as the captain put it, "We'll be out soon, men."

"Hello, Fellows, Here We Are!"
McCann Rescue Chamber, Atlantic Ocean
1130, 24 May 1939, Twenty-Six Hours after the Sinking

"All right, we're ready!" Commander McCann shouted to two crew members standing next to the rescue chamber, eight feet wide and ten feet high. With anticipation mounting, scores of small boats swarmed around the *Falcon* at a distance. Airplanes with photographers, reporters, and sightseers buzzed overhead. Momsen and Admiral Cole watched intently as McCann gave final orders to the rescue chamber's operators, experienced divers TM1 John Mihalowski and GM1 Walter E. Harmon. "Keep us fully informed of your progress," McCann demanded as the two lowered themselves into the chamber through the topside hatch.

At McCann's signal, a boom lofted the 18,000-pound vessel out over the sea and lowered it into the Atlantic, where it bobbed. Two air hoses and electrical cables for the chamber's telephone and bright interior lights ran from the top of the chamber back to the *Falcon*. The operators remained at the controls in the pressurized upper compartment encircled by fourteen auxiliary cans filled with water to be used as seats for the survivors; the water was to be dumped for each passenger taken on board in order to maintain neutral buoyancy. Also stowed on board were extra blankets, flashlights, a pot of hot coffee, a five-gallon milk can filled with hot pea soup, and several cans of carbon dioxide absorbent for delivery to the *Squalus*. Below the upper chamber was a narrow lower compartment open to the sea with a rubber gasket, designed to create a watertight seal over the hatch of the stranded sub, around its lower lip. A horizontal bulkhead with a watertight hatch and a glass view port separated the lower and upper chambers. A ballast tank around the lower compartment controlled buoyancy. The downhaul cable from the reel inside the lower chamber connected the rescue chamber to the *Squalus*. An air-driven control shaft from the winch ran up through the bulkhead to an air motor in the upper compartment. There the operators would control the descent by taking up the line and adjusting ballast through multiple valves. A heavy uphaul safety cable shackled to the top of the chamber ran to the *Falcon* and would play out during the descent.

Harmon powered up the air motor. The chamber's winch started taking up slack in the downhaul cable. McCann and Momsen watched as the rescue chamber crept across the ocean surface about a hundred feet from the *Falcon*. "Then it gradually submerged looking like some sea monster as it sank from sight," Momsen later noted.

The vessel progressed with stops and starts, giving the operators a chance to adjust the ballast and make sure the reel was winding properly. Thirty minutes into the descent, Mihalowski squatted over the view port. He reported the shadowy form of the submarine coming into view. Gradually, it became more distinct, turning from a brown to black, until he clearly saw the deck grate. "The hatch cover is in sight," he told McCann, listening in on the open telephone line to the *Falcon*. The winch pulled the craft gently down around the hatch. With a blast of compressed air, Harmon squeezed seawater from the open end of the chamber and equalized the pressure between the upper and lower chambers. The enormous weight of the ocean at 175 tons per square inch now produced a watertight seal between the chamber and the sub. Mihalowski, the smallest diver in the Navy at five feet five inches tall, opened the hatch leading to the lower compartment and stepped down onto the sub's deck in ankle-deep water. There he attached four steel bolts to rings around the forward hatch as a safety measure. Harmon then slackened the downhaul cable so that Mihalowski could open the torpedo room hatch. The diver had practiced the maneuver many times. But now he was about to free the crew of a stranded submarine for the first time in history.

Unbeknownst to him, however, the survivors had closed a secondary hatch at the egress of the escape trunk after a message from the *Falcon* told them to expect some water to drain down on top of them when the rescuers opened it. Swinging a latch on the deck hatch, Milhalowski let the cover fall open below. As expected, seawater swirled down into the sub. Leaning into the opening, he and Harmon shouted in unison, "Hello!" There was no reply, just an echo. Both men were mystified.

Unable to see the bottom of the trunk leading into the torpedo room, Mihalowski grabbed a flashlight, looked into the orifice and saw the lower hatch. He worked his way down to it, pulled out a wrench, tapped the hatch several times, and cranked the cover open. Again, residual water spilled below. Persico, who got drenched, was ecstatic seeing the diver's shoes. "They were black, torn sneakers which were wet. To me, they were the prettiest sight in the world."

Bending down to look below, Mihalowski viewed the collective faces of beaming *Squalus* crew members. "Hello, fellows, here we are!" he announced.

The sudden blast of fresh air from the rescue chamber revived the men. Mihalowski remained perched overhead in the trunk so that he could lower the hot coffee and soup Harmon passed to him. Someone cracked, "Where in the hell are the napkins?" After Mihalowski handed down carbon dioxide absorbent and other supplies, Lieutenant Nichols motioned to the six crew members chosen to go up first. "OK, let's go," he said. Weakened by the long ordeal, the men stood and nearly fell. "Good luck," said a survivor who would stay behind. "See you in Portsmouth," came the reply. Another shouted to the operators, "Tell them topside to send us down a quart and I don't care whether it's a quart of soup, ice cream, coffee, or whiskey." To which another chimed, "Make mine a blonde."

"All right, Preb," said Nichols, "you're first man out."

"Just a moment, John, I want to get something," replied Preble. All eyes turned to him as he fumbled with a flashlight, looking for articles on a bunk. His fingers sorted through them until he found what he was looking for—personal items brought on board and stowed in the forward battery by General Motor's Don Smith, who was lost in the engine rooms. Carefully, Preble placed them in his pocket to give to Smith's widow. The poignancy struck the survivors, three of whom cleared their throats; Isaacs bit his lips. The divers helped

Preble climb up through the hatch and into the rescue chamber. The others followed with little conversation. Harmon yelled down to those left behind, "We'll be back before you know it."

Mihalowski closed the hatch at 1256. With the seal broken with the *Squalus*, the chamber moved off as the operators unrolled the downhaul cable. They maintained a close eye on pressure gauges so that the chamber did not gain too much buoyancy, which might cause it to break away from the cable. The climb took thirty minutes.

"Who Could Remain Calm?"
USS *Falcon*, Atlantic Ocean
1330, 24 May 1939, Twenty-Eight Hours after the Sinking

People leaned over the rails, watching the gray roof of the chamber slowly come into view and halt, still underwater but illuminated in bright sunshine. McCann, riveted to the action throughout the drama, could be heard over the telephone, "You're almost out; blow the lower compartment dry." He turned to those on deck and said, "Take up the slack of the lines. They're coming up!"

At 1333 on 24 May, the chamber bobbed to the surface next to the *Falcon* and two men leaped onto the overhead as McCann called out over the telephone, "All right, inside the chamber, open the hatch!" The cover flipped open. At first no one emerged. Finally, the ghostly, unshaven face of a survivor appeared through the chamber's hatch. "It's Nichols!" shouted a sailor on the *Falcon*. Momsen was beside himself. "In the eyes of the outside world this was a miracle," he later said. "We tried to appear calm and maybe others were but to me this was the most exciting moment of my life. Eleven years of preparation, combating skepticism and constructing imaginary disasters, all telescoped into one moment. Who could remain calm?"

Nichols winced as sunlight fell across him. Two seamen helped him climb topside, one gripping him around the waist to steady him. Others reached down to pull him on board. Another seaman placed a blanket around his shoulders. On ships and planes above, cameras rolled, recording every moment to be shown around the globe. One at a time, six survivors followed the lieutenant. The fresh air was so intoxicating that one fell backward in a faint and was carried on deck. The "lucky" seven were given first aid, including warm towels placed around their abdomens, and then they entered the *Falcon*'s decompression tank.

Below the *Falcon*, twenty-six remained entombed in the *Squalus*. McCann wasted no time redeploying the rescue chamber to get them. Diver BM1 William Badders and Harmon made the second descent. McCann had contemplated bringing up more men on each trip and had asked Harmon and Mihalowski on their way up with the first load how much reserve buoyancy they had. Plenty,

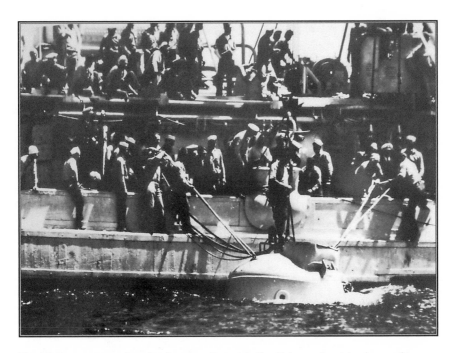

The McCann rescue chamber in seas alongside the *Falcon*, about to descend to the stricken *Squalus* to make history's first rescue of a submarine crew from great depth.

Naval History and Heritage Command, Washington Navy Yard, Washington, D.C.

came the reply. Knowing this, Badders decided on a change in plans: "I got to thinking that I had operated this chamber probably more than anyone else in the Navy, and I knew it could handle more than seven passengers and two operators. I decided I was going to bring more men up. The weather was fair when we started the rescue, but I knew how quickly squalls could spring up, and the havoc they would wreak on this operation. Also, there was the danger of a bulkhead giving way in the submarine and flooding the area where the men were."

The second descent went smoothly over the next two hours. The chamber brought up nine survivors. "I hadn't said a word to anybody topside about this, I just came up—with no difficulty—with nine men," said Badders. "Momsen was on the deck when I came up. He said, 'You brought out too many men on this trip, but do it again,' which I did."

At 1624, the third trip down began. Two hours later, nine more men emerged from the rescue chamber and boarded the *Falcon*. Eight more survivors remained, including Captain Naquin. At 1841, with the sun setting, James H. McDonald, a chief petty officer from the Washington dive unit, and Mihalowski were chosen for the fourth descent.

"Something's Wrong"
USS *Squalus*, Atlantic Ocean
1841, 24 May 1939, Thirty-Three Hours after the Sinking

Captain Naquin had moved the men in the control room forward to the torpedo room. They used their Momsen lungs to cross through the forward battery compartment to avoid breathing the chlorine gas leaking from the cells. Doyle, Persico, and Bryson were among the last men left in the boat. The skipper, who had supervised the loading of survivors on the second and third trips, now waited as seven more survivors climbed up into the rescue chamber. He cast a glance back at dank *Squalus* and then became the last man to leave the sub. He closed the lower escape hatch behind him, entered the upper chamber, and seated himself on one of the emptied water cans next to his men. The operators flooded the lower compartment and partially blew the ballast, enough to establish positive buoyancy and break the seal with the *Squalus*. At least they thought so.

They started backing off the air motor, which began feeding the downhaul cable from the winch into the lower compartment. After a short period, the men realized the chamber was not ascending but rather was still on the sub's hatch combing. "Something's wrong," McDonald said to Mihalowski. At that moment, they made the wrong decision, according to McCann, by again blowing the ballast tank. The vessel jerked free, swiftly taking up the slack in the downhaul cable until the chamber came to a jarring halt at 160 feet, sixty feet above the submarine. McDonald reversed the motor, forcing a descent of a few feet. When he put it in forward motion, the chamber came to an abrupt halt at 155 feet, where the air motor failed. The rescue chamber remained stuck, unable to move up or down.

McCann, over the telephone link, directed the men to try different methods to undo the jam, but without success. Worse, unbeknownst to anyone, the force of the accident had caused strands of the uphaul cable attached to the top of the chamber to rip near the surface and begin to uncoil.

Rescuers in the *Falcon* faced a grave situation. McCann determined that there was only one recourse: Lower the chamber by flooding the ballast to slacken the cable connecting it to the *Squalus*, and then send a diver down to unlatch the downhaul wire or cut it. Once the chamber was free of the sub, the uphaul line could be used to winch the survivors to the surface.

As instructed, the operators took the rescue vessel down to 210 feet, where it began to list slightly from the slack in the downhaul wire to the *Squalus*. The chamber remained there to await a diver. Momsen selected ChTorp Walter H. Squire. The mission would be extraordinarily dangerous given the depth and darkness. McCann gave Squire final instructions as crew members worked to fit him with his equipment, including his bulbous hard hat, air hoses, and cables. "Unshackle that wire to the *Squalus* if you can," McCann told the diver. "Otherwise cut it."

Sliding down the line from the *Penacook*, Squire landed heavily on the deck of the submarine. He could see light emanating from the glass port of the rescue chamber floating off to the side. Moving forward in slow motion across the sub's deck, he reached the rescue hatch and trained his light on it. He located the downhaul wire but could not unlatch it. He reached for the wire cutters dangling from his belt and cut the line, releasing the rescue chamber. The chamber swung like a pendulum from the uphaul wire into the side of the *Squalus*, crashing hard against her and rattling the survivors. McDonald tried to lighten the mood. "Well, I'll be darned if that isn't the first time a collision like that ever happened," he said with a grin. "You fellows have really got something to talk about now. A collision between a rescue bell and a submarine at more than 200 feet! It isn't everybody that can tell a story like that."

With the chamber at negative buoyancy and dangling heavily at the end of the uphaul cable, crew members on the *Falcon* began drawing it in with a winch at McCann's direction. The chamber had just begun its ascent when those on the *Falcon* noticed the frayed strands of the cable and shouted an alarm. Stunned, McCann ordered the cable released to prevent it from breaking and ripping away air, light, and telephone hoses and suffocating the men inside the rescue chamber. The chamber fell precipitously, hitting the seafloor with a thud 240 feet down. Fortunately, it didn't topple over. Those inside knew something was wrong, but what? Bryson, who grew up in rural South Carolina, muttered to Persico, "I should have followed my old man's advice when he said to use a mule's ass for a compass and you won't get lost." The operators feigned there was nothing to be concerned about. "Here we are nice and steady on the bottom and we've got plenty of good air and lots of light and everything," Mihalowski said cheerfully. Both divers kept up the conversation, straying to thoughts of the comfort food they'd eat once they were free and trading jokes.

Topside, Cole, Momsen, and McCann decided to send a diver down to attach a new uphaul cable to the rescue chamber's topside. TM1 Jesse E. Duncan was chosen but got caught on the frayed line on the way down. Working himself free, he relayed stunning news that a single strand of the six-strand steel cable held the chamber. Resuming his descent, Duncan landed atop the chamber. There his lines became entangled with the chamber's air and electrical cables. In the struggle to untangle himself, he nearly slipped. If he had, because of the weight of his helmet, he would have plunged headfirst to the seafloor and been killed. After the struggle, Duncan was nearly incoherent because of the exertion and depth, so *Falcon* crew members hoisted him back to the surface for decompression. Another diver was sent down. M1 Edward Clayton landed on the chamber without incident, but he too became entangled owing to dim illumination. Inside the chamber, Mihalowski slid a steel plate slightly open over the chamber's glass view port on the side of the vessel in hopes that ambient light would help. He couldn't risk opening it fully, should the diver slip and kick in the glass.

For more than a half hour, Clayton squirmed to free himself while trying to shackle the new uphaul line. The exertion nearly caused him to black out. Alarmed, Momsen ordered him back to the surface and called off further attempts. "It's hopeless at this time of night; the divers are in too great a danger," he told McCann. Clayton came up to fifty feet, and because Duncan still occupied the *Falcon*'s decompression chamber, he remained there to complete a lengthy decompression.

In McCann's mind, only one possibility for rescuing the rescue chamber remained, and it would be extremely challenging. By carefully controlling the ballast, the operators would give the vessel a neutral buoyancy, allowing the frayed cable to be pulled up by hand from the *Falcon* so as not to put any strain on it. The risk was that the chamber could shoot to the surface, perhaps smashing into the wooden hull of the *Falcon* and sinking both the ship and the rescue chamber.

Calculating how to adjust the air pressure, McCann relayed orders to blow ballast at fifteen-second intervals while six men topside gripped the uphaul line with a slight tug. Once the chamber came to neutral buoyancy, the lift would begin.

At four minutes past midnight on the third day of the rescue, McCann telephoned the operators to begin. He stayed on the line, a stopwatch in hand, and yelled "Stop!" after every fifteen-second blast of compressed air into the ballast tank. The pattern was sustained until the six handlers on deck could move the chamber with a light pull. Admiral Cole, leaning far over the rail, kept a keen eye on the cable. It began to move. "Slowly now, men, until we get the stranded part on deck, and remember there's only one strand left," McCann cautioned them.

Inside the chamber, the survivors fixed all eyes on the depth gauge as it tracked the ascent just past midnight. At 0005, 228 feet. At 0006, 215 feet. 0008, 200 feet. 0012, 190 feet. 0013, 180 feet. 0014, 170 feet. 0019, 110 feet. 0023, 50 feet. Exhilaration replaced tension on board. "I'm practically eating a steak right now," joked one of the survivors.

Clayton, decompressing in the icy ocean while suspended on lines like a marionette, watched as the dimly lit rescue chamber floated past him like some ethereal sea creature.

"Never Any Doubt"
USS *Falcon*, Atlantic Ocean
0025, 25 May 1939, Thirty-Nine Hours after the Sinking

The chamber bobbed to the surface, and the hatch opened. Bryson, Persico, and the other enlisted men emerged one at a time under the bright floodlights of the flotilla. Momsen was there to greet each one of them. Once on deck, they were aided by the ship's physicians who led them inside. Doyle and Naquin were next, the skipper being last. After poking his head from the hatch, the captain ducked back in, then returned, grinning. He had left his logbook inside. On reaching the deck of the *Falcon*, Naquin looked up at Momsen's beaming face. "Welcome aboard, Oliver!" Momsen said. "I am damn glad to be aboard," replied the captain.

The last group from the *Squalus* proceeded to the decompression chamber, where they would remain for a few hours. Meanwhile, their identities and the identities of those lost were announced in Portsmouth. Emotional reunions

Survivors of the *Squalus* gather for a group photo shortly after their rescue by the McCann rescue chamber. Lt. Cdr. Oliver Naquin, the captain, holds a silver sailboat given to him by his grateful crew for what he did to preserve hope and morale in the desperate hours of entombment in the submarine.

Private collection of Carl LaVO

with family members occurred as each group of survivors came ashore and were taken to the hospital for examination. Others grieved. Naquin arrived in the last group on board the Coast Guard cutter *Harriet Lane*. To observers, he seemed the quintessential Hollywood sub captain with his tall, erect stature. He waved but wouldn't repeat the gesture at the urging of photographers. Rather, he started toward his wife, who fretted that the cameras would spoil a private moment. As he approached, she mouthed, "Don't kiss me, don't kiss me." He kissed her anyway. Both stepped into an awaiting sedan for the trip to the hospital, where they addressed the media. Preble praised Admiral Cole for his fast response to the tragedy and the instinctive actions of Lawrence Gainor. "In my estimation," he said, "Gainor's quickness in noting the high rate of discharge and his bravery in entering the battery tank and pulling the switches to prevent fire in the forward battery can by no means be overlooked." Maness told of closing the bulkhead door to the after battery after letting a few men slip through. Naquin praised Maness for saving the lives of those in the control room. Maness also insisted that he was confident of rescue: "There was never any doubt in my mind at all that we would come up, especially after we heard from the *Sculpin* that the *Falcon* (with the McCann Rescue Chamber) was underway."

"Well Done!"
House of Representatives, Washington, D.C.
26 May 1939

A day after the miraculous rescue, Rep. Allen T. Treadway of Stockbridge, Massachusetts, drew thunderous applause at the regular session of Congress when he mentioned Allan McCann's name:

> Mr. Speaker less than 48 hours ago the country was shocked at the terrible tragedy of the sinking of *Squalus*. When the news came to us we received it with great sorrow in that the probability was that all these valuable lives had been lost. This morning we learned that 33 out of the 59 were rescued. The submarine bell used in rescuing these heroes was invented by the first candidate whom I appointed to Annapolis after I came to Congress in 1913. [Applause.] This young man, because of his energy and ability and because of the education he received at the Naval Academy and later under other naval auspices, gave this country and the world an invention that undoubtedly will continue to be used in future years to save the lives of the men who go down under the sea in ships. Certainly it is a credit to the Naval Academy and to the Navy Department and it is a credit to my district that Allen

Rockwell McCann invented the very intricate bell by which the lives of these 33 heroes were saved yesterday.

McCann was hailed a hero in his hometown. But as a modest man who preferred to defer credit to others, the commander was uncomfortable in the spotlight. He asserted at every occasion that the chamber was "a bureau development," that it shouldn't be named for him. But the name stuck and was recognized in every ocean where one of the devices was stationed.

Internationally, praise for what the Navy had accomplished spilled over in the days following the rescue. "A splendid page in the annals of the U.S. Navy," noted the *Illustrated London News*. "The American Navy has accomplished a feat of seamanship which deserves universal acclaim," trumpeted *Boerson Zeitung* in

Cdr. Allan R. McCann (left) and Cdr. Charles B. Momsen look on as Acting Secretary of the Navy Charles Edison reads a letter of commendation from President Franklin D. Roosevelt following the rescue of the *Squalus* survivors and the successful salvage of the submarine. The boat was refitted, was rechristened the USS *Sailfish* (SS-192), and achieved great valor in World War II, surviving the entire war. The bridge of the boat is now enshrined at the Portsmouth Naval Shipyard.

Naval History and Heritage Command, Washington Navy Yard, Washington, D.C.

Germany. *Deutsche Allgemeine Zeitung* joined the chorus: "The achievement of the rescue crew in those tense hours will be counted among the most impressive peacetime accomplishments of the United States Navy."

The rescue was all the more remarkable given the loss of 329 lives in submarine tragedies within days of deliverance off the Isles of Shoals. In the Bungo Channel of southeast Japan, eighty-one perished in the Japanese I-63. Sixty-three others died when the French boat *Phoenix* was lost at a depth of three hundred feet off Indochina. And only six days after the *Squalus* rescue, HMS *Thetis* sank in 160 feet during a practice dive in Liverpool Bay. There was no way to reach the ninety-nine crew members, who either drowned or suffocated. Scorn was heaped on the British navy for not having developed a rescue chamber. The plans had been offered to any country who wanted them. Germany, Russia, France, Japan, Denmark, the Netherlands, Norway, Sweden, Yugoslavia, Poland, Argentina, Brazil, and Peru received them. But submarine powers Italy and Great Britain preferred to go their own ways.

After the rescue, McCann remained attached to an unprecedented effort to raise the *Squalus*. The Navy was intent on salvaging its state-of-the-art investment. Because divers needed to work for long hours at a depth of 240 feet, Momsen authorized them to begin using the experimental breathing mixture in which helium replaced nitrogen. It alleviated the major threat of nitrogen narcosis, the effect of nitrogen in normal air causing a narcotic effect on the brain at depth. Now divers could think clearly and remain down longer while doing many strenuous tasks to prepare the submarine to be lifted and towed back to Portsmouth. They attached air hoses to the *Squalus* to blow seawater from her water-filled compartments and tunneled under the hull so that steel chains could be threaded from one side to the other. They created slings out of the chains and anchored them to gigantic, water-filled pontoons, each the size of a small house that could be blown dry to lift the boat. The work involved fifty-eight divers who overcame many obstacles. The plan was to raise the sub halfway to the surface and then tow it toward port until she grounded in shallower water, where conditions would be more advantageous to divers in preparing for a final lift. During the first lift on 13 July 1939, the sub's tail remained stuck in the mud. Blowing the main ballast on the boat freed her suddenly. Preceded by the pontoons, the boat soared to the surface. The *Squalus* survivors, working with the salvage crew, watched in horror. Said one, "There was a tremendous roaring of air coming up. The water was just boiling from the air. Then the pontoons started coming up. It was frightening." The bow of the submarine rose thirty feet into the air and then slid back into the depths, slipping her harness and releasing the pontoons that flopped around on the surface out of control. Crew members on the *Falcon* used axes to chop air lines to the pontoons as divers used small surf boats to chase them, climb on board, and close valves to keep them from sinking. None of the divers was injured, but one of the pontoons sank and was lost.

With a new harness fastened around the *Squalus* on the seabed, subsequent lifts finally brought the submarine back to the surface. She was towed into Portsmouth on 13 September, after 113 days and 628 hard-hat dives. After the sub entered dry dock at the Navy yard, the bodies were removed. A court of inquiry visited the craft and discovered that the induction valve worked flawlessly. The court had earlier heard from Naquin, his officers, and his crew and ultimately concluded that no one was at fault, that the accident was caused by a mechanical malfunction. It also praised Naquin's leadership through the crisis. Charles Edison, acting secretary of the Navy, accepted the findings but faulted the skipper for not training his men to always close inboard inductions prior to a dive. For Naquin, the reprimand was devastating because so many other boats operated no differently than his.

Because of the accident, all fleet submarines were built with bulkheads dividing the engine room into two compartments. Also, hand-cranked valves on induction lines were replaced by quick-closing flapper valves to prevent a repeat of what happened to the *Squalus*. The boat would undergo a $1.4 million refit over a year's time and then be rechristened USS *Sailfish* in hopes of diminishing her previous reputation. The *Squalus* survivors, except Naquin and Doyle, who were reassigned to the surface fleet, continued in the undersea service.

In its probe of the accident, the court of inquiry had called McCann to testify. He impressed the judges by describing the rescue chamber's development and how it performed. Asked directly what recognition he had received, the commander replied that he had been given none except a letter commending him for disregarding his own safety in testing the device as it neared completion. President Franklin D. Roosevelt righted that by presenting a commendation to McCann and others involved in the rescue and salvage, noting, "Your determined and efficient efforts have held the attention of the entire nation and the successful completion of this unprecedented task merits the highest approval and admiration. . . . Well done!"

McCann had little time to dwell on the *Squalus*. Detached from the salvage operations, he returned to the Bureau of Navigation as planning officer in July. War with Japan and Germany, then on the offensive in China and Europe, respectively, was imminent. The entire U.S. Navy went into readiness mode. By May 1941 McCann had assumed command of Submarine Squadron 6 of the Pacific Fleet. As fate would have it, he would be at the sub base in Pearl Harbor on the very morning Japan attacked.

CHAPTER 9

UNBELIEVABLE

USS *Pelias* (AS-14)

Pearl Harbor, Hawaii

0730, 7 December 1941

*A*llan McCann had rehearsed the eventuality of war in his mind many times throughout his twenty-five-year military career: on guard in the Chesapeake and coastal Atlantic in World War I for possible German submarine intruders, on guard against surprise attack on both sides of the Panama Canal in the 1920s, standing ready from ports on the West Coast for possible deployment to the Far East after Japan invaded Manchuria in the 1930s, and now on guard in Hawaii in case Japan made a move against U.S. territories in the western Pacific. McCann had left his wife and teenage daughters behind at the family home in Washington when he was assigned command of Submarine Squadron 6 in May 1940. At age forty-five, he had never seen war up close and hoped he never would. On 7 December 1941, a peaceful Sunday morning, on a ship anchored in a tropical paradise, McCann could hardly imagine that hostilities would come at him in mind-numbing fury in a matter of minutes.

The weekend was one of relaxation for many of the thousands of sailors, soldiers, and airmen assigned to Pearl Harbor. Officers and their families could relax on pristine Waikiki Beach, a playground for wealthy Americans, while enlisted men enjoyed the city's shops, shows, bars, and brothels on Hotel Street. "Cinderella liberty" for them meant that they had to be back on base by midnight, and many woke with inevitable hangovers on Sunday morning.

McCann had risen early in his cabin on board his 8,000-ton sub tender. USS *Pelias* (AS-14) was moored at the sub base with a clear view of Battleship

Row. Moored on the far side of the harbor's Southern Lock, the dreadnaughts USS *Nevada* (BB-36), USS *Arizona* (BB-39), USS *Tennessee* (BB-43), USS *West Virginia* (BB-48), USS *Maryland* (BB-46), and USS *Oklahoma* (BB-37) were lined up end to end on the interior side of Ford Island in the center of the harbor. From *Pelias*, McCann had command of twelve modern fleet submarines in Squadron 6: *Tautog* (SS-191), tied up at a finger pier near the tender; *Tambor*, *Thresher* (SS-200), *Triton*, *Trout*, and *Gudgeon* (SS-211), out on patrol; and *Tuna*, *Gar*, *Grenadier*, *Grayling*, *Grampus*, and *Grayback*, back in the States for repairs or on shakedown cruises. Another nine boats of Squadron 4 were also based out of Pearl, but only the *Cachalot* (SS-170), *Dolphin* (SS-169), and *Narwhal* (SS-167) were in Pearl that Sunday morning.

As was his habit before breakfast, McCann methodically powered through the steps of the Navy's physical fitness program while in his pajamas. He followed a regimen designed by world heavyweight boxing champion J. J. "Gene" Tunney, a Marine veteran of World War I and U.S. Expeditionary Forces boxing champion of 1921. Tunney was the "thinking man's" pugilist; he was known for analyzing the fighting ability of his opponent in the first few rounds of a match. That skill and lightning-fast foot speed made him formidable; he won all but one of his sixty-eight official bouts. Tunney had developed a conditioning regime that had attracted national interest. Promoted to lieutenant commander and head of the Navy's physical fitness programs, he popularized a fifteen-minute daily exercise routine that could, in his words, "remove puffy inches off your waistline, recondition unused muscles, [and make one] feel better, work better and live longer." To him, there was nothing worse than poor posture and a flabby constitution, especially in the military. McCann did Tunney's calisthenics religiously each morning, fifty each of four exercises that maintained the commander's tall, lean frame.

During these solitary workouts, McCann often thought about his life and especially a military career that began in World War I, in which he saw no action, and then extended into decades of peacetime submarine, surface craft, and shore duty. He was frequently on the frontier of plans for a second conflict. He and the rest of the fleet had thoroughly practiced elements of the War Department's War Plan Orange and War Plan Red. The two plans anticipated conflict with Japan and England as far back as 1900, following the successful U.S. war with Spain, in which the United States took possession of Guam, the Philippines, and other islands in the western Pacific. With no means to properly administer or defend the territories, the United States worried that both Great Britain and its new ally, Japan, might conspire to seize the islands. President Theodore Roosevelt's administration created the Joint Army and Navy Board to formulate a defensive strategy. When Japan's Imperial Navy emerged victorious over the powerful Russian fleet in 1904–5, the Red and Orange battle plans took on greater urgency under the assumption that Japan's need for natural resources, including oil, might compel it to seize the Philippines as a staging point for a further advance on oil- and mineral-rich Malaysia. The Joint Board envisioned a two-theater war in which the Army and Navy would first win the Battle of the Atlantic with England under Plan Red and then deploy the fleet through the Panama Canal to defeat Japan in a climactic Pacific battle under Plan Orange. Between 1921 and 1924 the plan evolved under the assumption that Japan would attack the canal and U.S. bases in California and Washington. As a result, the Army and Navy strengthened their presence in the Philippines and on the West Coast. In the 1930s anxiety grew as Japan invaded Manchuria and China, withdrew from the League of Nations, closed access to islands in the western Pacific mandated to Japan for helping Britain in World War I, and abrogated naval arms limitation agreements, giving Tokyo freedom to greatly enlarge its navy. In the summer of 1940 the U.S. Pacific Fleet, including all its battleships, relocated from fleet headquarters in San Pedro, California, to Pearl Harbor to send a message to Japan not to attempt a move against the Philippines or any other American possessions. By the fall of 1941 Japan had 10 aircraft carriers, 10 battleships, 35 heavy and light cruisers, and 111 destroyers, compared to 3 aircraft carriers, 8 battleships, 24 heavy and light cruisers, and 80 destroyers in the combined U.S. Pacific and Asiatic Fleets. Odds favored the Japanese Empire if war came.

On McCann's arrival at Pearl Harbor from the Navy Department, tensions between Japan and the United States were near the breaking point. By then War Plan Orange and War Plan Red had settled on one scenario: Germany had replaced Great Britain in Plan Red, and Japan remained the enemy in Plan Orange. The strategy was first to win the war with Germany and its ally Italy, which were overrunning Europe and North Africa while threatening England and the Soviet Union. The Pacific forces of the Army and Navy would have to stiffen in a holding pattern to stall Japan if it invaded the Philippines. The Joint Board, concluding that Japan would succeed in taking the islands, envisioned the Navy responding with the massed fleet at Pearl Harbor in a progressive campaign of island hopping, slowly moving west over several years and ending in a climactic sea battle somewhere off Japan. McCann's long-range fleet submarines and other sub squadrons would be used immediately to harass and sink Japanese ships.

For Commander McCann, Plan Orange warfare still seemed over the horizon as he focused on his calisthenics on board the *Pelias*. The *Pelias* towered over the submarines nested at nearby finger piers, the boats tiny slivers in contrast to the former West Coast passenger liner with her complement of 925 officers and enlisted sailors. Tied up near the submarines was USS *Widgeon* (ASR-1), the primary rescue ship in the area of Hawaii. From the *Pelias*, McCann could clearly see the gray cylindrical rescue chamber named for him, strapped to the fantail of the *Widgeon*.

On the *Pelias*, McCann lived closer to the nerve center of the harbor. Yet there was no hint of the slaughter heading his way on the morning of 7 December. Below deck, breakfast was being served to the crew. The ship's large cargo doors were open to the fresh air and stunning views of the island's palm vegetation and the spiny Koolau Mountain Range, running north–south along the eastern edge of the big island of Oahu. George Kelley, a *Pelias* plank owner, and his buddies had just begun to eat when they saw a massive formation of planes coming directly at them from the direction of the Hawaiian highlands. Topside, Robert Eakin was chatting with an officer on deck when both noticed the aircraft flying low and heading for the harbor. "We thought the approaching aircraft was the Army Air Force practicing weekly maneuvers," he later recalled. "We didn't think anything of it until we started hearing machine guns and bombs."

McCann heard the explosions. Still in his pajamas, he rushed to the bridge and issued a general quarters alarm that sent submariners racing to their battle stations. As the senior commanding officer present, McCann couldn't believe what he was seeing. The initial wave of Japanese dive-bombers flew by the *Pelias*, swung around the ship, and turned west to jettison torpedoes at the battleships. The *Arizona* exploded in a fireball. As McCann later described it, "It turned my stomach upside down . . . unbelievable." He added that Japan's surprise attack against a country not at war was "shabby . . . absurd."

The sky above the tender soon swarmed with enemy aircraft coming in from the southwest, bombing and strafing ships in the harbor plus aircraft hangars and planes on Ford Island. The *Pelias* was especially vulnerable because she had not yet been fitted with her full array of antiaircraft weapons. Momentarily, McCann held off return fire in fear that many of his gunners hadn't had target practice and might hit other Navy ships. He also considered getting under way to clear the harbor, but the escape route quickly became clogged by exploding ships and flaming wreckage. McCann feared the worst as a flight of torpedo bombers roared directly at the *Pelias* as if intent on blasting the ship. But they flew right over the tender and continued on to attack Battleship Row.

As the severity of the aerial assault became clear, *Pelias* gunners opened up with every available weapon—from handguns to rifles, machine guns, and antiaircraft batteries. Seaman Kelley was a loader for one of the ship's .50-caliber machine guns. Realizing that the ammunition was in a padlocked container and that the key was in the possession of an officer on liberty in Honolulu, twenty-seven miles away, Kelley found a bolt cutter, broke the lock, retrieved the ammunition, armed the machine gun, and rattled off shots at the marauders overhead.

SN Warren Hewett, eighteen, was serving breakfast when he felt an explosion and scrambled topside. "The Japanese bombers flew right beside us, turning to get to the battleships," he later recounted. "We had a ringside seat."

At the nearby barracks of the sub base, eighteen-year-old SN Edward "Dutch" Gaulrapp, who was a baker in USS *Pompano* (SS-181), which had returned to the West Coast for repairs, was in the middle of a card game. "We heard a loud explosion and looked at each other like 'what the hell is that' so we all went outside. At first we thought the Navy was practicing, but when we saw the *Arizona* go up in flames and they started sinking the ships beside her, we knew we were under attack." Base officers issued Gaulrapp and others .30-caliber rifles and ordered them to shoot anything they could fire upon. "It scared the hell out of us," Gaulrapp recalled.

Lt. Bernard Clarey, executive officer of the submarine *Dolphin*, was eating breakfast with his family at his hillside home, about a ten-minute drive from the sub base, when he noticed smoke rising from aircraft hangars at the Army's Hickam Field and antiaircraft bursts from Hickam and Pearl Harbor. Hopping in the family car, he, his wife, and his fifteen-month-old son sped toward the base. He recalled, "We took the back road which in a few minutes gave us an overview of the horrible sight of Battleship Row and the smoke and fire from burning planes and buildings. Concerned for my wife and son, I got out of the car on the highway leading to the Pearl Harbor Gate and told my wife I would call home as soon as I could. I hitchhiked to the base about a mile away." When he arrived on the *Dolphin*, he found that duty crew members had manned all machine guns and small arms and were shooting at enemy planes as they passed about four hundred yards astern of the boat at a finger pier.

The disbelief over what was happening deepened as battleships, destroyers, and cruisers took a pounding for two hours from two waves of 353 Japanese dive-bombers, torpedo bombers, high-altitude bombers, and fighter aircraft launched from six aircraft carriers 230 miles to the north. Within minutes the harbor was an inferno.

In its counterattack, the *Pelias*' two forward and two aft antiaircraft guns fired two hundred rounds of ammunition. Her two forward and two aft .50-caliber machine guns expended five thousand rounds. Under the combined fire of the *Pelias*; the submarines *Tautog*, *Cachalot*, *Dolphin*, and *Narwhal*; a destroyer at the submarine dock; and a group of patrol torpedo (PT) boats anchored behind the tender, one dive-bomber was brought down. It fell into the sea just off the finger piers before it could launch its torpedo. Gunners on *Tautog*

A rescue craft approaches the inferno on the USS *West Virginia* (BB-48) to rescue survivors after the 7 December 1941 surprise attack on Pearl Harbor by Japanese torpedo bombers. Commander McCann was on board the submarine tender USS *Pelias* (AS-14) at anchor within sight of the battleship. As the senior commanding officer in *Pelias*, he organized a counterattack against incoming bombers as well as rescue efforts to bring injured officers and crew members to the sub base for treatment.

U.S. Naval Institute photo archive

claimed the score. Another enemy craft was turned away in its bombing run. It began to stream smoke and fly low over the officer's club, and then it crashed. The four submarines of Squadron 4 and Squadron 6 kept up antiaircraft fire and were complemented by sub base personnel manning 250 rifles, 15 automatic rifles, and 15 machine guns.

Amazingly, enemy aircraft did not attack the *Pelias*, the submarines, or commander, Submarine Fleet, U.S. Pacific Force (ComSubPac) headquarters. Also left untouched were scores of nearby oil storage tanks containing 4.5

million gallons of volatile fuel to resupply the fleet. Nevertheless, the attack dealt a devastating blow as revealed in numerous deck logs of besieged and ill-prepared ships:

> Planes heard and sighted attacking Ford Island hangars. . . . *Oklahoma* struck by 3 torpedoes on port side; rapid heeling of ship. . . . Airplane with large red disks on bottom of wings; sounded general quarters and made attempts to locate ammunition. . . . Torpedoes dropped from about 50 feet after submarine base pier passed. . . . Observed BBs [battleships] attacked from astern by about 10 dive bombers. . . . Two heavy shocks felt on hull of *West Virginia*; ship begins [to] list rapidly to port. . . . Last explosion flashed a flame about 15 feet high forward on *Arizona*. . . . Wall of flame advancing toward *West Virginia* and *Tennessee* from *Arizona*. . . . Oily water around stern burning. . . . Canvas awning on stern on fire; some so thick, cannot see. . . . *West Virginia*'s quarterdeck and planes on fire. . . . . Squadron of planes diving on Navy Yard. . . . Abandoned station too hot. . . . *Oklahoma* seems to be capsizing. . . . *California* down by the stern. . . . *Tennessee* hit twice. . . . *Nevada* underway to clear channel but struck by torpedo or mine. . . . *Utah* attacked by torpedo plane and bombing plane; severe underwater hit. . . . *Arizona* on fire. . . . Tugs trying to pull overturned *Oklahoma* clear. . . . *Nevada* underway and standing out, dive bombed, hit several times and beached. . . . Enemy pilots directing fire at civilians. . . . Damage repair party sent to capsized *Utah* to cut men out of hull. . . . Two destroyers in dry dock with *Pennsylvania* hit. . . . Both destroyers heavily on fire; no hose available for fighting fire. . . . Superstructure on *West Virginia* on fire; 4 or 5 men trapped, trying to escape by crane. . . . Bow blown away on *Arizona*.

By noon, the attack was over and the harbor was ablaze. McCann helped direct rescue efforts from the *Pelias*. Crews in small boats headed into the channel to assess the wreckage and effect rescues. "We got in the patrol boats to pick up the bodies and it was awful looking down in that oily water," Gaulrapp recalled. "There were times when I would reach out for an arm, and only half of one would come out of the water. I never could wear my whites again after that day." From his battle station, Kelley watched the horror of it all as deckhands in the patrol boats brought in dead and wounded to the sub base. One sailor lifted a corpse from the harbor. It was half a body. The hips and legs were gone. Burned skin tore loose from other bodies brought ashore.

The *Widgeon*, off-loading its McCann chamber and taking on its own divers and those at the sub base's Momsen lung escape training tank, motored over to Ford Island to try to save more than four hundred trapped sailors in the overturned *Oklahoma*. The *Widgeon* encountered burning oil spewing from ruptured tanks on the *Arizona* and threatening the *Oklahoma* and *West Virginia*. Under orders from the battle force commander, the *Widgeon* joined the *Tern* (AM-31) and *YG-17* in battling the fire to keep it from spreading. Afterward, the sub rescue ship moved in on the ravaged battleships. Divers entered the mangled interiors in search of survivors. At the overturned *Oklahoma*, they could hear tapping from inside the hull and proceeded to cut through the metal with welding torches. Unfortunately, rescuers discovered after breaking through that the torches burned up oxygen inside the ship, suffocating some survivors. The release of air pressure inside the ship also caused water levels to rise, possibly drowning others. Realizing what had occurred on recovering the bodies of men previously alive in one of the compartments, salvage workers turned to hammers and chisels to pound their ways inside the ship, and thirty-two sailors eventually were saved.

Back at the sub base, submariners worked with hospital and ambulance crews or aided rescue parties returning from Ford Island. All facilities at the base were made available to survivors, who were fed and clothed. More than fifteen hundred blankets and two thousand mattresses were distributed on the lawn to make sailors coming in off the sunken ships comfortable. Wounded were treated at the base dispensary.

By day's end, the toll on the Navy was overwhelming. The Japanese had sunk the battleships *Utah*, *Arizona*, *West Virginia*, *Nevada*, *California*, and *Oklahoma*. Suffering serious damage were the battleships *Tennessee*, *Pennsylvania*, and *Maryland*; the cruisers *Helena* and *Raleigh*; the destroyers *Shaw* and *Downes*; and the service ships *Vestal* and *Curtiss*. Navy and Army Air Forces lost 188 combat aircraft, and another 159 were damaged. Bunched together at Oahu's Hickam, Wheeler, and Bellows airfields to prevent attack by possible saboteurs before the raid, the planes were easy targets for enemy bombers. Most sobering was the human toll—2,335 military and civilian personnel killed and 1,143 wounded.

In the attack on Pearl, the Japanese succeeded in immobilizing most of the U.S. Pacific Fleet. They had hoped to achieve a coup de grâce by sinking the aircraft carriers *Saratoga*, *Lexington*, and *Enterprise*, but they were not in port. *Saratoga* was on the West Coast, and the other two had left Pearl a few days before the attack to deliver aircraft to U.S. bases on Midway and Wake Islands. Japan's failure to hit the carriers was about the only saving grace for the U.S. Navy. Yet there were two others: The nation's undersea fleet in the Pacific had escaped mostly unscathed, and the fuel depots at Pearl had avoided bombardment.

"Ground to Powder"
White House, Washington, D.C.
1300, 7 December 1941

Word of the Pearl Harbor disaster arrived at the White House while President Franklin D. Roosevelt was eating lunch. British prime minister Winston Churchill soon called to encourage the president to enter the war. Churchill recalled, "To have the United States at our side was to me the greatest joy. Now at this very moment I knew the United States was in the war, up to the neck and in to the death. So we had won after all! . . . Hitler's fate was sealed. Mussolini's fate was sealed. As for the Japanese, they would be ground to powder."

Roosevelt addressed an emergency session of Congress, urging the legislators to declare war on Japan and its Axis partners, Germany and Italy, terming 7 December "a day that will live in infamy." With Congress' quick acquiescence, the War Department ordered the Navy and Army to wage unrestricted air and submarine warfare against Japan. Yet quick retaliation depended mostly on the nation's submarine fleet. The twenty-one submarines based in Pearl Harbor and the twenty-nine of the Asiatic Fleet out of Subic Bay were the only real hope of blunting Japan's lightning-fast offensive threatening the Philippines and points south. The gravity of the Pearl Harbor destruction would ramp up within hours as news arrived that Manila and the Navy base at Cavite in Subic Bay had been bombed and that a massive stockpile of submarine torpedoes and the fleet sub *Sealion* (SS-195), in dry dock, had been destroyed. Japanese bombers also obliterated the Army's air force based near Manila. Dozens of B-17 Flying Fortress bombers under the command of Army general Douglas MacArthur, who had been recalled from retirement to head American and Filipino ground forces, could not get airborne in time and were destroyed. Worse, a Japanese invasion force of 2 battleships, 3 carriers, 45 destroyers, and 100 transports, bearing 43,000 Army troops and supported by 500 land-based aircraft, was about to land on northern Luzon, and another large force swept south along the Malaysian Peninsula, threatening British Singapore, Indonesia, Borneo, and northern Australia.

With Cavite in ruins, Adm. Thomas C. Hart, commander of the U.S. Asiatic Fleet, withdrew most of his fleet to Australia. That included the heavy cruiser USS *Houston* (CA-30), the light cruiser USS *Marblehead* (CL-12), and thirteen World War I–era destroyers. Left behind was Hart's force of twenty-three modern submarines, including the former *Squalus*, renamed the *Sailfish*, and the *Sculpin*, to fight it out with the advancing Japanese navy. The situation deteriorated for the U.S. Army in the Philippines by late March, and President Roosevelt ordered MacArthur to evacuate to Australia and from there become Supreme Allied Commander of the South West Pacific Area. With Germany and Italy in military alliance with Japan, the United States faced the grim reality of exactly what War Plan Orange and War Plan Red had envisioned—fighting wars in the Atlantic and Pacific simultaneously while depending on the immense industrial base of the United States to replenish what had been lost. It would take time. Meanwhile, the War Department counted on Navy and Army forces spread across the Pacific to hold the line, to stall the Japanese any way possible.

CHAPTER 10

DEAD ISSUES

ComSubPac Headquarters
Pearl Harbor, Hawaii
7 December 1941

*T*he Pacific high command was determined to strike back hard against Japan, a sentiment shared by American submariners throughout the Pacific. Said William B. Sieglaff, duty officer in the *Tautog*, about to make her first war patrol, "After the carnage at Pearl Harbor—a sneak attack—who could have moral qualms about killing Japanese. Every ship they had, combat or merchant, was engaged in the war effort one way or the other."

ComSubPac officers convened a meeting within six hours of the attack to develop a strategy for employing the undersea fleet against the enemy. Four subs moored at Pearl had not been damaged. Five others outside the harbor made it in safely to create a rather meager combined force of nine. Attending the conference were Rear Adm. Thomas "Tommy" Withers, fifty-five, ComSubPac and a kindly, soft-spoken veteran of World War I sub duty; Lt. Cdr. Charles "Gin" Styer, Withers' chief of staff; Rear Adm. Freeland Allan Daubin, Squadron 4 commander, in charge of six old V-boats (*Argonaut*, *Nautilus*, *Narwhal*, *Dolphin*, *Cachalot*, and *Cuttlefish*) and three of the latest fleet boats (*Pompano*, *Plunger*, and *Pollack*); and McCann, commanding Squadron 6, consisting of a dozen submarines, only two of which were in Hawaii at the time, *Gudgeon* and *Tautog*. Their task was to decide how to best deploy seven of the nine subs that were armed and ready to go from Pearl. "Plan Orange was a dead issue," McCann later said of that strategy session. "There would be no cruise to the Philippines for a decisive blow against the Japanese fleet. The submarine force was left on its own, to do what it could against the Japanese sea lines of communication. Fortunately the fleet boat was ideally suited for this new and completely unexpected mission."

As the officers considered their options, Adm. Husband E. Kimmel, commander of the Navy in the Pacific, interceded, worried that the Japanese might be mobilizing for a second strike at Pearl from the Marshall Islands, two thousand miles southwest of Hawaii. Kimmel ordered Withers to send most of his boats to the Marshalls to scout for the enemy and sink any enemy vessels they came across. Withers sent four—*Pompano, Dolphin, Thresher,* and *Tautog*—speeding to the Marshalls, while three others—*Gudgeon, Plunger,* and *Pollack*—cast off to patrol the coast of Japan. Two others would delay departure to effect repairs.

Despite the low numbers, ComSubPac and commanders of subs in the Southwest Pacific, based in Manila, were supremely confident of success. The most modern of the subs, the fleet boats, were equipped with radical new weapons that the Navy thought would make them quite lethal with a single torpedo launch. Among each boat's armament of twenty-four torpedoes were improved Mark 14 torpedoes with warheads containing top-secret Mark 6 magnetic exploders, developed by the Navy's Bureau of Ordnance. The "fish" were longer, faster, and heavier and had twice the explosive power of previous models. Most important, the magnetic feature worked on the principle that all steel-hulled vessels create a magnetic field in the sea around them—enough to trigger the exploder as it penetrated that field, breaking the ships' lightly armed keels and sending them to the bottom. No longer would it be necessary to make direct contact to sink a vessel. At least that was what those at the Bureau of Ordnance believed. The technology was so secret in the late 1930s that only just before war broke out did the Navy authorize sub commanders and their torpedo officers to learn of its existence and be provided manuals concerning its operation. The reason: the Navy feared that if Japan learned of the magnetic feature, it would alter construction of its ships to strengthen their keels.

After learning the secret, some sub skippers remained skeptical because none had witnessed a live test. Lt. Cdr. Lewis Parks of Squadron 4's *Pompano* asked for a demonstration, but the Navy turned him down, explaining that the ordnance factory in Newport, Rhode Island, could produce only ten of the incredibly complex weapons per month owing to prewar budgetary constraints. The Navy did not have the luxury to "waste" any in target practice. Instead, a laboratory test in Hawaii was arranged for the skipper and his executive officer, Slade Cutter. "The way they demonstrated its effectiveness was to set one up in the torpedo shop at Pearl Harbor and pass a charged wand over it," explained Cutter. "It would go 'click,' and they would say, 'See, it works.' This was supposed to simulate a torpedo going through the magnetic field of a ship." The demonstration left Parks and Cutter doubtful. Nevertheless, the simulated tests were enough to convince higher-ups that the weapon would be decisive.

Top commanders, including McCann, were resolutely convinced that the torpedoes would do what was intended. They could hardly wait for the initial results of war patrols.

Unfortunately, critical anomalies had not shown up before the war because of Bureau of Ordnance miscalculations and faulty testing. So now, with World War II under way and U.S. submarines closing in on enemy ships with expectations of sinking them, officers were in fact sailing into jeopardy with defective weaponry. There would be profound consequences.

"His Face Turned White"
USS *Sailfish*, Lingayen Gulf, Philippines
13 December 1941

USS *Sailfish*, the former *Squalus*, under the command of Lt. Cdr. Morton Claire Mumma Jr., had been deployed from Pearl Harbor the previous October to fortify the Asiatic sub force. Mumma had been chosen to shake the sub's reputation as a "ghost ship," a reputation earned after her tragic sinking years earlier. The Navy had renamed her *Sailfish* after her recommissioning in order to erase her past. But sailors in the fleet scoffed, referring to her as the "Squailfish." It took a brave man to join a sub that had sunk with loss of life in 1939. Nevertheless, many did. And now, on the third day after the Japanese attack on the Cavite Navy base and the bombing of Manila, the boat was in position with its Mark 14 torpedoes to sink Japanese warships approaching the Lingayen Gulf with an invasion force of thousands of soldiers.

Contact with the enemy came at 0230. Lt. Joseph R. Tucker, the officer of the deck, confirmed sighting three ships on the dark horizon. Because of the sub's silhouette in the moonlight, the warships spotted *Sailfish* and turned toward her, dropping depth charges as they charged. "We dove and began listening on sound," said COB Lester Bayles, referring to hydrophones extended into the ocean below the boat. "According to the soundman, there were three sets of propellers. We knew then that three destroyers were operating together. Our soundman was very experienced."

Mumma used the sound bearings to set up an attack. At 0250, with the boat at periscope depth, he fired two Mark 14s.

"I was in the conning tower after the first 'exploded,'" recalled SM Claude Braun.

> Mumma was on the periscope at the time. But there were no breaking-up noises of any vessel going down. Mumma says to me, "Braun, see if you can see anything." So I stepped into the

periscope and he said, "Leave it right there. We haven't moved that much. You will see one of two destroyers up there."

"I see a shape up there, sir, but I don't see any fire or explosion. Nothing." I looked right at Mumma and his face turned white. Then the second torpedo hit at a longer range without exploding. When the second one was a dud and the guy on the hydrophone said he had a hit, Mumma said, "You got a hit?!" And nothing happened, no explosion. His knuckles stood out as he gripped the periscope ears. And that's when he put the ears up, lowered the scope, and said, "Take her down!"

Sailfish evaded the destroyers and lived to fight another day. But the failure of the new torpedoes had unnerved Mumma, who would relinquish command to another skipper back in Manila.

"What It Was Like to Face Death"
USS *Pompano*, Marshall Islands
11–16 January 1942

Skipper Parks had just arrived off Wotje Island in the Marshalls when he discovered the 16,500-ton former luxury liner *Kamakora Maru*, now a troop transport, at anchor in a narrow channel. The *Pompano* lay in wait offshore overnight. At dawn, as the liner left port, Parks was in excellent position to sink the ship from close range and gave the order to fire four torpedoes. "We heard the hits and Parks saw the splash of water through the periscope, so he assumed that it was going to be sunk and went to deep submergence," said Cutter. The torpedoes, however, proved to be duds. The liner accelerated, quickly leaving the scene. Crew members in the sub mistook the noise of the ship's propeller churn as evidence of the vessel breaking up.

For four days, Parks, who was known for his aggressiveness—what some considered reckless command tactics—lingered outside the harbor, looking for other targets. On the fourth, two destroyers on patrol drew his interest. He decided to go after one of them. As Cutter explained, "We fired two torpedoes with magnetic exploders, and both of them exploded before they could hit the target." Parks readied for a third shot. "Jeez, I'm on TDC [torpedo data computer] and I got from Parks, 'Range twelve hundred yards, speed 25, angle on the bow 2 degrees port, stand by.' And I put on the solution light. 'Fire!' About this time Parks came down, 'Slade did you ever have so much fun before with your clothes on?' And over the loudspeaker system. Well, I wasn't worrying about having fun with clothes on or off about that stage of the game."

The third shot also detonated prematurely, enabling the destroyer to bear down on the *Pompano* by tracking back on the torpedo wake. There was little time to escape. A dozen depth charges exploded around the boat, battering it and terrifying the crew. One blast raised the bow several degrees. The swoosh of seawater through the boat's superstructure frayed nerves. "I knew then what it was like to face death," said Cutter. "We thought we had been holed. So I thought, that's the end and you don't feel anything."

The *Pompano* made a narrow escape. It had launched seven torpedoes at two targets from close in, resulting in four duds and three premature explosions. The boat would be the first to return to Pearl Harbor from an extended war patrol and would be mistakenly credited with sinking the troop transport. Cutter's cryptic note in the patrol log about the "utter unreliability" of the magnetic torpedoes in the attack on the destroyer was dismissed by senior officers who blamed the crew for improper maintenance of the weapons. Squadron 4 commander Daubin oppugned Cutter's note about the torpedoes. "If the above torpedoes were unreliable," the rear admiral wrote in his assessment of Parks' patrol, "the *Pompano* had ample time to find it out before the torpedoes were fired. After the torpedoes were issued, the *Pompano* gave the torpedo shop no indication that the torpedoes were found to be unreliable. The Torpedo Officer of the *Pompano* commented to the effect that the torpedoes were fine, but that there were two and possibly three premature explosions. The shop is taking steps to prevent premature explosions of the exploders."

Suspicions about torpedo reliability among *Pompano* officers and crew members were just the latest in a growing body of evidence from all over the Central and Southwest Pacific that the new torpedoes were a colossal failure. Most believed they traveled too deep. Others blamed the magnetic exploder. Sub captains, including Parks, begged Withers in Pearl to allow them to deactivate the magnetic feature. But the admiral refused. He cited a critical shortage of torpedoes and the Navy's belief that one magnetic warhead could sink a ship, whereas it would take two or three contact torpedoes to do the same job.

"Total Failure"
USS *Grenadier* (SS-210), Tokyo Bay
7 March 1942

Lt. Cdr. Allen Raymond Joyce's fleet boat, assigned by Allan McCann to scout the bay for enemy targets, was submerged in daylight when the commander made periscope contact with a freighter. The crew went to battle stations, and Joyce fired four torpedoes. Although he believed he got one hit, the skipper noticed the ship sailing on. The crew reported hearing three "thuds" as if the torpedoes hit without detonating. Joyce fired two more torpedoes. They too did no damage. Discouraged and noting in his report that he was "tired," Joyce broke off patrol early to return to Pearl Harbor empty-handed.

McCann and other top base commanders were irate, terming the patrol a "total failure" and appending stinging comments to Joyce's official patrol report. McCann was especially critical of Joyce firing six torpedoes at a single, slow-moving freighter. "The torpedo supply does not warrant such a prodigal use of torpedoes," McCann noted, adding, "Torpedoes must be fired to hit and the results must not be left in doubt." None of the commanders noted the "thuds" in Joyce's report, possible evidence of torpedo duds. Joyce was relieved of command, never to serve in submarines again.

"Demoralized"
USS *Sculpin*, Kendari, South East Sulawesi
31 March 1942

Lucius Chappell, commander of USS *Sculpin*, the sub that located *Squalus* on the ocean bottom off New Hampshire in 1939, patrolled off the Indonesian city of Kendari in the Indian Ocean, looking for the whereabouts of Japanese Carrier Division 5. Intelligence reports indicated that the warships had sortied from the Philippines for a suspected raid on northern Australia, thought to be the next aim of Japan. *Sailfish* and *Sculpin* were among the boats now operating out of Fremantle on the coast of Western Australia. The boats were positioned to help defend the subcontinent from attack.

Capt. John Wilkes, commander of the Fremantle base near the city of Perth, had received word from code breakers that the carrier division—six carriers and two battleships—had anchored in Kendari's port and were about to leave for Australia. As *Sculpin* lay in wait, the task force never appeared. Rather, the warships veered west for a raid on India. Nevertheless, *Sculpin* intercepted a 5,000-ton enemy freighter and fired three torpedoes at extremely close range. All three missed. Chappell couldn't believe it. Over the next six days, the submarine had ideal setups on two more freighters. Chappell fired three torpedoes at each target. Again they all missed. Furious, the skipper decided something was wrong with the torpedoes and obtained permission to break off the patrol and head back to Fremantle. Appending a note to his official patrol report, Chappell described his frustration after a particularly arduous patrol: "It seemed impossible that they [the torpedoes] could miss, yet no explosions were heard, no hits were observed and the target was heard to continue to run without pause. If the truth must be told, the Commanding Officer was so demoralized and disheartened from repeated misses he had little stomach for further action until an analysis could be made and a finger put on the deficiency or deficiencies responsible and corrective action taken."

Corrective action was slow in coming, however, despite a change of command at Pearl Harbor. Among the changes was a decision to send McCann's Squadron 6 fleet boats in a staged deployment to Fremantle to strengthen offensive actions against the enemy in Malaysia. McCann and the *Pelias* would follow in July. Meanwhile, Rear Adm. Robert English succeeded Tommy Withers as ComSubPac in April, the latter detached to take over the Portsmouth Naval Shipyard in New Hampshire to oversee construction of new fleet boats. English was the officer who had braved fire on board the *O-5* in 1918 to rescue the boat's trapped commander in the Brooklyn Navy Yard. His appointment at first breathed new life into the Pacific Fleet. Yet, to the chagrin of sub captains, he soon fell into line with others who defended the Bureau of Ordnance from criticism and blamed the sub captains even as reports of premature explosions and duds continued to stream in.

"Bitter Dose"
USS *Skipjack* (SS-184), Cam Ranh Bay, Indochina
17 May 1942

Lt. Cdr. James W. Coe, known as a methodical and courageous skipper, had become increasingly skeptical of the new torpedoes on his boat, USS *Skipjack* (SS-184), currently patrolling Cam Ranh Bay. Days earlier he and his crew had made numerous sightings and some successful attacks, but mostly they witnessed torpedo duds and premature explosions. Two torpedoes fired at a 6,000-ton former passenger liner exploded too far away from the target to do any damage. A third passed under it with no hit. On another occasion, two darted under a deep-draft vessel with no detonation. "These fish were set at 10 feet but must be running mighty deep," Coe anguished in the sub's patrol log. "This was a bitter dose and I now have little confidence in these torpedoes!"

On the evening of 17 May, the commander had another perfect setup on a heavily loaded enemy troop transport at a range of seven hundred yards. He wrote of the incident, "I was so sure of a hit that I had not fired a second fish to save it. Watched as smoke from the wake passed directly under the stern of the target. No explosion." Coe, completely disillusioned, saved his last torpedo to be examined back in Fremantle by Rear Adm. Charles Lockwood, the new commander whose appointment was intended to "fire up the troops" of a sub force deep in despair over all the torpedo misses. Recently detached as a naval attaché in London, fifty-three-year-old "Uncle Charlie" was outgoing, energetic, and known for his optimism and for being the submariners' submariner, given his extensive experience as a boat skipper dating back to 1914. Lockwood's first order of business was to give pep talks to buoy morale. Along those lines, he arranged for bands to herald the arrivals and departures of all sub crews. In keeping with the Old West ambiance that existed in Western Australia, the bands played Gene Autry tunes: "Empty Saddles in the Bunkhouse" when the boats departed and "Back in the Saddle Again" when they returned. Meanwhile, Lockwood thoroughly investigated why subs based in Fremantle were not performing up to expectations. He was attracted at once to Skipper Coe's careful analysis of the woeful performance of *Skipjack*'s Mark 14 torpedoes. The admiral dispatched a letter to the Bureau of Ordinance to see if it was aware of any defects that would cause torpedoes to run too deep. The bureau fired back that there were none, that sub skippers were guilty of poor marksmanship. It wasn't the weapon, it was the submariners—an allegation that rankled officers and enlisted who were fighting amid incredible risk.

Frustrated by the bureau's sense of infallibility and reluctance by both the bureau and commanders in Pearl, including Withers, McCann, and Styer, to arrange tests, Lockwood decided to take personal action. He reasoned that in the six months following the attack on Pearl Harbor, American subs had fired eight hundred torpedoes, yet none had been launched in a controlled test because of the Bureau of Ordnance's resistance. That was about to change.

"Restore Their Confidence"
USS *Skipjack*, Frenchman's Bay
20 June 1942

Lockwood arranged for a test firing in the calm waters of Frenchman's Bay near the old whaling port of Albany on the south coast of Australia about two days' sailing time south of Fremantle. Participating with him was Rear Adm. James Fife Jr. on his sub tender, USS *Fulton* (AS-11), stationed in Albany. The problem was how to recover the torpedoes; they were limited in supply and too valuable to waste by losing them in the depths of the ocean. Fife noticed a brilliantly white, sandy beach at a resort town on the bay and conceived stringing a net for the test between the beach and a submarine offshore. Torpedoes fired by the sub would hit the net and then continue on to a landing on the beach. There their black shapes would easily be seen on the white sand, and they would be retrieved for reuse. Fife got four Portuguese fishers to make him five hundred feet of netting for the tests and strung it between buoys six thousand yards offshore. Those on the *Fulton* would witness the test. Skipper Coe brought *Skipjack* to within 850 feet of the netting on the surface. Crew members loaded the suspect Mark 14 into a bow firing tube. The live warhead had been removed and replaced with enough sodium chloride to equal the weight of the original explosive. Set to run at a depth of ten feet, Coe launched the Mark 14 at Fife's command and it raced for the net. When it was pulled up, there was a hole ripped open at exactly twenty-five feet.

It was a revelation—proof of what sub commanders had been arguing for six months. Fife wanted more tests the next day because a single launch did not represent a "scientific sampling." Subsequently, Coe fired two more torpedoes with dummy warheads at the net from closer in, seven hundred yards. One was set to run at ten feet and the other set to run on the surface. Both cut a hole at eighteen feet. No longer did Fife, Lockwood, Coe, or those on board *Fulton* have any doubt that the Mark 14s were defective. By Fife's calculations, the torpedoes ran an average eleven feet deeper than intended, which would cause them to miss the magnetic field of target ships.

These simple tests at Albany could have been accomplished by previous base commanders in Pearl Harbor, Fremantle, and Brisbane who had been informed by the Bureau of Ordnance early in the war that Mark 10 torpedoes on older S-boats tended to run four feet deeper than designed. Fleet boat captains suspected the Mark 14 similarly ran deep, but no one authorized any tests.

On 22 June Lockwood forwarded the results of his trials to the Bureau of Ordnance. Eight days later, the bureau rebuffed him, saying "no reliable conclusions" could be drawn because the torpedoes' trim conditions were improperly adjusted to compensate for the dummy warheads. The admiral, furious, vowed to repeat the tests with proper trim. He also suggested the bureau do its own test and send him the results—which it never did.

Fife reanchored the net in the bay. On 18 July, five days before McCann arrived on board the *Pelias*, the sub *Saury* (SS-189) fired three fish at the net from between 850 and 900 yards. Set to run at ten feet, all three pierced the net at twenty-one feet. Lockwood considered the case closed; the torpedoes ran too deep. He quickly transmitted the results back to the Bureau of Ordnance and waited for a reply.

Meanwhile, other commanders weighed in. In Washington, Fleet Adm. Ernest J. King Jr., after reading Lockwood's field test results, had Adm. Richard Edwards, his deputy chief of staff, undertake an exhaustive study of torpedo attacks. Edwards' review concluded that at least half of all torpedoes fired by U.S. subs missed their targets for some mysterious reason. King ordered the bureau to recheck data from all torpedoes, stressing "it was of utmost importance not only to supply submarine personnel with correct data but in addition to take steps to restore their confidence in the reliability and accuracy of the performance data furnished them." On receipt of Edwards' report, ComSubPac English ordered his sub skippers to subtract eleven feet in calculating running depth for their torpedoes—but to continue to rely on the magnetic warheads.

On 1 August the Bureau of Ordnance at last tested the Mark 14s, launching them from the submarine *Herring* (SS-233) off Newport, Rhode Island. Six weeks later, in mid-September, the bureau admitted design flaws in the depth mechanism and issued instructions to boat commanders everywhere as to how to modify the torpedoes to run within three feet of depth settings. Although some commanders, like Lewis Parks in the *Pompano*, had grave suspicions about the magnetic warheads and had deactivated them without permission, fleet commanders in the Pacific, including McCann, insisted they be used since the depth control issue had finally been rectified. The Mark 14s now were primed and ready to pierce the magnetic fields of enemy ships and destroy them with a single shot—as intended.

It did not work out that way, however. The torpedoes continued to misfire. And the sub that proved the Mark 14s were running too deep would also provide hints of yet another major fault.

"Most Disappointing"
USS *Saury*, off the Island of Rabaul
18 November 1942

The submarine under the command of Leonard "Tex" Mewhinney had received reports of an approaching convoy of several big ships, including the 7,500-ton aircraft carrier *Hosho*, making preparations for the pivotal Battle of Guadalcanal, the costly turning point of the war for the Allies. The night was brightly lit by the moon when Mewhinney's *Saury* came across the convoy. The sub moved in from 2,200 yards in perfect position to sink the *Hosho*, built in 1922 as Japan's first carrier. Mewhinney fired a spread of four torpedoes at 0206. The first exploded prematurely, scattering the convoy. Screened by destroyers hunting for the *Saury*, the *Hosho* and the cruisers made a safe getaway.

Four days later Mewhinney targeted a 5,000-ton cargo carrier with four torpedoes from nine hundred yards. None exploded. Then on the night of 26 November, the skipper took aim at a 4,000-ton cargo ship and launched a spread of three torpedoes from seven hundred yards. All ran straight and normal. Again, no explosions. One torpedo was seen to run right under the transport. The ship sailed on.

Disappointed, Mewhinney and the *Saury* headed for Pearl Harbor for an overhaul. On arrival, Admiral English blamed the skipper for bad judgment for firing so many torpedoes without success, terming it "most disappointing." Mewhinney later recounted, "In my post-patrol interview with Admiral English, I told him that some of our torpedoes were exploding prematurely or not exploding at all. He replied that SubPac had never had a premature explosion."

Resolving the Mark 14s' depth control problems had obviously not corrected the situation. Something else was wrong.

"Duds!"
USS *Trout* (SS-202), off Borneo
11 January 1943

Skipper Lawson "Red" Ramage of the *Trout* had received intelligence from code breakers that a 17,000-ton tanker, the *Kyokuyo Maru*, was being loaded with oil in the port of Miri on the west coast of Borneo. After dark, the *Trout* slipped in unnoticed on the surface to within three thousand yards of the tanker, and Ramage launched four torpedoes. Two hit amidships, causing a tremendous explosion. But the third exploded prematurely and the last was a dud.

The *Trout* returned to the open sea and proceeded to Cam Ranh Bay, where the boat sank a 3,000-ton freighter before accurately attacking a destroyer with three torpedoes from nine hundred yards. All three failed to explode as the warship chased the *Trout* under. Ramage later fumed in his patrol log, "Duds!"

Returning to Borneo, Ramage continued his aggressive patrol off Balikpapan, where he found a 2,000-ton freighter, which he attacked with two torpedoes from seven hundred yards. The first blew off the bow of the ship, but the second hit without exploding. Another dud. Ramage surfaced and closed on the ship, which maneuvered wildly to get away. Japanese gunners opened up with devastating accuracy, spraying the submarine's deck and injuring seven of the boat's gunnery crew. Ramage broke off the engagement, gathered up the wounded, and eased them below; he then took the boat down and escaped.

The skipper was boiling mad by the time he reached Fremantle on 24 February 1943. Of the fourteen torpedoes fired, one had exploded prematurely and five didn't explode on contact. McCann expressed concern but suggested that all the failures could not be blamed on the magnetic warhead. He noted "control errors or firing at too close range might have accounted for them." That aside, continuing disparagement of the torpedoes by sub skippers every-where convinced McCann and Lockwood that something else must be wrong. But what? The Bureau of Ordnance continued to do nothing to determine the warheads' defects.

A reshuffling of the submarine command in Pearl, however, offered hope that something would be done. The changes came in the wake of a tragic plane crash on the coast of Northern California that claimed the life of Rear Admiral English and other officers. Their Pan Am clipper aircraft ran into a fierce storm on its approach to San Francisco, where the admiral had hoped to inspect submarine repair facilities at Mare Island. The plane smashed into a cliff and exploded in a fireball, killing everyone on board. Admiral King facilitated the appointment of Lockwood to replace English in Pearl. Rear Adm. Ralph Christie, former commander of submarines based in Brisbane, was recalled to replace Lockwood in Perth-Fremantle. Christie had been detached from

Brisbane in 1942 to go back to Newport to resolve the torpedo problems. He campaigned to return to Brisbane, where the sub base was growing exponentially and included three tenders. The plum position went to Admiral Fife rather than Christie, earning him Christie's undying enmity. The irony of the move was obvious. Christie had directed development of the Mark 6 exploder before the war and never lost faith in it.

Under Christie, McCann remained commander of Squadron 6 and the *Pelias* in Fremantle. The arrival of a second tender, the *Otus* (AS-20), made it possible for Christie to carry out a plan envisioned by Lockwood before he was detached: to establish a second sub base farther up the west coast of Australia to shorten the travel time to enemy shipping lanes in Indonesia. Although Lockwood had considered the port of Darwin on the north coast, Japanese bombings made that location impractical. So, he settled on Exmouth Gulf and gave the base the code name "Potshot." It was 750 miles north of Fremantle, which enabled submarines to remain on patrol an extra two days.

McCann and others vigorously opposed the idea. To veterans, Exmouth was a terrible place to rest weary submariners coming off war patrol. Its notoriously rough waters made it difficult for subs to moor alongside a tender for any length of time. Vicious windstorms known as "wily willies" also ravaged plains and villages around the gulf. Millions of flies besieged Quonset huts set up to quarter the crews on mud flats, creating misery for the sailors. Given the ardor of war patrols, as McCann viewed it, they would hardly get any rejuvenation in a place like Potshot—especially compared to what Perth had to offer with its young women, pubs, and better quarters. Nevertheless, Navy vice admiral Arthur S. Carpender, commander of Allied Naval Forces in Australia and based in Brisbane, was anxious to remove off-duty submariners from Perth. Like those in Brisbane, the enlisted men in Perth tended to be rowdy from heavy drinking coming off war patrols and caused many problems for shore police. Carpender thus endorsed the Potshot plan and ordered Christie to execute the experiment. The *Pelias* with McCann sailed for the gulf as April turned to May, and the *Otus* stayed in Fremantle to service submarines there.

"Tipped Off"
Potshot, Australia
Early May 1943

The *Pelias* arrived in Potshot in what locals called the "good weather" month. Hardly. High winds whipped the gulf, making it extremely difficult to refit incoming submarines. Ashore, the flies and the dust storms created hell on earth. Fortunately for the submariners and McCann, a twist of fate would spare them a long stay; the relocation of the squadron had not gone unnoticed by the enemy. On the night of 20 May, a Japanese reconnaissance aircraft out of Timor flew over under a full moon. McCann passed orders not to fire at the plane to keep from revealing the anchorage. However, the antiaircraft gunnery crews didn't receive the order and sent tracers up in an attempt to shoot down the aircraft. They missed. The next night a dozen Japanese bombers attacked, dropping 150-pound bombs close to the ack-ack batteries. The jig was up; it was too dangerous for the *Pelias* and, especially, the lightly armored subs to remain. With Carpender's okay, Christie withdrew his force, to McCann's great relief. Said one wag facetiously, "The Japanese were probably tipped off by McCann or the people on *Pelias*."

Back in Fremantle, Red Ramage was stifling bitterness over torpedo failures as he prepared for his fourth war patrol in the *Trout*. The plan was to lay mines off Borneo to interdict enemy oil shipments. Christie asked the skipper how many torpedoes he would be carrying. Ramage said sixteen. Jokingly, the admiral replied, "I want you to sink sixteen ships with those torpedoes." Ramage exploded: "If I get 25 percent reliable performance on your torpedoes, I'll be lucky, and you will bless me." Christie, his ire rising, ripped the skipper for creating an air of distrust and suspicion regarding the weapons. The two went nose to nose. Afterward, Ramage admitted the altercation was "a little bit rough. Tex McLean [Squadron 16 commander] grabbed me by the neck and pulled me out of there, saying, 'It's time to leave.' When we got outside Christie's office, McLean said, 'You're god-damned lucky to be going to sea.' I said, 'It's the other way around, Tex. With these torpedoes you're giving us, I'll be goddamned lucky to get back. If you think I'm so lucky, how about packing your bag and coming along with me?' That cooled him."

The *Trout* survived the patrol, but four other boats did not.

Not His Fault
New Farm Wharf, Brisbane
June 1943

Across the continent from Perth, Admiral Fife in his quarters at the Brisbane submarine base was smarting from the loss of four fleet boats in the first three months of the year—the *Argonaut*, *Amberjack*, *Grampus*, and *Triton*—plus the death of Skipper Howard Gilmore in the *Growler*. Injured by gunfire on the bridge after *Growler*'s collision with a small Japanese ship, Gilmore had issued his immortal words—"Take her down"—to save the boat at the sacrifice of his own life.

Fife, a Lockwood favorite, was his complete opposite in temperament. Bespectacled with the aura of a professor, Fife obsessed over undersea war tactics night and day and stayed aloof from submariners. He lived an austere existence in a Quonset hut, which he seldom left. His patrol report endorsements were long, extremely detailed, and harsh toward boat skippers, whom he often relieved of command after what he considered a less than aggressive patrol. To one of his division commanders, Lt. Cdr. Chester Bruton, the admiral was "a strange, solitary, almost lonely figure. He didn't drink or fraternize. He never seemed concerned about people. When a submarine came in from patrol, he wanted to know about the condition of the battery or the engines or the periscopes or electrical equipment." His lack of compassion came through in a letter he sent to Lockwood in Pearl Harbor after the loss of the four boats: "Tough luck but you can't get Japs without taking chances," Fife wrote. "I don't think the time has arrived to inject caution into the system because it is too difficult to overcome again."

From Fremantle, Christie saw an opportunity to return to Brisbane by calling into question Fife's tactic of forcing his skippers to take chances on patrol. He proposed an investigation into how the boats were lost and sought permission from Carpender to fly to Brisbane to conduct it. The vice admiral turned him down flat, telling him it was none of his business and to butt out. Instead, Carpender sent for McCann, whom he viewed as impartial and who was senior to Christie by a year. He gave McCann free reign but told him not to disclose the results of his investigation to Christie. Rather, he was to deliver a single report to Carpender, who would consider its findings and tuck it away.

Christie was miffed. In a dispatch to Lockwood in Pearl, he expressed his displeasure. Lockwood replied with a diplomatic tone: "Naturally I am surprised at the method selected for handling the investigation of Jimmy's losses. Certainly a thorough investigation should be made and certainly it would appear that you should be a party. . . . I hope that you and Jimmy [Fife] will not let any friction grow up between you. I realize you are not pals but I trust that you will not let that interfere with cooperation. God knows there are enough personnel problems in the Southwest Pacific without letting them creep into the submarine service."

McCann flew to Brisbane and conducted a thorough investigation. He interviewed Fife; the admiral's staff, including Bruton; and many others in the sub force. Christie never saw the report, just as Carpender intended. It would be years before McCann would reveal the rough outlines of it: "I exonerated Fife completely. The losses were in no way his fault. The boats may have been sunk by our own aircraft. There was no way to tell."

Fife offered to resign during the investigation, but Carpender refused. Christie, meanwhile, conducted his own impromptu investigation and argued openly that Fife's frequent radio communications with sub skippers on patrol may have compromised their whereabouts, resulting in their destruction. That argument came to naught, however.

Many submariners believed that the performance of the Mark 14 torpedoes on Fife's four ill-fated boats could have just as easily been the culprit. Indeed, duds and premature detonations continued unabated. For instance, in thirty-two torpedo attacks made by the *Trout*, in which she fired eighty-five torpedoes, there were five confirmed premature explosions, five confirmed duds, and twenty-five suspected duds. Lockwood and others, including McCann, had long been aware that Germany and England had deemed their own versions of magnetic warheads unreliable during the Battle of the Atlantic in 1941. The two enemies discovered that a ship's magnetic field changed unpredictably, sometimes flattening out depending on where it was. Magnetic triggers inside the warheads either didn't engage the field below a ship because it was too shallow or detonated too far from the vessel to cause any damage. Because the Bureau of Ordnance's design was somewhat different, relying on electrical induction coils and vacuum tubes instead of a compass to detonate the charge, the bureau and Christie clung stubbornly to their belief the warheads would work. Still, the evidence of malfunctions kept piling up in war patrol reports. Lockwood's cynicism grew at the rate of his skippers'. At a wartime conference in Washington, he let loose. "If the Bureau of Ordnance can't provide us with torpedoes that will hit and explode," he said, "then for God's sake, get the Bureau of Ships to design a boat hook with which we can rip the plates off a target's side."

Finally, on 24 July 1943, Lockwood had had enough. He ordered all sub captains to deactivate the magnetic mechanism at once and rely instead on contact detonators. The Bureau of Ordnance could not do anything to stop them. That same day, however, even that decision would not be enough to resolve the problem.

"Incomprehensible"

USS *Tinosa* (SS-283), near Truk Atoll

24 July 1943

Lt. Cdr. L. R. Daspit had been alerted by code breakers that a 19,000-ton whale factory ship, the *Tonan Maru No. 3*, which had been converted into one of the largest tankers afloat, was en route to Truk, the major Japanese fortress island in the Central Pacific. With the ship cruising at thirteen knots, Daspit moved USS *Tinosa* (SS-283) into favorable firing range so that his torpedoes would smack the hull dead on at a perpendicular angle. Daspit launched a spread of four. Only two hit; both sent up geysers of seawater but yielded no explosions. The ship turned to escape. Daspit fired two more torpedoes at an oblique angle. Amazingly, both exploded and left the ship dead in the water and settling by the stern. The skipper maneuvered the submarine around the tanker and prepared a final salvo from 875 yards away. The crew of the *Maru* could do nothing except fire ammunition on the tracks of any incoming torpedoes and shoot at the periscope when it appeared. The *Tinosa* fired a single torpedo that ran straight and normal. There was a splash on contact but no explosion. Bewildered, Daspit ordered remaining torpedoes inspected. All were in perfect condition. The skipper tried again. Another hit without exploding. Then another. Seven pelted the stationary target over the next hour and a half. Still no explosions. The skipper watched in disbelief through the periscope as one hit aft of midship, sent up a geyser of water, "and then was observed to have taken a right turn and to jump clear of the water about 100 feet of the stern of the tanker. I find it hard to convince myself I saw this." The skipper, down to his last torpedo, was beside himself and didn't launch it. Rather, he decided to take it back to Pearl for examination.

Daspit was not a happy man when he arrived. As Lockwood recalled the moment, "I expected a torrent of cusswords, damning me, the bureau of ordnance, the Newport Torpedo Station and the Base Torpedo Shop, and I couldn't have blamed him—19,000 ton tankers don't grow on trees. I think Dan [Daspit] was so furious as to be practically speechless. His tale was almost unbelievable, but the evidence was undeniable." Daspit at one point compared use of the Mark 14s as "banging against the sides of enemy ships like toothless sharks."

The commander of Submarine Squadron 14, J. B. Longstaff, expressed astonishment concerning the attack on *Tonan Maru No. 3*. "It is a disheartening experience to fire fifteen torpedoes at an unescorted tanker at good range, observing thirteen of them hit the target, and still fail to sink her," he wrote in his endorsement attached to Daspit's war patrol report. "It is hoped that some reason for this destructive effort can be found by a careful examination of the remaining torpedo." Even the skipper's division commander, Leo L. Pace, was flummoxed: "The subsequent series of torpedo failures is incomprehensible."

"Chunks of TNT Lying Around"
USS *Muskallunge* (SS-262), Kahoolawe Island, Hawaii
31 August 1943

Admiral Lockwood discussed with his commanders possible means of finding out why *Tinosa's* torpedoes were such an utter failure. Capt. Charles Momsen, commander of Sub Squadron 2 in Pearl and the man McCann had worked closely with to develop the submarine rescue chamber, suggested an idea: Load previously inspected torpedoes, including *Tinosa's* remaining unused fish, into the launch tubes of a submarine and fire them at a ninety-degree angle against the vertical cliffs of Kahoolawe, the small island south of Maui that was being used as a Navy test range. The launch would mimic the broadside manner in which *Tinosa* attacked the tanker. Divers would retrieve the first dud so that the Navy could carefully examine it to find out what went wrong.

The newly arrived USS *Muskallunge* (SS-262) was chosen for the experiment. Accompanied by the escort ship *Chalcedony* (PYC-16) and sub rescue ship *Widgeon* (ASR-1), the sub sailed for Kahoolawe. *Muskallunge* fired three torpedoes into the cliff. The first two exploded, but the third hit in the familiar manner of a dud: with a geyser of seawater and compressed air but no fireworks. At great risk, Lockwood, Momsen, and a group of Navy skin divers in swimming trunks boarded small boats and headed to the base of the cliff, where they dove into the sea with goggles and began looking for the dud in the clear waters. As Lockwood later put it, it would be very risky: "I suspected we would find ourselves shaking hands with Saint Peter when we tried to examine a dud warhead with six hundred and eighty five pounds of TNT." BM John Kelly from the *Chalcedony* spotted it fifty-five feet down. The warhead was split open with chunks of explosives lying around on the seabed. Kelly dove down and looped a tether around the torpedo. It was hauled gingerly on board the *Widgeon*, where Momsen could see that the warhead's firing mechanism was intact but severely deformed by impact. Back in Pearl, the fractured warhead was painstakingly dissected under Momsen's direction. The cause of the problem soon emerged. The firing pin was jammed and bent in its guide track, just short of striking the primer with enough force to detonate the explosive. It was clear what had caused the defect: The entire triggering mechanism was designed for an earlier model torpedo, the Mark 10, which reached a maximum speed of thirty-six knots after launch. The 3,000-pound Mark 14, on the other hand, accelerated to forty-six knots. It made contact with a target at such velocity that the warhead's firing spring was not strong enough to speed the pin along the stud guides to detonate the charge before the channel collapsed, trapping the pin.

Lockwood arranged for additional tests at the Navy yard by dropping dummy warheads containing live exploders along a wire atop a ninety-foot crane onto steel plates at the bottom of an empty dry dock. A direct hit at a ninety-degree angle produced duds in seven out of ten tests. The 70 percent failure rate was cut in half by landing the warheads on plating tilted at a forty-five-degree angle. At a greater angle, the exploder went off without fail in every test. Knowing this, Lockwood immediately ordered all sub captains to fire their torpedoes at oblique angles until corrected torpedoes became available.

Once they had discovered the problem, Momsen and his men found a rather easy solution. They machined replacement firing pins with light, high-strength aluminum alloy made, ironically, from the propellers of Japanese fighter aircraft shot down during the attack on Pearl Harbor. The pins were shorter in order to cut down on friction inside guide tracks that were strengthened and equipped with heavy-duty, powerful springs to launch the pin against the explosive. The submarine USS *Halibut* (SS-232) fired six torpedoes with modified warheads into the cliffs of Kahoolawe at Lockwood's direction. All six detonated on impact. The solution—known as the Pearl Harbor modification—subsequently was carried out on every torpedo in the current inventory. It was also adopted in all new production back in the States.

At last all problems with Mark 14 had been resolved except one—occasional circular runs of the torpedoes that would cause the future loss of at least two submarines, USS *Tang* (SS-306) and USS *Tullibee* (SS-284). The later Mark 15 torpedoes would prevent this defect with metal collars that kept the torpedoes from turning back. It had taken twenty months to discover and correct the major problems, and the delay had seriously hampered the effectiveness of American submarines. But the undersea fleet, a mere 2 percent of the entire Navy, would rally and deal a decisive blow against the Japanese fleet with the corrected Mark 14s and a new breed of wakeless electric torpedoes. By war's end, U.S. submarines would destroy more than 1,178 merchant ships and 214 warships totaling 5.6 million tons—55 percent of all Japanese vessels. The toll on submariners would be high, however—374 officers and 32,131 enlisted lost on 52 submarines, the highest fatality rate of any branch of the service in the Pacific.

For Allan McCann, the Pacific submarine war was over by mid-1943. He was awarded a Navy Legion of Merit for his service in Pearl Harbor and Australia, the citation in part reading, "Demonstrating exceptional ability and untiring devotion to duty as Squadron Commander, [he] inspired the officers and men under his command to the successful completion of dangerous and vital missions. . . . His brilliant leadership and proficient execution of many difficult tasks were reflected in the splendid material conditions of all units of this task force and the excellent morale of his men, resulting in a tremendous toll in enemy shipping."

Captain McCann now had a new mission: assume command of Sub Squadron 7 in the Atlantic, where he would help the legendary Navy admiral Francis Stuart "Frog" Low formulate unusual tactics that would become the key to defeating the German U-boat offensive.

CHAPTER 11

BERMUDA COLLEGE

Submarine Squadron 7 Headquarters
Ordnance Island, Bermuda
April 1943

*A*llan McCann arrived on Ordnance Island, a 1.7-acre outcropping in St. George's harbor on the eastern edge of Bermuda, to help engage the final frontier in the battle between the U.S. Navy and Adolf Hitler's Nazi U-boats. His mission: knit together two divisions of submarines into a new squadron to help teach destroyer crews how to hunt and destroy U-boats.

For many months, enemy subs in growing numbers had ravaged Allied convoys trying to resupply Britain with desperately needed war matériel. The Nazi raiders were on the verge of winning the Atlantic struggle. In the previous year, they had destroyed 876 Allied ships totaling 4.6 million tons—an overwhelming blow to American efforts to buttress England. U-boats, operating with near impunity off the U.S. coast, were sinking ships at the rate of nearly one every day. Debris from shattered oil tankers and freighters and bodies of drowned crew members washed up regularly along the Eastern Seaboard.

Who would win the Battle of the Atlantic in many ways hinged on technological breakthroughs—moves and countermoves that first favored one side, then the other. When the Germans developed wolf packs to concentrate attacks on convoys, the Allies developed hedgehog depth charges, which could be lobbed ahead of destroyers, and Mark 9 depth charges, which were streamlined to swiftly sink to their targets. When German scientists perfected torpedoes that homed in on the sound of ship propellers, the Allies countered with noisemakers towed behind merchant ships to divert the weapons. When the Allies refined their sonar capabilities, the Nazis covered submarine hulls with rubber to absorb sonar pings. They also invented *Pillenwerfer*, effervescent chemical pellets that created disturbances in the sea to confuse sonar operators. When radar-equipped, land-based bombers began effectively hunting U-boats coming and going from bases in Europe, the Germans countered with oil tanker submarines that resupplied U-boats at sea. The U.S. Navy responded with small escort carriers that brought hunter-killer aircraft armed with homing torpedoes and 500-pound depth bombs into the midocean. The Germans, meanwhile, stepped up production of U-boats to the rate of one every day. British prime minister Winston Churchill commented on how complicated the war in the Atlantic had become—"a war of groping and drowning, of ambuscade and strategem, of science and seamanship," as he put it.

By early 1943 the Allies seemed to be gaining. Whereas Germany lost only six U-boats in January, the tally rose to twenty in February and another fifteen in March. However, also in March, German grossadmiral Karl Doenitz organized three wolf packs of thirty-eight submarines to attack four Allied convoys of 208 transport ships traveling in close proximity and guarded by thirty destroyers. The U-boats fanned out to confuse the Allies and used decoy subs to draw off the escorts before the wolf packs struck from all directions during a seven-day engagement culminating in the sinking of scores of ships. "This is the greatest success ever achieved in a convoy battle and is all the more creditable in that nearly half the U-boats involved scored at least one hit," touted a German communiqué decoded by the British. Doenitz was equally ecstatic, noting, "After three and a half years of war we had brought British maritime power to the brink of defeat in the Battle of the Atlantic."

The success was short lived. As Doenitz unleashed his attacks on the four convoys, U.S. Fleet Adm. Ernest J. King Jr. summoned top British, Canadian, and American commanders to a high-level conference in the Federal Reserve Building in Washington to review how the war against the U-boats had been waged and what improvements could be made. King emphasized the gravity of the situation. "A ship saved is worth two built. Think it over!" he challenged the group. The officers concluded that one of the big impediments to fighting U-boats was a lack of uniform procedures, tactics, and gunnery instructions among the various warships trying to provide cover for convoys. Admiral King came to the same conclusion and decided on a new course of action centered around small aircraft carriers operating with many destroyers on the convoy routes, all directed by a command post in Washington. What he had in mind was unparalleled.

"The Fleet with No Ships"
Navy Department, Washington, D.C.
May 1943

Admiral King would be the face of a whole new Navy fleet dedicated to hunting U-boats. The flagship of his antisubmarine command would not be at sea but rather in crammed office space in a third-floor wing of King's Navy Department headquarters in Washington, D.C. He tapped Navy captain Francis Low to helm the new operation. Low was King's assistant chief of staff, a brilliant, debonair officer who had a knack for putting the admiral's rough ideas into a coherent plan. In this case, he supervised daily operational command of the Navy's mysterious Tenth Fleet. Shrouded in secrecy, this "fleet with no ships" was actually an electronic operations center with tentacles stretching to all corners of the Atlantic. By King's ultimate authority, all carriers, destroyers, destroyer escorts, aircraft, and smaller sub-hunting vessels were at Low's beck and call wherever they were stationed in the Atlantic. In Washington, the captain directed operatives around a plotting table that showed fresh intelligence from code breakers in Britain that needed to be analyzed quickly. A tactical plan then was executed, putting warships into motion within a moment's notice against U-boats wherever they were detected.

The cerebral Low was very much the key decision maker of the Tenth Fleet. A veteran submariner, he knew all the eccentricities of undersea warfare dating back to World War I. To many, he was an enigma. "There are two mysteries about Francis Low," said one observer. "One is why he is called 'Frog.' The other is who he really was." The son of a naval officer from an affluent Boston family, he graduated from the Naval Academy in 1915, two years ahead of McCann. In Annapolis, Low derived his nickname from his deep, rolling baritone voice, which to midshipmen conjured up the croaking chorus of frogs from the comedy *Frogs* by ancient Greek playwright Aristophanes. In addition, his studies of French made him a "frog" in midshipman parlance. After graduation, Low served in submarines in World War I and later conducted submarine and torpedo research. In the late 1930s he commanded Submarine Division 13, after which he joined Admiral King's staff at the outbreak of World War II. He made an immediate impression for his seminal ideas, including launching Army lieutenant colonel James "Jimmy" Doolittle's B-25B raid on the Japanese home islands from a Navy carrier. The raid, just five months after the attack on Pearl Harbor, was a major boost to U.S. morale. Low later assumed command of the heavy cruiser USS *Wichita* (CA-45) in Operation Torch, the Allied invasion of North Africa. Amid the chaos of U-boat attacks on Allied convoys, Admiral King had recalled him.

The first thing Low did as King's chief of staff was review a large archive of often conflicting American and British antisubmarine literature in order to formulate a plan for the admiral. The captain's report—"Appreciation of the Antisubmarine Situation"—recommended detailed steps, including improving training of destroyer personnel and deploying many more ships and planes flown from carriers. "The prosaic answer to the problem is *enough* escorts *and* aircraft, recognition of fundamentals and pressure to make them work," the captain concluded. He further recommended a top-to-bottom reorganization of the antisubmarine effort. Admiral King endorsed the report and the Combined Chiefs of Staff followed up by urging Allied nations to centralize control of antisubmarine warfare and join together in integrating the effort.

Named operational commander of Admiral King's new fleet, Low got the most out of his subordinates. He contrasted markedly with King in temperament. The admiral was brusk, often sending back memos he disliked with a curt "No, K." Low, preferring face-to-face discussions, would write "See me about this" on memoranda he did not approve of. Although unusually kind and respectful in his relationships with staff, he nonetheless was a tough taskmaster who worked the same around-the-clock schedule he demanded of his subordinates at Tenth Fleet headquarters. Low cultivated close bonds and insisted that no artificial barriers persist between regular and reserve officers. In his mind, like submarine crews, they were all in this together. He attracted experts in destroyer, submarine, and aircraft operations from around the world. He rotated the heads of the various divisions of the fleet in order to encourage new ideas.

In his recruitments, Low bypassed existing antisubmarine specialists whom he thought too rigid in their thinking, given the few accomplishments so far in the war against German subs. Instead, he chose a small group of officers known as rugged freethinkers to lead the Tenth Fleet's five divisions—operations, antisubmarine measures, convoy and routing, civilian scientific council, and air antisubmarine development. Among the men selected to head the divisions were Capt. William Dodge Sample, one of the Navy's greatest aviators; Capt. John Meade Haines, famous for commanding the submarines that smuggled Carlson's raiders ashore on Japanese-controlled Pacific islands; Capt. Ross Forrester Collins (Ret.), a Navy Reservist and investment broker from Kansas City, Missouri; and Dr. John T. Tate, a professor of physics at the University of Minnesota who was King's scientific adviser. Although Low's organization developed a strategy to defeat U-boats, it would rely on ships commanded by Atlantic Fleet Adm. Royal E. Ingersoll to carry out the battle plan. Admiral King and Ingersoll had worked seamlessly for some time and were in close contact.

Low, who eschewed using aides and lieutenants as personal assistants, had a single secretary, Mary Elizabeth Cummings, who held a degree in secretarial studies from Carnegie Tech. Also joining the command was Lt. (jg) Virginia Mildred Louise Hill, a former Chicago newspaper reporter. She had been attending Waves Midshipmen's School at Smith College in Massachusetts when Low recruited her to edit the fleet's influential *U.S. Fleet Anti-Submarine Bulletin*, a lively periodical distributed monthly to skippers of escort carriers and destroyers plus the pilots who flew off the flattops. Popularly known as "Yellow Peril," the bulletin was written with verve to attract attention and to disseminate up-to-date information about weapons development, tactics, and the capabilities of U-boats and about new doctrines and thinking about antisubmarine warfare. Another of Lieutenant Hill's publications was the immensely popular *Tenth Fleet Incidents*, which reconstructed in dramatic narrative the most successful attacks on U-boats.

With operational leaders in place in Washington, the next step for Admiral King was to put the grand plan into action. The strategy would evolve from the Navy's training centers and would bring Allan McCann back from the Pacific.

Antisubmarine University
Camp Allen, Norfolk, Virginia
Late May 1943

Rear Adm. Donald D. Beary, from his headquarters at Camp Allen, near the Chesapeake Bay, would become vitally important to the success of the Tenth Fleet. To him fell the job of taking over all existing training schools and centers used by the Atlantic Fleet. Training would become intensified in antisubmarine operations—and only that.

Beary approached his task by remodeling the schools into a de facto "U.S. Antisubmarine University." He rewrote the curricula of scores of sonar sound schools and antisubmarine training and refresher schools—the campuses of his university—which were spread out all along the Atlantic coast, from Argentia in Newfoundland in the far north to Recife in Brazil and to Casablanca. Among new specializations was the Aircraft Antisubmarine Development Detachment at Quonset Point, Rhode Island, where naval pilots, crew members, technicians, and scientists came together to improve aircraft capabilities in antisubmarine warfare. King suspended the normal Navy practice of shifting officers around to broaden their experience in a variety of commands. "In view of the urgency of building up quickly a large and efficient antisubmarine element," Admiral King explained, the Navy needed "personnel especially trained for and experienced in antisubmarine operations and activities."

Utmost in Admiral King's mind was to avoid the kind of situation that prevailed at the Subchaser Training Center in Miami. To him this center typified the haphazard development of antisubmarine operations to date. Although proficient in training officers and enlisted sailors for service on small antisubmarine surface craft, the center didn't have facilities to handle destroyers and destroyer escorts. That forced destroyer and escort personnel to move from port to port, seeking adequate facilities and instruction and delaying deployment for weeks. To correct this oversight, Admiral Beary created a major base in Bermuda, designed exclusively to school destroyer officers and sailors in antisubmarine operations.

DD-DE Shakedown Task Force
Tucker Island, Bermuda
June 1943

With work under way to build a large seaplane hangar and other facilities on Tucker Island, a 260-acre island near the western tip of Bermuda, the USS *Hamul* (AD-20) arrived under the command of Capt. James L. Holloway Jr. The destroyer tender was accompanied by the newly commissioned escort destroyer USS *Andres* (DE-45), the first of 348 destroyers that would pass through DD-DE Shakedown Task Force, informally termed "Bermuda College." Holloway had chosen the island as a training site because of its location near the battle zone and his previous experience there with his destroyer squadron. The locale, on one of the most beautiful islands in the Atlantic, was ideal, not only for the psychological benefit to the sailors but also for the tight control the Navy could exert on sailors on leave.

Destroyer crews arriving from shipyards on the East Coast and in the Gulf of Mexico had gotten a classroom introduction to antisubmarine warfare in the United States. But few had experienced practice at sea. In Bermuda, base personnel assumed control of each destroyer on mooring alongside the *Hamul*. Captain Holloway's personnel provided all logistics, repairs, and mechanical adjustments in order to free up commanders to concentrate on training their sailors. The crews shifted to the tender and facilities at the base, which featured attack-teacher trainers. Employing what they learned at sea in battle with real submarines was quite another matter. That's where Allan McCann came in.

Killer Groups
Ordnance Island, Bermuda
June 1943

McCann had worked expeditiously to forge a new squadron of subs that would serve as practice targets for the destroyers. As commander of Sub Squadron 7, he took charge of Submarine Divisions 71 and 72 consisting of older S- and R-boats that had been homeported in Bermuda since 1942. The squadron would eventually be augmented by captured Italian and French submarines. McCann administered the squadron from Ordnance Island, which had a single pier, a whitewashed, three-story administrative headquarters, and a grove of about a dozen palm trees. The island had served the Royal Army Ordnance Corps since the nineteenth century. The British had created it from the sands of three former islets in the harbor that were once used for executions. Predating Ordnance Island, a storage depot for gunpowder was within the town of St. George and had earned a nefarious reputation during the American Revolution. At the request of Gen. George Washington, subversives stole a hundred barrels of the munitions and smuggled them to the colonies for use against British troops.

McCann's steel sharks operating out of Ordnance were manned by veteran American officers and sailors. The subs became practice prey for the freshly minted destroyers and destroyer escorts in azure waters around Bermuda. The ships, as many as two dozen at a time, drilled in mock battle with McCann's subs over a five-week period. The destroyers formed units that operated with aircraft in practice attacks on the squadron. The crews also fired on towed targets and practiced gunnery, communication, and radar skills. To be avoided was the habit of dropping depth charges too early in an attack. Sonar operators became adept at differentiating the evasive maneuvers of McCann's subs at depth. They also learned to "sweep" a submerged target with sonar to give conning officers an idea of what edge of the sub they had located so that they could better calculate depth-charge runs. The destroyer crews drilled on ship-to-ship and ship-to-plane communications, which would be critical in coming engagements with the enemy.

The sailors drilled day and night, perfecting their use of all weaponry and systems on board. The success of the program was such that Canadian corvettes and destroyer escorts of the Royal Navy later enrolled in Bermuda College.

At the end of the training period, the warships set sail for their assigned escort carriers and their aircraft already on patrol in the Atlantic. Fleet Admiral Ingersoll was particularly adept at organizing the ships into what he called "killer groups." The destroyers created an ocean-searching electronic network that could span many miles as carrier aircraft patrolled overhead. From May to July, the Tenth Fleet exerted itself. In May alone, forty-one U-boats met destruction. Success was exemplified by what happened in mid-July to one particular U-boat.

Atlantic Wall
U-487, Seven Hundred Miles Southwest of the Azore Islands
13 July 1943

Ominous signs preceded the arrival of U-487, a 1,600-ton oil supply sub, in the mid-Atlantic southwest of the Azore Islands. Known as a "milk cow" for its ability to ferry fuel to boats at sea, U-487 was under the command of reservist Helmut Metz. The sub, making its second resupply mission, had sailed from a bomb-hardened concrete pen on the coast of occupied France in Bordeaux. Coming off its first voyage in May, the boat was crossing the Bay of Biscay en route to Bordeaux when Royal Air Force aircraft sandwiched it with three bombs at a distance of fifty yards before Metz could dive. He took the boat down with only minor damage—a close call. While in port for overhaul alongside a half dozen other boats, the skipper had the sub's after deck gun replaced by a three-foot-high platform dubbed the "Atlantic Wall." A triple-mount 20-mm antiaircraft battery was installed on the platform connected to the con by a catwalk.

On 14 June the sub cast off for the mid-Atlantic after taking on fuel from a small oil tanker. The sub arrived in its patrol sector on 1 July. In succeeding days, it resupplied five U-boats to extend their patrols. The skipper of one of them was suffering from a nervous breakdown that required U-487's physician to go on board to treat him.

At sea, Metz required his crew to rehearse crash dives daily; he didn't want to be caught off guard as in the first war patrol. Whereas land-based aircraft frequently patrolled the Bay of Biscay, no Allied aircraft had appeared in the Atlantic. During a lull, the skipper allowed groups of eight to ten to take a swim off the boat and sunbathe on deck. Having completed his mission, Metz received orders from the German high command to rendezvous with a large outbound submarine, U-160, which was to transfer to U-487 all the fuel and provisions that it could spare to enable Metz to stay at sea.

At dawn of 13 July the submarine proceeded at twelve knots on the surface to meet U-160. Unbeknownst to either boat, Allied cryptologists working with the Tenth Fleet had intercepted radio messages between them, decoded them, and relayed them to Low's operatives in Washington. Promptly, the escort carrier USS *Core* (CVE-13), operating near the Azores, received orders to launch seven aircraft to search for the U-boats.

Lookouts on the bridge of U-487, unaware of the search under way by aircraft from the *Core*, studied the skies for any sign of approaching planes. There were none. At midday crew members on deck noticed a crate bobbing about nearby and snagged it. It was lofted to the bridge for inspection and found to be filled with cotton, which could be useful. As the box was lowered down the hatch to the control room, the lookouts on deck were distracted by a commotion. They had made a fatal mistake.

"One-Man U-Boat Killer"
Grumman Avenger Bomber, off USS *Core* (CVE-13)
13 July 1943

Pilot Lt. Robert Pershing Williams had been at the controls of his three-man aircraft for more than two hours after liftoff from the *Core*. He, his radioman, and his turret gunner had been scanning the ocean for signs of enemy subs to a distance of two hundred miles forward of the carrier. Escorting Williams' Grumman Avenger dive-bomber was a Grumman Wildcat fighter flown by Navy lieutenant (jg) Earl H. Steiger. Williams was a decorated pilot, having earned accolades for heroism during the Battle of the Coral Sea the previous year.

Unable to see any sign of U-487 or U-160, Williams had turned back for the carrier just as his turret gunner noticed the frothy wake of a submarine about ten miles distant. It was U-487. Both planes veered to port and used cloud cover to disguise their fast approach. Williams signaled to Steiger to make a strafing run from the U-boat's starboard bow. The Avenger would then come in low at 250 feet. The planes caught the sub by complete surprise. Ten seconds after Steiger's strafing attack, Williams jettisoned four Mark 47 depth charges, which bracketed the sub and exploded with terrific force, crippling the boat. Williams' radioman filmed the blasts as the bomber flashed by.

Barely making headway and unable to dive, U-487 took a pronounced list to starboard. Skipper Metz rushed to one of the 20-mm guns on his Atlantic Wall and opened fire. Simultaneously, bomb fragments ignited the cotton bale in the control room. Although crew members successfully snuffed the fire with their bare hands, smoke drifted below into the compartments.

Above, the two aircraft circled, observing the scene from 3,500 feet. The U-boat circled, slowed, and came to a standstill. Leaking oil spread in a broad circle around it. Lieutenant Williams radioed the *Core*, which catapulted four Avengers and one Wildcat to race to the scene. The *Core* also sortied the destroyer USS *Barker* (DE-190). Meanwhile, Steiger made another strafing run—his third—and was shot down by antiaircraft fire from the sub. The plane plunged into the ocean a hundred feet off the U-boat's starboard beam and disappeared.

There was no letup in the attacks, however. Arriving Avengers blistered the submarine with bursts of .50-caliber ammunition, strafing the topside and dropping additional bombs, two of which exploded near the bow and foredeck. Metz, mortally wounded and realizing he could not save the boat, ordered his crew to abandon ship. Crew members inflated three rubber boats and tossed them overboard; one was sunk by gunfire. Half of the fifty-eight officers and crew members swam for the dinghies. Some watched as their skipper, unable to get off the deck, bled to death.

Avenger aircraft swarmed over the boat. One bombing run caused the sub to lurch upward about ten feet by the bow and then drop back into the foam and begin a death slide by the bow into the depths at a forty-five-degree angle. Later the *Barker* arrived to pick up thirty-three survivors clinging to the two rubber boats.

The attack on U-487 was significant because it ended Germany's attempt to resupply its U-boats at sea. Of nine "milk cows" put into service in June 1943, seven, including U-487, had been sunk by the Tenth Fleet by August. Williams would be credited with sinking three U-boats, including U-487, within four days in operations with the Tenth, earning him wide press coverage in the United States as a "one-man U-boat killer."

The Big Stick
Navy Department, Washington, D.C.
September 1943

Allan McCann's command of Squadron 7 came to an end in September with his transfer back to the United States for a year's shore duty in the Fleet Maintenance Division of the Office of the Chief of Naval Operations at the Navy Department in Washington. By midwar, the Navy's combined fleets, fighting in two oceans, had grown exponentially. The fleet grew larger than the combined navies of all other nations involved in World War II with 6,768 ships, including eighteen carriers and eight battleships, by war's end. Fleet Maintenance governed the material readiness of the ships, including any design changes to the vessels, their armament, and their equipment.

In Washington, McCann was able to reconnect with his wife, Katheryne, and his young daughters, Barbara, Lois, and Alyn, at the family home in town. But by July 1944, McCann was on the move again with his pending elevation in rank to rear admiral. His orders: take command of a battleship on the other side of the world. That warship—"The Big Stick"—soon would face off with the Japanese in Tokyo's struggle to hold the Philippines.

CHAPTER 12

KURITA'S BLUNDER

Battleship *Iowa*

Philippine Sea, East of Samar Island

0600, 24 October 1944

*A*llan McCann was on the navigation bridge when an urgent message arrived from Navy admiral William "Bull" Halsey. Pilots of reconnaissance planes from USS *Intrepid* (CV-11) had sighted a Japanese armada of five battleships, seven heavy cruisers, two light cruisers, and thirteen destroyers. The fleet was crossing the central Philippines' Sibuyan Sea from the west in the direction of San Bernardino Strait. Among the warships were *Yamato* and sister ship *Musashi*, the largest battleships ever built, which were now on a collision course with the USS *Iowa* (BB-61) and other elements of Halsey's Third Fleet—six battleships, eight cruisers, forty destroyers, and ten carriers with more than a thousand aircraft—guarding the eastern egress of the strait between Luzon and Samar Islands. Halsey's job was to prevent Japanese vice admiral Takeo Kurita's warships from exiting the strait and heading south along the coast of Samar to attack Gen. Douglas MacArthur and more than 132,000 soldiers of the Sixth Army off-loading on the east coast of Leyte Island to begin the fight to retake the Philippines.

As a precursor, Halsey, in the *Iowa*'s sister ship, USS *New Jersey* (BB-62), ordered his entire fleet to prepare for surface action and launched hundreds of aircraft to attack Kurita's fleet some three hundred miles to the northwest and closing. "Strike! Repeat: Strike!" Halsey barked from the bridge of the *New Jersey*. Fighters, dive-bombers, and torpedo planes from USS *Enterprise* (CV-6) were the first to lift off into the morning mist. They were joined by dozens of others in multiple waves. If the Japanese somehow managed to survive the

Japanese navy vice admiral Takeo Kurita led Japan's Central Force—an armada that included the two largest battleships ever built—on a collision course with Navy admiral William "Bull" Halsey's Third Fleet on the eve of the Battle of Leyte Gulf in October 1944. Halsey's fleet included the new battleship USS *Iowa* (BB-61) under the command of Capt. Allan McCann.

U.S. Naval Institute photo archive

swarm and kept coming, a decisive confrontation between Kurita and Halsey would occur as early as nightfall.

For McCann, the new commander of the *Iowa*, anticipation couldn't have been higher. He and his 133 officers and 2,400 enlisted sailors had dreamed of a duel with the vaunted *Yamato* and *Musashi*. The clash of such powerful dreadnaughts on both sides would be unprecedented. The two Japanese warships, completed in 1942 and able to attain twenty-seven-knot speeds, were equipped with nine 18-inch guns, each capable of lobbing one-ton shells at targets twenty-six miles away. Secondary batteries and 25-mm machine guns numbering well more than a hundred made the two ships formidable to air attack. The *Yamato*-class warships were also impervious to torpedo attack, each being reinforced with heavy steel hull "blisters" to absorb impacts. Japanese naval architects declared the "super-battleships" indestructible.

Despite such reputations, McCann was confident that the *Iowa*, displacing 57,600 tons, could outmaneuver and outgun her 72,800-ton counterparts in an open sea shootout. Although she didn't have the range of the *Yamato*-class guns, the main batteries of the *Iowa* class—two forward and one aft, each with three 16-inch .50-caliber guns—could fire one-ton armor-piercing shells at tremendous velocity at targets twenty-three miles away with radar-controlled, pinpoint accuracy. The *Iowa*, the length of three football fields, also was nimble and much faster than her Japanese counterparts. She could make thirty-five-plus knots, easily outrunning all other warships afloat, including cruisers and destroyers, the greyhounds of the sea. The $100 million *Iowa* was the most modern, most potent warship in the world. Her starboard and port decks were crowded with 40-mm antiaircraft guns and 20-mm single-barrel close-in weaponry capable of throwing up a carpet of explosives that made attack by aircraft extremely difficult.

In command of all this weaponry was Captain McCann, now on the fast track to becoming rear admiral. Taking command of the *Iowa* in August, he and the Third Fleet sortied from Eniwetok, where the *Iowa*'s big guns supported amphibious landings on Peleliu on 17 September and then brought them to bear once again on Japanese airfields in the Philippines prior to the Leyte invasion. Otherwise the ship had seen no action in a somewhat checkered career. In August 1943, after her commissioning the previous February, she sailed for Norway in hopes of tracking down and sinking the German battleship *Tirpitz*, thought to be hiding in a fjord. The dreadnought turned out not to be there. In November, with President Franklin D. Roosevelt and the Navy's top brass on board en route across the Atlantic to midwar conferences with France and England in Cairo and Tehran, the *Iowa* was accidentally fired upon by an accompanying destroyer during a training exercise. Warned of the incoming torpedo launched by USS *William D. Porter*, the *Iowa* managed to narrowly evade the 500-pound warhead. After ten months in the Pacific, the *Iowa* had yet to encounter the Japanese fleet. Until now.

From his captain's chair on the port side of the enclosed navigation bridge, McCann surveyed the sweeping, 180-degree view of the forward guns and the sea in all directions. Dead ahead was the entrance to San Bernardino Strait, through which Kurita's battleships soon might emerge. McCann and others on the bridge could envision the coming cataclysm with Japan's near mythic battleships, braced by destroyers and cruisers in a do-or-die clash with the U.S. Navy. "The battle flags were flying," recalled EM1 George Graham standing bridge watch near McCann. "Everyone was expecting a fight with the battleships. We were antsy, you might say. And confident. We were the fastest and had the best guns and the best range finders of any battleship in the world."

If the *Iowa* were to come under intense bombardment, McCann could take cover within the armored-plated conning tower encircled by the bridge and just aft of where the captain was seated. Inside, crew members controlled the steering and speed of the *Iowa*. With a circular bulkhead seventeen inches thick, the con stretched upward three flights—from the weather bridge on Deck Three past the navigation bridge to the flying bridge used by lookouts on Deck Five. The con offered a protected view through slotted ports to the ocean outside and the ship's forward turrets.

Prior to the Battle of Leyte Gulf, McCann directed the *Iowa*'s 16-inch guns at Philippine airfields to soften up enemy defenses before Marines came ashore on the Leyte beachhead.

U.S. Naval Institute photo archive

Fortunately, Kurita's approach had been predicted. American submarines on patrol the night before on the west side of the Philippines had discovered and attacked his force as it passed through Palawan Passage to the Sibuyan Sea. USS *Darter* (SS-227) and USS *Dace* (SS-247) torpedoed and sank the heavy cruisers *Maya* and *Atago*. Undeterred, the fleet pressed onward toward San Bernardino Strait.

So it was that Captain McCann found himself at the crossroads of history once again. He had come a long way from his youth in North Adams to command of the world's most advanced warship about to engage in one of the greatest naval battles in history. He, like Halsey, had every reason to believe the Third Fleet would prevail through its sheer numbers. But at what cost? Where were the Japanese carriers, a much more lethal threat? None had been spotted with Kurita's fleet. They had to be lurking somewhere. But where?

"Meat for the Enemy"
Battleship *Yamato*, Sibuyan Sea, Central Philippines
1020, 24 October 1944

The loss of two cruisers and damage to another in the attack by the two American submarines was a serious blow to Admiral Kurita's Central Force. The admiral also suffered the ignominy of swimming away from the torpedoed *Atago* in Palawan Passage with the loss of 360 men. The destroyer *Kishinami* had fished him from the oily sea and transferred him dripping wet to the deck of his new flagship, *Yamato*. The admiral, known for his bravery in action, did not believe in dying in vain and was openly critical of the time-honored practice of a captain "going down with his ship." He judged that a waste of invaluable experience and leadership. In terms of his current mission, he remained confident of success given the size of his force.

His still powerful fleet continued across the Sibuyan at fifteen knots, fully expecting to acquire ground-based air coverage in the final push through six-mile-wide San Bernardino Strait. The first planes sighted, however, were not Japanese. They were from Halsey's carriers. The fleet increased speed to twenty-four knots and began evasive maneuvers as aircraft swarmed the *Yamato* and *Musashi*. Gunners on the battleships blazed away, knocking torpedo bombers and fighters out of the sky. Other planes evaded fire to score torpedo hits, although protective hull plates absorbed the explosions with little damage to *Yamato*. The heavy cruiser *Myoko* wasn't so lucky. Damage caused the ship to slow, drop back, and finally withdraw to the west. Pilots continued the furious assault for twenty-four minutes before breaking off to fly back to their carriers in the Philippine Sea.

A lull fell over the Central Force. But it didn't last long. A second wave of Navy aircraft zoomed in from the east just past noon. Torpedo bombers scored three hits on *Musashi*, staggering it. A third wave arrived. Fighters raked the battleship with gunfire. Five hundred–pound bombs ripped apart the superstructure, mangling bodies and producing fireballs and columns of smoke. Torpedoes finally penetrated the hull, causing an engine room to flood. The giant vessel began to list. Sixty-five more aircraft from the carriers *Enterprise* (CV-6) and *Franklin* (CV-13) poured in on the crippled monster, whose 18-inch guns belched fire to little effect. A message radioed to Kurita in *Yamato* described conditions: "Listing to port about 15 degrees. One bomb hit first bridge; all members killed. Five direct bomb hits and twelve torpedo hits."

There was no letup. Seemingly endless numbers of dive-bombers and fighters pressed the attack as the fleet drew closer to San Bernardino Strait. By midafternoon, planes from *Intrepid* (CV-11), *Cabot* (CVL-28), and *Essex* (CV-9) bore in on *Musashi* with devastating hellfire. Ten bombs and nineteen torpedoes wreaked havoc. The battleship sent out a desperate message to Kurita: "Speed 6 knots. . . . Damage great. What shall we do?" He ordered the ship to turn back toward Brunei with a cruiser and two destroyers.

Smarting over the lack of air support promised from Japanese shore bases, Kurita decided to pull back temporarily to the middle of the Sibuyan Sea, where the fleet circled just as the attacks ended. In the respite that continued the rest of the day, the vice admiral sent a message to Combined Fleet Admiral Teijiro Toyoda in Tokyo. Without Japanese aircraft to protect his fleet, Kurita wrote with bitterness, passage through San Bernardino Strait would be futile. He added, "Under these circumstances it was deemed that were we to force our way through [the strait], we would merely make ourselves meat for the enemy, with very little chance of success."

For Kurita, the carefully crafted plan to obliterate U.S. forces in Leyte Gulf was in grave doubt. *Sho Ichi Go*—Operation Victory One—was designed to stave off disaster in the Philippines, which would cut off natural resources to Japan. Coastal observers had reported Navy warships arriving in the gulf to protect a vast array of troop carriers, landing craft, and small escort carriers. Admiral Toyoda conceived an intricate pincer movement in which two surface battle fleets attacked the Seventh Fleet while a decoy carrier fleet drew the more powerful Third Fleet away from Leyte Gulf. The Southern Force—four older battleships, a heavy cruiser, and four destroyers commanded by Vice Admiral Shoji Nishimura—would sail from Brunei in the west, cross the Sulu and Mindanao Seas, and then enter Leyte Gulf from the south through Surigao Strait. Nishimura would meet up with a second battle group of two heavy cruisers, a light cruiser, and four destroyers carrying troops to engage the Americans on Leyte. At precisely the same time, Kurita's more powerful Central Force would debouch from San Bernardino Strait and attack from the north. Both fleets would combine their firepower to destroy the Seventh Fleet and trap MacArthur's soldiers between the Japanese army in the mountains overlooking the beachhead and Japanese battleships and cruisers offshore.

The most critical element of *Sho-1* involved a third Japanese fleet—Vice Admiral Jisaburo Ozawa's Northern Force of six aircraft carriers, including the large carrier *Zuikaku*, which had attacked Pearl Harbor; three light cruisers; and nine destroyers. The fleet had moved into position several hundred miles north of Leyte. There it would be sacrificed to draw Halsey's Third Fleet away from San Bernardino Strait so that the Central Force could come through unmolested. At a briefing to go over the plan with fleet commanders, Kurita acknowledged the great risks. "Would it not be shameful to have our fleet remain intact while our nation perishes?" he asked the commanders rhetorically. "You must remember that there are such things as miracles. What man can say that there is no chance for our fleet to turn the tide of war in a decisive battle?"

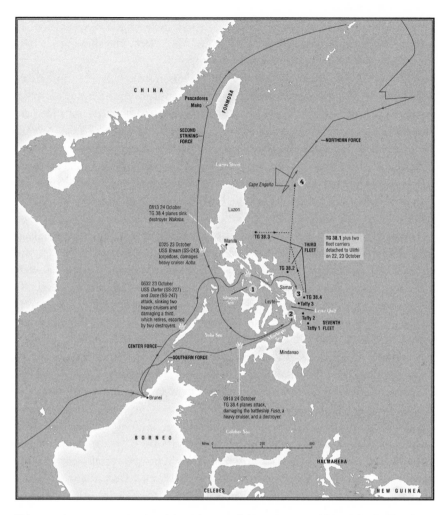

This map traces movements of American and Japanese naval forces in the Battle of Leyte Gulf, including Kurita's Central Force and Halsey's Third Fleet.

Graphic by Kelly Erlinger

The only part of *Sho-1* known to the Americans from intelligence intercepts was the decoy operation. But naval intelligence found it preposterous that Japan would willingly sacrifice its most valuable carrier fleet. Admiral Toyoda, however, was wagering an all-or-nothing gambit in a battle against a far superior American navy that could count on 1,712 aircraft launched from 30 carriers protected by 12 battleships, 24 cruisers, and 141 destroyers. Although all Japan's remaining carriers might be lost, Toyoda reasoned that annihilation of the Seventh Fleet via a surprise attack and destruction of General McArthur's army ashore had the best chance of forcing the United States to the peace table for a negotiated end to the war.

Sho-1, however, wasn't working out exactly as planned. U.S. submarines and patrol aircraft reported that the Southern Force was sailing east through the Mindanao Sea toward Surigao Strait. Navy admiral Thomas Kinkaid, commanding the Seventh Fleet's 738 vessels engaged in amphibious operations at the Leyte beachhead, responded by deploying most of his destroyers, cruisers, and battleships into the strait more than sixty-five miles south to sink the Japanese as they came through. Far to the north, Ozawa was trying to fulfill his role in *Sho-1*, but no one noticed he was out there. And now, Kurita seemingly had lost his nerve and turned back into the Sibuyan Sea.

"I Expected Complete Destruction"
Carrier *Zuikaku*, East of Luzon
1440, 24 October 1944

Vice Admiral Ozawa's hope in the coming battle was that the Third Fleet would attack with full force his nearly defenseless carriers. He had lost most of his airpower the previous June in the lopsided victory of the U.S. Navy in the Battle of the Philippine Sea. Now he was inviting attack. As he later told confidants, "I expected complete destruction of my fleet but if Kurita's mission was carried out, that was all I wished." Ozawa's orders from Toyoda were to "lure the enemy to the north" away from San Bernardino Strait. Two days earlier he had broken radio silence from *Zuikaku* to reveal his location. Yet no one was listening. He sent out patrol aircraft, hoping Halsey's pilots would follow them back to the carriers. It never happened. Now, having ordered seventy-six planes to attack the Third Fleet from 190 miles away, the admiral expected a quick counterattack. Again nothing happened. A forward task force within the Third Fleet easily deflected Ozawa's planes. Survivors fled inland rather than back to sea, reinforcing a belief that they had come from land bases. But some Navy pilots noticed the planes were of a carrier type with landing hooks on their tails.

"Start Them North"
Battleship *New Jersey*
1500, 24 October 1944

Capt. Doug Moulton, Halsey's air operations officer, was agitated. "Where in hell are those goddam Nip carriers?" he demanded, bringing his fist down on the chart table of the *New Jersey*. He had sortied snooper aircraft north and east to search for the mystery fleet. Finally, at 1540, Ozawa's wish to be discovered came true. Two pilots spotted the Northern Force. An hour later, another got a clear view of four carriers, two light cruisers, and five destroyers sailing west at sixteen knots. He radioed the coordinates back to Halsey at 1640.

The admiral faced a difficult choice. He had just issued his battle plan to McCann and other commanders to prepare for the coming clash with Kurita. The strategy directed four battleships, two heavy and three light cruisers, and nineteen destroyers at his signal to take position in a surface striking force to counter the Central Force should it come through San Bernardino Strait. Accordingly, Task Force 34 (TF-34) would "engage [Kurita] decisively at long ranges." On the receiving end of Halsey's communication was Combined Fleet Adm. Chester Nimitz, three thousand miles away in Pearl Harbor. Admiral Kinkaid, Seventh Fleet commander, intercepted the message as well. Both concluded that Halsey had formed TF-34 to seal off the strait while major portions of the Seventh took up station in Surigao Strait to handle Admiral Nishimura's Southern Force.

Halsey had no such intention now that Ozawa's carriers had been located. He believed that Kurita's force had been destroyed as an effective fleet by ear-

Admiral Halsey on the bridge of the *New Jersey*. His misjudgments were costly; they enabled Kurita's fleet to enter Leyte Gulf undetected, attack American escort carriers and destroyers, and then escape.

Naval History and Heritage Command, Washington Navy Yard, Washington, D.C.

lier bombardments, so there was no need for the task force to hang around. Navy pilots erroneously had reported major damage to four, perhaps five, battleships. At least one had been sunk, as had three heavy cruisers, a light cruiser, and a destroyer. Another heavy cruiser was seriously damaged. The fact that Kurita's "badly mauled" fleet had turned back into the Sibuyan Sea strengthened that view. For Halsey, the more urgent task now was to attack Ozawa's Northern Force.

Many times he and his staff had rehearsed on a game board the possibility of an ultimate showdown with the carriers. As Halsey described it, "If the rest of the Navy did not then know it, we, in the Third Fleet, were thoroughly cognizant that the carrier had replaced the battleship, and was potentially the strongest and most dangerous naval weapon our opponents possessed." Although the Navy had triumphed in the Battles of Midway, the Coral Sea, the Eastern Solomons, Santa Cruz, and the Philippine Sea, more than half of Ozawa's fifteen carriers had survived. Those ships would not escape this time, if Halsey had his way.

Indeed, the admiral was the fiery fleet commander that Admiral Nimitz had been looking for in the aftermath of Pearl Harbor. Then commander of the *Enterprise*, Halsey had boasted after the attack, "Before we're done with them, the Japanese language will only be spoken in hell." His carrier task force launched the famed Doolittle raid on Japan that had helped restore the Navy's morale in the early stages of the war. His slogan, "Hit hard, hit fast, hit often," became the motto of the entire fleet. Rising to command of South Pacific forces, Halsey's aggressive style, including risky deployment of his fast battleships in the confined seas of the Solomons, earned victories over the Japanese at Guadalcanal. His carriers also blunted the Japanese onslaught in the Coral Sea and Eastern Solomons.

Promoted by Nimitz to command of the new Third Fleet the previous May, Halsey now considered his options while standing off the coast of Samar. He could divide his fleet so that TF-34 would stand by at San Bernardino Strait while his carrier arm went after Ozawa. Or he could keep the entire fleet in position guarding the strait. A third option would be to attack the Northern Force with all his forces, leaving the strait unguarded. He rejected the first option because it would deprive TF-34 of adequate air cover should it be needed. He was mindful of how Japanese heavy air attacks sank the carrier USS *Princeton* (CVL-13) off the coast of Luzon four days earlier. Halsey also ruled out the second option; Ozawa's carriers could not be allowed to operate with impunity while the Third Fleet did nothing to stop them. The third option was the only reasonable choice in Halsey's mind: attack the Northern Force with his entire fleet to ensure that Ozawa did not escape and perhaps hasten an end to the war. Even if Kurita were able to sortie the remainder of his ships through

San Bernardino Strait, Halsey reasoned, Kinkaid would be able to handle them. Above all Halsey was mindful of his initial orders from the beginning of the war: "In case opportunity for destruction of a major portion of the enemy fleet is offered or can be created, such destruction becomes the primary task." Eliminating Ozawa's Northern Force was now that primary task.

Halsey left the bridge of the *New Jersey*, entered the flag plot behind the conning tower, and thrust a finger firmly on the table denoting Ozawa's position. "Here's where we are going, Mick," he said to Rear Adm. Thomas Carney, his chief of staff. "Start them north."

On board *Iowa*, McCann ordered speed increased to thirty knots. Halsey wanted his fast battleships out in front of the carriers when the aerial attack began so that they could prevent Ozawa's ships from escaping. The sudden acceleration riveted the sailors below decks. "All of a sudden we changed course at flank speed," recalled EM1 Grier Sims, battleship plank owner. "At that high a speed, the fantail just shudders from the four big propellers. You realize, 'Wow, he's got his foot on it. He's really moving fast.' We really didn't know why. But we knew we were fully engaged to meet the Japs somewhere."

"Heavenly Guidance"
Battleship *Yamato*, Sibuyon Sea
1700, 24 October 1944

Admiral Kurita had been circling, surprised that Navy aircraft had made no further attacks. Most of his fleet was intact and fully able to fight, contrary to what Halsey's pilots had told him. Yet, there was the dismal spectacle of the mortally wounded *Musashi*, which Kurita's fleet had overtaken and passed during its retreat. The "unsinkable" battleship had lost steering control, its bow was awash, and it was leaking vast quantities of oil. Escorts flanked the ship as it rolled to port and sank in a great whirlpool. Only half the 2,200 crew members had been rescued. Kurita, knowing *Sho-1* had no chance of success without his fleet, again reversed course at 1714, heading east toward San Bernardino Strait. With no aircraft to thwart him, Kurita intended to pass through in darkness and then attack Leyte Gulf after dawn. Toyoda in Japan was ecstatic. "With confidence in heavenly guidance, all forces will attack!" he radioed his vice admiral.

"A Brush Off"
Carrier *Intrepid*, Traveling North with the Third Fleet
2345, 24 October 1944

Disturbing news arrived for Adm. Gerald F. Bogan on USS *Intrepid* from Capt. Edward Ewen, commanding officer of the carrier. Routine night-flier patrols from *Independence* (CVL-22) for an over-the-shoulder look in the direction of San Bernardino Strait reported that channel lights were on. Further investigation to the west revealed the shocking sight of Kurita's Central Force plodding east into the waterway. Bogan drafted an urgent message to Halsey. He recommended detaching TF-34 to return to the strait. Halsey was asleep in anticipation of action against Ozawa in the morning, and his aide acknowledged receipt of the message but didn't wake the irascible admiral. To Bogan, it seemed "a brush off."

Staff officers on USS *Washington* (BB-56), tracking north with the other battleships of the Third Fleet, were also worried about leaving San Bernardino Strait unguarded. They suggested to Vice Adm. Willis A. Lee that Ozawa's carriers could be decoys. Lee, commander, Battleships, Pacific Fleet, agreed with them, especially after receiving news that channel lights had blinked on in the strait. Lee was convinced that TF-34 needed to be detached. He sent three separate messages to Halsey asking him to give the order. Each came back with a simple "Roger" but no change in course. Lee gave up.

In *Lexington* (CV-16), Chief of Staff Commo. Arleigh A. Burke also had growing concern. He couldn't understand why Japanese carriers would be operating separately from Kurita's fleet. Reports of channel lights going on in the strait and of Kurita's ships approaching from the west persuaded Burke and Cdr. James Flatley, staff operations officer, to wake Vice Adm. Marc Mitscher, commander of the carrier striking force. The admiral, perhaps irritated that Halsey had bypassed his authority during the initial attacks on the Central Force, asked one question: "Does Admiral Halsey have that report?" Flatley replied, "Yes, he does." Mitscher shrugged. "Admiral Halsey has all the information we have. He may have more. . . . If he wants my advice, he'll ask for it." With that, the admiral turned over and went back to sleep. The entire Third Fleet continued north.

"We've Never Asked Halsey"
Amphibious Command Ship *Wasatch* (AGC-9), Leyte Gulf
0400, 25 October 1945

Admiral Kinkaid met with his staff on board USS *Wasatch* (AGC-9), the flagship of the Seventh Fleet, to review the outcome of the battle in Surigao Strait earlier that night. Rear Adm. Jesse Oldendorf's six battleships, four heavy cruisers, four light cruisers, twenty-eight destroyers, and thirty-nine motor torpedo boats had trapped and clobbered Nishimura's battle fleet in its attempt to force its way into Leyte Gulf. Harassed in the initial stages by the PT boats, Nishimura's two battleships, heavy cruiser, and four destroyers closed on Surigao Strait before midnight without waiting for the second battle group reinforcements. Once inside the passage, the enemy warships passed through a gauntlet of destroyers positioned to ambush them. Defying broadside fire from the battleships, the escorts roared in all guns blazing, launched their torpedoes, turned, and fled. The battleship *Fuso*, holed by three torpedoes, exploded and capsized. The damaged *Yamashiro* steamed on with the rest of the force, reduced to the cruiser *Mogami* and destroyer *Shigure*. Oldendorf's battleships and cruisers lay in wait, strung out across the mouth of the strait. It was no contest. At 0316 the *West Virginia*'s radar detected the oncoming fleet and began firing ninety-three armor-piercing shells from her 16-inch guns at thirteen miles. The first salvo hit the *Yamashiro*. Within an hour, the battleship sank with Nishimura on board. The cruiser *Mogami* was reduced to a burning hulk. The *Shigure* had turned back with the Seventh Fleet in pursuit.

As Kinkaid pondered the situation from Leyte, he posed a question to his staff: "Is there anything we have forgotten to do or anything that we are doing that is wrong?"

"Admiral, I can think of only one thing," replied Capt. Richard H. Cruzen, Kinkaid's operations officer. "We've never asked Halsey directly if Task Force 34 is guarding San Bernardino Strait."

"Well, my lord!" exclaimed another officer. "We ought to find out about this thing."

Kinkaid got off a message to Halsey. The admiral also dispatched "Black Cat" night reconnaissance aircraft to see if Kurita's fleet could be located. Unfortunately, the pilots flew west, missing the strait and the oncoming fleet.

"God Has Come to Our Assistance"
Battleship *Yamato*, East of San Bernardino Strait
0400, 25 October 1944

Vice Admiral Matome Ugaki, commander of Japan's First Battleship Division, embarked on the *Yamato* with Kurita as his operational commander, earlier had expressed foreboding. He feared a concentrated attack by Halsey after dawn. "All of our fighting strength will be reduced to nothing at the end," he worried. For the moment, however, fortune favored the fleet. The nocturnal passage through the strait had been accomplished with no opposition. Now entering the Philippine Sea off Samar, Admiral Kurita again appealed for support from Japan's land-based aircraft in the Philippines. "Braving any loss and damage we may suffer," he added, "the First Striking Force will break into Leyte Gulf and fight to the last man."

Tension was high. Every man was at his battle station, anticipating that the Americans would pounce. They didn't.

"God has come to our assistance," exulted Kurita's chief of staff as the fleet turned south down the Samar coast. Younger officers brushed back tears.

Kurita, exhausted, showed no visible sign of surprise or relief. He merely issued orders for the fleet to move into formation, his battleships and cruisers in the center and the destroyers in columns to each side in a front extending more than thirteen miles.

The fleet pushed south unopposed. Lookouts maintained a close vigil for submarines and aircraft. None appeared. It was baffling—and unsettling. How was this possible? At 0623 radar on the *Yamato* detected distant aircraft. Lookouts soon sighted the masts of ships off the southern tip of Samar. Kurita assumed it was Halsey's fleet. The Battle East of Samar was about to begin.

"Where Is Task Force 34?"

Battleship *New Jersey*, Outbound Two Hundred Miles
North of Leyte Gulf
0700, 25 October 1944

The speedy *New Jersey* and *Iowa* had slowed during the night so as not to pass Ozawa's carriers in darkness. Now, with the Northern Force about to come under aerial attack, the two battleships were on an intercept course to lay waste to the enemy. Halsey, eager for the battle-to-be, was interrupted by a message from Kinkaid, informing him that the Seventh Fleet had engaged enemy forces at Surigao Strait. Kinkaid concluded with a rather strange question: "Is TF-34 guarding San Bernardino Strait?" Hours earlier Halsey had radioed that he was heading north with his entire fleet. Why the question? Certainly enough firepower was at Leyte to pick off any Kurita stragglers. Halsey replied that TF-34 "is with our carriers and engaging enemy carriers" off Cape Engano, about 250 miles to the north.

An hour passed. Another coded message arrived from Kinkaid. The Surigao battle had gone well. A third message followed. Urgent. An enemy battleship and cruiser had opened fire from fifteen miles astern on one of three lightly defended escort carrier groups stationed at the mouth of Leyte Gulf. Halsey was perplexed. Kurita had obviously gotten through San Bernardino Strait with substantial firepower. Still, he wasn't alarmed. Kinkaid's eighteen carriers with their destroyers and destroyer escorts certainly could put up enough of a fight until Oldendorf's forces at Surigao came to the rescue. Eight minutes passed. Another directive from Kinkaid: "Urgently need fast BBs Leyte Gulf at once." In Halsey's mind, that was Oldendorf's responsibility, not his. After all, the Third Fleet was fully engaged with Ozawa's fleet and too far away. Yet another incoming message from Kinkaid revealed the full impact of the attack at Leyte: "Our CVEs being attacked by 4 BBs, 8 cruisers, plus others." Stunned that such a large force had materialized after the pounding in Sibuyan Sea, Halsey radioed his position to Kinkaid to emphasize that he was too distant to help. The admiral, growing desperate, radioed back, this time in plain English. "Where is Lee? Send Lee." Halsey, growing exasperated, was about to respond in the negative when another message arrived—this time from Admiral Nimitz. "Where is Task Force 34?" he asked. "The world wonders."

"We Can't Go Down with Our Fish Aboard"
Carrier *Fanshaw Bay* (CVE-70), Northeast of Leyte Gulf
0710, 25 October 1944

Rear Adm. Clifton "Ziggy" Sprague had just ordered the resumption of routine flight operations from the decks of eighteen baby carriers under his command and strung out north to south off the southern coast of Samar. The carriers were divided equally into three groups, each protected by three destroyers and three destroyer escorts and known as Taffy 1, Taffy 2, and Taffy 3, their radio voice call signs. The carrier-based aircraft were armed with either depth charges to hunt down enemy submarines or small bombs and ammunition to support troops ashore at Leyte. None were equipped to combat cruisers and battleships. What's worse, the flattops were slow. In the most favorable conditions, they could make only eighteen knots, easy prey to the likes of Kurita.

Sprague, who had planted his flag on *Fanshaw Bay* in the northernmost Taffy 3, had been watching aircraft take off from carriers in his group—*Kalinin Bay* (CVE-68), *White Plains* (CVE-66), *St. Lo* (CVE-63), *Kitkun Bay* (CVE-71), and *Gambier Bay* (CVE-73). He was not amused when a pilot reported four enemy battleships, seven cruisers, and eleven destroyers approaching at a thirty-knot clip from the northwest. The admiral assumed it was Admiral Halsey's task force. "Air plot, tell that pilot to check his identification," Sprague demanded. The answer came back instantly. "The pilot insists that these ships are Japanese. He says they have pagoda masts!"

Sprague's continence shifted abruptly. Jolted into action, he ordered the launch of all aircraft and recalled those sent to the beachhead to support the troops. Meanwhile, Taffy 3 carriers dialed up flank speed, pouring black smoke from their stacks and churning east away from the enemy. Kurita's fleet closed rapidly. At eighteen miles the battleships opened fire. The first salvo landed within two thousand yards of *Fanshaw Bay*, producing enormous geysers. The next round bore in closer. Just when it seemed hopeless, smoke from the carriers drifted down onto the ocean surface, temporarily hiding them. Unable to target the carriers, Kurita's ships turned their guns on the destroyer USS *Johnston* (DD-557) making a desperation run at the cruiser *Kumano*.

Lt. Cdr. Ernest Evans, captain of the destroyer, had made an instinctive decision to attack single-handedly. The *Johnston*'s 5-inch gunfire did little to thwart the charging *Kumano*. Evans plotted a zigzag course between Sprague's carriers and the enemy cruiser while spreading white smoke from the destroyer's smoke generator to help obscure a clear view of the Taffy 3 carriers. "We can't go down with our fish aboard," shouted Evans. "Stand by for torpedo attack!" The torpedo officer rattled off targeting data as the destroyer homed in. Evans deftly chased the splashes of incoming shells, correctly guessing that enemy gunners would compensate for a miss by firing at a new coordinate. He was right. The *Johnston* gained on the target. "Range thirteen thousand yards. Target speed two-five knots. . . . Range twelve thousand yards. . . . Range eleven thousand yards. . . . Range ten thousand yards. . . . Fire one," Evans ordered. In quick order, four more torpedoes—half a salvo—leaped from their firing tubes and raced away toward the *Kumano*. The *Johnston*, wheeling around, fled to safety in her own smoke screen while firing the ship's remaining five torpedoes at the battleships. Evans could hear distant explosions. The *Johnston* soon emerged into view of the cruiser; an inferno burned wildly on the enemy's fantail.

Sprague, seeing the *Johnston* racing headlong for the enemy, ordered four others into the fray in what became a furious shootout. In the chaos of the firefight, Kurita's battleships and cruisers dodged destroyer-launched torpedoes, while Sprague's destroyers darted from incoming shells with wild maneuvering. Two of the destroyers crisscrossed each other's paths, nearly colliding in the mayhem. The *Johnston*, gravely holed by 14-inch shells and on a single engine, kept returning fire, again wheeling around toward the enemy. The destroyers, each throwing out smoke to screen the carriers, managed to blunt Kurita's approach by doing exactly what the *Johnston* had done—launching half a salvo at the cruisers and half at the battleships. It worked by stalling the advance. The *Kumano* retreated owing to damage inflicted by the *Johnston*. Several torpedo hits on the *Yamato* caused Kurita's flagship to veer north. And the cruiser *Suzuya* backed off as well. Others, however, soon pressed the attack. The constant pummeling of heavy shells for nearly two hours took its toll on the Americans. The destroyer USS *Hoel* (DD-533) succumbed to forty rounds of heavy bombardment by two heavy cruisers and a battleship. The destroyer escort USS *Samuel B. Roberts* (DE-413), successful in putting several torpedoes into a cruiser, engaged in a duel to the death. Repeatedly armor-piercing shells passed through the destroyer, carrying away anything in their path. The *Johnston*, still under way, passed the *Roberts*, where Capt. Robert W. Copeland was assessing damage. From the bridge, Copeland looked down upon the *Johnston*'s fantail, from which Evans had resolutely directed his doomed destroyer toward Kurita's fleet. Copeland waved; Evans waved back. Enemy shells rained down with no letup. Copeland gave the order to abandon ship. The *Johnston*, still in the fight by Evans' sheer willpower, faced off with the battleship *Kongo* at five thousand yards, so close that the dreadnaught's big guns could not be lowered enough to target the tiny destroyer. Out of torpedoes, Evans kept up constant gunfire, chipping at the armored goliath as Japanese cruisers and destroyers moved in. Evans and his sailors were overmatched and went down fighting, disappearing below the seven-mile-deep Philippine Sea.

On board the *Fanshaw Bay*, Sprague directed the action as best he could. His 450 aircraft swirled over Kurita's fleet, dropping whatever firepower they had. Some of the torpedo bombers, lacking anything to drop, zoomed in as if they were about to launch to fake out the enemy and slow the chase of the carriers. Aircraft with live ammunition succeeded in damaging the battleships *Nagato*, *Haruna*, and *Kongo*, which nevertheless continued to pursue Taffy 3 in an erratic manner. The retreating line of carriers miraculously found sanctuary in a rain squall.

However, the respite didn't last long. Enemy fire quickly resumed. Sprague's flagship absorbed several hits but remained afloat and under way. Numerous heavy projectiles caused serious damage to the trailing *St. Lo* and *Kalinin Bay*, but the *Gambier Bay*, the most vulnerable during the retreat, took the brunt of the attack. The carrier was closest to Kurita's advancing fleet. Over a sixty-minute span, round after round of armor-piercing shells slammed into the thin-skinned carrier, passing completely through without exploding. One destroyer captain compared the carrier to a colander because of its numerous holes. A strike near the forward engine room breached the hull. Seawater poured into the doomed vessel. Slowed to eleven knots, she had no chance of escape. She capsized to port and sank at 0911, the first carrier lost to enemy gunfire in the entire war.

Southeast of Taffy 3, Rear Adm. Felix B. Stump launched the aircraft of Taffy 2 to help Sprague. The planes earlier had been loaded with torpedoes, rockets, and bombs in anticipation of action in Surigao Strait. Because Oldendorf did not need their help, Stump now sent them aloft to attack Kurita's fleet. Together with Taffy 3 fighters, Stump's aircraft swept over the enemy, adding a new element of chaos over the battle zone, in which dozens of Avengers and Wildcats were lost with their pilots.

Taffy 1 to the south came under attack from a new threat—the first organized kamikaze attacks of the war. Enemy planes, stuffed with explosives, had lifted off from land bases, their pilots intent on ramming destroyers and carriers wherever they could be found. The first salvo, however, caused minimal damage.

The five surviving Taffy 3 carriers steadily were losing their race with Kurita. The masts of his warships loomed ever larger. All that each of the carriers had left to fend off attack was a single 5-inch gun plus 40-mm and 20-mm gun batteries. As the battleships drew closer, an officer on *White Plains* admonished with black humor his idle gun crews, "Just wait a little longer, boys. We're sucking them into 40-mm range."

"Pull Yourself Together!"

Battleship *New Jersey*, Closing on Ozawa's Carriers
1000, 25 October 1944

Admiral Halsey had thrashed about angrily after receipt of Nimitz's "world wonders" message. Deep embarrassment set in. He knew the message was copied to Kinkaid and Admiral King in Washington. Sarcasm seemed to drip from Nimitz's interrogative, this from a man whom Halsey considered his friend and advocate. Nimitz, however, had intended only to get a clarification of where TF-34 was. A coding officer had added the words "the world wonders." Both the front of the message—"turkey trots to water"—and the end—"the world wonders"— were intended to confuse the enemy should the message be intercepted and decoded. However, Halsey's ensign had failed to remove the end words in decoding the message. The damage was done. Deeply humiliated, Halsey broke down in tears, flinging his hat to the deck in resignation.

"Stop it!" shouted Carney, the admiral's chief of staff, grabbing him by his shoulders. "What the hell's the matter with you? Pull yourself together!"

At the time, Halsey's battle fleet was well ahead of his carriers and within forty-two miles of Ozawa's fleet. The carriers had come under intense attack from Third Fleet aircraft as the Battle off Cape Engano got under way. Within the hour, *New Jersey* and McCann's *Iowa* would be within range to make certain Ozawa didn't get away. But now, blinded by his smoldering rage, Halsey believed Nimitz intended that TF-34 should be in action against Kurita. Thus, he ordered his force divided. Half would go after Ozawa under the command of Admiral Mitscher. The other half would target Kurita and include the two fastest battleships, the *Iowa* and *New Jersey*, and three cruisers, all under the command of Rear Adm. Oscar C. Badger. TF-34 turned and prepared to return to the coast of Samar, a six-hour voyage. Halsey directed a carrier group under Rear Admiral Bogan to provide air cover for the journey. If Halsey were lucky, he would be able to prevent Kurita from escaping through San Bernardino Strait after whatever carnage occurred in the gulf.

Not wanting to chance an encounter with the enemy without his destroyers, Halsey also assigned eight to the task force. The destroyers, however, required refueling from the battleships. It would take nearly three hours. The delay would prove decisive.

"Goddammit, They're Getting Away!"

Battleship *Yamato*
1030, 25 October 1944

Admiral Kurita could see the carrier *Gambier Bay* go under. The report from the *Kongo* was that it was an *Enterprise*-class carrier, the largest in the American arsenal. The doomed destroyer *Hoel* likewise was mistaken for a cruiser. And there were reports that another carrier had been torpedoed and sunk, with a third crippled. Kurita nevertheless was somber. He had lost the cruisers *Kumano*, *Suzuya*, *Chikuma*, and *Chokai* to aircraft and destroyer attacks. He also was certain that Halsey's task force was lurking on the horizon. He sent up two search aircraft from the *Yamato* to find out—one to the north and one to the south. Neither returned. However, the pilot of the northern recon radioed that he could find no sign of any American warships. To Kurita, this was proof that Halsey's Third Fleet was in Leyte Gulf, waiting to attack.

Kurita had one other major concern. His fleet was short on fuel, a situation exacerbated by the wild maneuvering in the fight with the Taffy 3 destroyers and aircraft. The admiral also believed that his fleet was making little progress in overtaking the carriers. To many, the opposite was true. However, the destroyers' effective smoke screen, the frantic battle, Navy aircraft, and his own fatigue had combined to make the admiral doubtful that he could prevail. Admiral Ugaki, sharing the *Yamato* on the same bridge with Kurita and his staff, didn't agree with the battle plan—cruisers and battleships at the forefront in the attack while destroyers followed. "The fleet's attacking directions were conflicting and I feared the spirit of all-out attack at short range was lacking," he noted in his shipboard diary. Ugaki worried that Kurita "lacked fighting spirit and promptitude" because he had not directed an all-out frontal assault, destroyers leading. However, Ugaki did nothing to countermand his commander. Thus, just when Kurita should have pressed his advantage to the maximum, he ordered a ceasefire. The Central Force turned north.

Those in Taffy 3 were astounded. "I could not believe my eyes, but it looked as if the whole Japanese fleet was indeed retiring," said Captain Sprague on the *Fanshaw Bay*. "However, it took a whole series of reports from circling planes to convince me. And still I could not get the fact to soak into my battle-numbed brain. At best I had expected to be swimming by this time." Indeed, most of the officers and sailors of the Taffy 3 carriers had been resigned to death or drowning before the jaws of the oncoming enemy fleet. A *Fanshaw Bay* signalman, seeing the battleships turn back to the north, chortled to fellow crew members, "Goddamit, they're getting away!"

The fighting was not over for Taffy 3, however. Kamikaze pilots targeted Sprague's carriers. At 1100 a Japanese Zero crashed into the deck of the *St. Lo*, penetrated it, and then exploded. A series of secondary detonations caused the ship to sink at 1125. Before the suicide blitz was over, four other escort carriers in the Taffys were to sustain damage.

In calling off the engagement, Kurita had decided to focus his attention on another U.S. carrier force erroneously reported to be north of Samar. Like Halsey earlier, Kurita believed that he had done substantial damage to the carriers in Leyte Gulf and that it was now his priority to go after the other carrier group. Plus, he had another motive for breaking off his attack on the Taffys: he didn't believe in wasting any more lives in what had become a futile effort. He had received the news that Japan's Southern Force had been annihilated in Surigao Strait and that the Northern Force was under attack and had lost four carriers. As he later put it, "I wanted to be at San Bernardino Strait at sunset to get through and as far to the west as possible during the night."

"The Gravest Error"
Battleship *New Jersey*
1345, 25 October 1944

Time was of the essence if Halsey's battleships were to have any influence on the outcome of the Battle of Leyte Gulf. It had taken several hours to concentrate his surface fighting group. Plus, refueling the destroyers that would accompany TF-34 had taken nearly three hours, an interminable slowdown. During the refueling, the admiral listened in on communications from the rest of his fleet attacking Ozawa's Northern Force. Under Admiral Mitscher, Navy aircraft made 527 sorties in attacks that would continue into the evening, sinking four carriers, a cruiser, and two destroyers. Yet, with the swift *Iowa* and *New Jersey* no longer on the scene, the rest of Ozawa's fleet—three carriers, two battleships, and seven destroyers—sailed off to the north and escaped. It was a bitter outcome for Halsey, who would later note, "I made a mistake in bowing to pressure and turning south. I consider this the gravest error I committed."

TF-34 arrived in the vicinity of San Bernardino Strait three hours too late to prevent Kurita's escape. The Central Force entered the waterway at 2200. The surviving ships of the enemy fleet—four battleships and five heavy cruisers—passed through the waterway and scattered to safety in the Sibuyan Sea under cover of darkness. All that was left for Halsey near the strait was the crippled destroyer *Nowaki*, quickly sunk.

Admiral Ozawa, who would survive the Battle off Cape Engaño, would later look back on the Leyte operations as an unmitigated disaster for the Imperial Navy: "After this battle the surface forces became strictly auxiliary, so that we relied on land forces, special [kamakaze] attack, and air power. . . . There was no further use assigned to surface vessels, with the exception of some special ships." Japan's navy minister, Admiral Mitsumasa Yonai, noted that the defeat at Leyte "was tantamount to the loss of the Philippines" and that in a larger context, "I felt that it was the end."

The results of the Leyte naval battles told the story. In the three-day period, Japan sustained more than 10,500 deaths plus the loss of three battleships, one large carrier, three light carriers, nine cruisers, twelve destroyers, and

Newly promoted Rear Adm. Allan McCann off duty at home in Washington in the fall of 1944 with his three daughters—(from the left) Barbara, Lois, and Alyn. Returning from the Pacific after the Battle of Leyte Gulf, he assumed operational command of the Navy's Tenth Fleet. His mission: to stop German U-boats from attacking American cities with suspected sea-launched missiles.

Courtesy of McCann family (Edie Sims)

more than five hundred aircraft. On the other hand, the casualty toll for the U.S. Navy was about three thousand deaths plus the loss of one light carrier, two escort carriers, two destroyers, a destroyer escort, one submarine, and about two hundred aircraft.

Despite the lopsided victory for the U.S. Navy, the Pacific war would continue another year. Ahead were the bloody battles of Iwo Jima and Okinawa. For Allan McCann, commander of the nation's most potent battleship and a participant in the greatest naval engagement of world history, there would be no guns fired, no claims of extraordinary valor at Leyte Gulf. Although battles raged all around TF-34—the submarine action in Palawan Passage, the Battle of the Sibuyan Sea, the Battle of Surigao Strait, the Battle East of Samar, and the Battle off Cape Engano—the *Iowa* and *New Jersey* saw no action. Such are the vagaries of war. The *Iowa* would remain in Philippine waters to screen carriers in air strikes against enemy strongholds on Luzon and Formosa (Taiwan). In mid-December, Captain McCann was promoted to rear admiral and returned to Washington to take operational command of the Tenth Fleet. There he would be engaged in a conflict with which he was more familiar—the war against Adolf Hitler's U-boats. The goal: to prevent a new breed of submarine from attempting to launch rockets into New York City to topple skyscrapers.

CHAPTER 13

OPERATION TEARDROP

Tenth Fleet Headquarters
Navy Department, Washington, D.C.
16 April 1945

*A*t age forty-eight, Allan McCann looked haggard from loss of sleep. Lines of worry etched his weatherworn face as his tall frame bent forward to survey a large plotting table showing the position of the Tenth Fleet's forty-two destroyers, four escort carriers, and four air wings with a total of seventy-six planes. Half were deployed in a defensive line south of Iceland to prevent seven German U-boats from launching a suspected missile attack on New York City. The other half was standing by to create a second barrier force south of Newfoundland over the Grand Banks and Flemish Cap. Two of the Seewolf submarines had been found and destroyed. But five others remained unaccounted for in their steady trek southwest from Norway toward the United States. Two days had passed with no sightings, causing heightening drama at the Navy Department.

The Seewolf group, augmented by several U-boats operating independently to attack shipping along the East Coast of the United States, had cast off in staged deployments from secret bases on the Norwegian coast beginning in late March. Thanks to code breakers in London who had deciphered the plot the previous November, the admiral knew the routes the Seewolf subs would take to cross the Atlantic. To counter the threat, McCann had mapped out their projected tracks and Atlantic Fleet Adm. Jonas Ingram had devised the type of defensive force—planes, carriers, and destroyers working in tandem—that had been effective in thwarting U-boat attacks on Allied convoys in the Battle of the Atlantic in 1943–44. McCann's predecessor, Rear Adm. Francis

Stuart "Frog" Low, had pioneered the concept: a network of carrier-destroyer hunter-killer groups stretched in a "barrier" line in the Atlantic. Navy aircraft flying off the carriers and U.S. Army planes joining in from land bases used radar and visual sightings while destroyers scanned the depths with sonar. At the first contact, aircraft and destroyers would head for the position in a concentrated attack. The tactic had been a resounding success, raising the "kill" ratio of sunken U-boats from 86 in 1942 to 243 in 1943 and 289 in 1944. Admiral Low was the inspiration for the Tenth Fleet, an intelligence nerve center based in Washington that had direct access to all U.S. warships and aircraft in the Atlantic. Although Fleet Admiral King was technically in charge of the "fleet with no ships," it was his operational commander—first Low, now McCann—who directed daily operations.

As the U-boat threat diminished in late 1944, King relieved Low, who returned to the Pacific to take charge of a cruiser division, and McCann took the helm of the Tenth in early January 1945. By then, U-boat sightings were rare in the western Atlantic. Said one frustrated carrier commander, "A contact now is a precious thing. Only a few will occur in any cruise and they must be developed and held onto with every ounce of skill and endurance it is possible to muster."

Admiral King had started the process of demobilizing the Tenth until there was "a marked renewal of U-boat activity in Atlantic areas of U.S. responsibility," as he put it. As a result, barrier force carriers spent much time in training exercises or ferrying aircraft and supplies during the winter of 1944–45. McCann, cool of temperament and highly respected throughout the Navy for his efficient command, seemed ideal to succeed Low during the drawdown. As a storied submarine veteran, he was well versed in undersea tactics and had helped set up Tenth Fleet antisubmarine training operations in Bermuda. If the U-boats made another thrust at the United States, King considered the admiral best able to deal with the challenge.

By early January, the plan for handling the Seewolf threat had been worked out. Relying on McCann's daily intelligence plots, derived from intercepted U-boat commands radioed to and from Europe, Admiral Ingram would deploy his destroyers, carriers, and aircraft as twin barrier forces, the second backing up the first and focused to the east to locate and destroy the Nazi subs. The First Barrier Force, under the command of Capt. John R. Ruhsenberger in the *Croatan* (CVE-25), was the more northern group consisting of the *Mission Bay* (CVE-59) and *Croatan*, each protected by a screen of four destroyer escorts. Another twelve destroyer escorts were strung out 40 to 50 miles to the east of the carriers in a 120-mile-long line northeast of the Azores. The forward destroyers were spaced five to ten miles apart. The force was to remain deployed from 11 to 21 April, and then the Second Barrier Force, under the command of Capt.

George J. Dufek in the *Bogue* (CVE-9), would form in relief west of the Azores near Newfoundland in the area of the Grand Banks and Flemish Cap. The force, to be on station from 20 April to 2 May, would consist of the carriers *Core* (CVE-13) and *Bogue* and their twenty-two escorts. Rather than have the escorts hug the carriers, as in the first barrier, the destroyers would be stretched out in a single line with the carriers at the two ends. Five miles separated each of the warships, creating a nautical Maginot line south of St. John's, Newfoundland, along the 45th meridian. If the U-boats got past the first barrier, the second would be in place "to bar off the entire eastern seaboard of Canada and the United States to a phalanx of snorkel boats," as Ingram put it. Because McCann calculated the submarine advance at approximately a hundred nautical miles per day, the First Barrier Force maneuvered slowly to the southwest to stay ahead of the supposed position of the Seewolf group.

The Type IX U-boats provided a formidable challenge. They were designed to travel 11,000 miles without refueling and typically were armed with twenty-two torpedoes. The subs were equipped with unique air breathing tubes that could be deployed to the surface, enabling the vessels to remain at depth while operating their air guzzling, nine-cylinder diesel engines to not only recharge batteries but provide forward propulsion. These revolutionary "snorkels" made the boats much harder to detect, especially to aircraft.

In the early stages, the strategy behind McCann's Operation Teardrop seemed to work well. On 15 April the destroyers USS *Stanton* and USS *Frost* in the First Barrier Force sank U-1235 after a three-hour battle south of Iceland. The next day the two again collaborated to sink U-880. Most alarming to Admiral McCann and others at Tenth Fleet headquarters were reports of the extremely violent explosions that had destroyed the two U-boats, so powerful they had knocked sailors to the deck in ships ten miles away. The blasts seemed clear evidence that the subs had missiles on board or were towing them.

Heightening McCann's worries was the ineffectiveness of aerial surveillance sent up by the First Barrier Force. Forty-knot winds, tumultuous seas, heavy rain, and fog had hampered the search. Sending pilots aloft for wave-top patrols had proven extraordinarily difficult. Even when B-24 Liberator and Avenger aircraft could fly, there were no contacts in the seething seas. Flying in such conditions in hopes of spotting a snorkel or intercepting a sub on the surface taxed even the bravest aviator whose gravest risk was returning to his carrier, pitching about in the most severe conditions imaginable. Crashes on board the flattops had resulted in two fatalities plus major damage or loss of returning planes.

Those in Washington thought that the remaining Seewolf subs might be slipping by the hunters and closing on the American coastline. By McCann's calculation, an attack could be expected by the end of the month or in early

May. There was little time left. All the admiral could do was wait and hope for a break. Fresh off the Battle of Leyte Gulf, he considered the strange twist of fate that found Frog Low going to the Pacific to command a cruiser division for the Okinawa invasion while he returned to Washington to wind down the operations of the Tenth Fleet. The new post should have been anticlimatic. After all, Germany was all but beaten. In March Gen. George S. Patton and the Third Army had crossed the Rhine River into Germany and were advancing toward Berlin while the Russian army moved against the Third Reich from the east. Adolf Hitler was desperate for a miracle, some victory that might give the Allies pause—or at least a measure of vengeance. A submarine-launched missile attack on an American city could be that kind of retribution, particularly coming in the aftermath of President Roosevelt's death from a cerebral hemorrhage on 12 April and the succession of Vice President Harry S Truman to the presidency. Thus, this possible last gambit of the dictator—a final battle of the Atlantic portending grave consequences for New York City—had fallen to McCann to prevent.

Creeper Attack
Coastal Command PBY Catalina, Atlantic Ocean
18 April 1945

A pilot on a scouting patrol for the First Barrier Force spotted what he thought was a Seewolf and radioed for assistance from USS *Mosely* (DE-321). The pilot in fact had spotted a U-boat. U-805 was headed for patrol duty off Long Island, New York. Richard Bernardelli, making his first war patrol as the boat's skipper, tracked north away from *Mosely*, warned off by all the radio noise. The destroyer raced to the coordinates reported by the pilot and began a careful search. It proved useless. Eventually, U-805 turned back on a different path, outwitting the barrier force screen and continuing toward Long Island.

On the night of 21 April, the carrier *Croatan* was about to be relieved by the Second Barrier Force when her four escorts made a final sonar sweep and detected U-805 again trying to pass the barrier. The destroyers attacked. Once more Bernardelli evaded the hunters by occasionally backing into the swirl of the sub's submerged wake to create a knuckle in the sea, confusing those manning sound equipment in the destroyers. U-805 escaped.

Less than an hour after the *Croatan* group lost contact with Bernardelli's U-boat, a Seewolf sub was spotted picking its way past the barrier. Skipper Hans-Werner Offermann at age twenty-two was one of the youngest of all the U-boat captains and a rising star, having sunk one ship and damaged another in attacks on convoys the previous year. Now making his second patrol, he had hoped mountainous seas would enable U-518 to find an opening in the barrier force. Offermann had taken the boat down, where the sub remained motionless amid sonar pinging by USS *Carter* (DE-112), which soon established a solid contact. Rather than attack immediately, destroyer captain F. J. T. Baker coached another, the *Neal A. Scott* (DE-769), in a "creeper attack" in a light fog barely illuminated by moonlight. The warship got a fix on the submarine at a depth of 150 feet and set depth charges accordingly. Hedgehog attacks by both destroyers blanketed the U-boat an hour after midnight. U-518 didn't have a chance. Offermann and his crew of forty-two perished.

Success for Operation Teardrop had come not from aircraft but from the tedious sonar and hydrophonic probing of the depths by surface ships. Not a single attack had been made by an Avenger bomber as had been expected. It was not for lack of trying. Said one flight leader on board *Croatan*, "No squadron in our experience had ever tried any harder."

With the First Barrier Force giving way to the second, force captain Dufek sent out night flyers on 20 April to a distance of 80 miles east and west of the 120-mile-long defensive line. It wasn't until 23 April, however, before the first apparent contact was made near the center of the force. As six destroyers worked to establish what to make of the contact at 0645, a low-flying Avenger off *Core* excitedly reported sighting the feathery wake of a U-boat snorkel. The pilot dropped multiple depth bombs and reported an explosion followed by the "motor noises" of a U-boat attempting to surface. The pilot jettisoned a life raft for any survivors and circled as two destroyers sped to the scene. What they found wasn't a U-boat or survivors. It was a dead whale.

"Stand by Guns!"
Avenger Aircraft VC-19, Atlantic Ocean
23 April 1945

Five hours after the whale sighting, another pilot had the first true fix on one of the hunted Seewolf boats. Lt. Cdr. William W. South had been flying seventy miles northeast of the *Bogue* when he saw U-546 breaking surface near the center of the Second Barrier Force. South attacked, but the sub dove to safety. Force captain Dufek ordered two destroyer screens into the chase, one following a clockwise rotation to the south and another a counterclockwise rotation to the north in hopes of finding the U-boat. Following a methodical nineteen-hour search, the *Frederick C. Davis* (DE-136) reestablished contact with U-546, which was passing down the ship's starboard side at two thousand yards. The destroyer's officer of the deck ordered a hard right rudder and sent sailors scrambling for hedgehog throwers and depth-charge racks. The crew was intent on adding a U-boat to the wartime score of the illustrious "Fightin' Freddie," one of the best-known destroyers in the Atlantic.

As an Edsall-class warship, the *Frederick C. Davis* had established a remark-able record for valor in the Mediterranean in 1943 while guarding convoys between North African ports and Naples. When torpedo and medium-range bombers attacked and damaged three ships on 6 November, intense antiaircraft gunfire from the destroyer drove the enemy away. Three weeks later, the *Davis* shot down two bombers while defending another convoy. A month later, the destroyer helped sink U-73 in the western Mediterranean. In providing cover during Allied landings at Anzio, Italy, on 22 January 1944, the warship remained on station for six months, fighting off numerous air attacks and using special jamming equipment to foil enemy attacks with rocket-propelled, radio-directed glider bombs. The battle was intense and at points led to the destroyer coming under fire from shore batteries. For the ship's accomplishment, officers and crew earned a Navy Unit Commendation.

After returning to the United States for overhaul, the *Davis* joined the Second Barrier Force and was now about to attack U-546. U-boat skipper Paul Just, however, struck first at a range of 650 yards at 0835. A torpedo exploded abreast of the destroyer's forward engine room, rupturing the compartment. The detonation flung the wardroom deck against the overhead, where offi-cers were eating breakfast, killing them all. Others on the flying bridge were thrown into the sea. Ruptured fuel lines fed an inferno in the area of the bridge. Within five minutes, the destroyer had split in two, and pandemonium was spreading. Three junior officers organized sailors to secure hatches and check depth charges to make sure they would not explode. Two could not be neutral-ized, their ignition caps and safety forks having been removed. Life rafts and floater nets were set adrift. A hundred crew members—who had been asleep in quarters aft of the engine room—swam for the rafts after the senior officer aft ordered abandon ship. The sea, rough and cold, claimed many of the sailors, some with no life jackets. Sharks also made their presence known. Two depth charges went off as the destroyer sank, causing more deaths.

Destroyer screen commander Frederick S. Hall, embarked in USS *Pillsbury* (DE-133), witnessed the explosions and sent USS *Hayter* (DE-212) and USS *Neunzer* (DE-150) to press the hunt for U-546 while USS *Flaherty* (DE-135) moved in to rescue survivors. Wary of becoming a second target, Capt. M. W. Firth proceeded carefully through the wreckage, plucking sailors out of the sea on the fly while tossing rafts and empty depth-charge canisters that could float to survivors. All the while Firth had his sonar operator maintain a vigil for any sign of the submarine. At 0917—forty-two minutes after U-546 attacked—the *Flaherty* found the U-boat lurking below the flotsam. Firth signaled the *Hayter* to take over rescue operations as the *Flaherty* began a creeper attack. But the *Pillsbury*, charging to the scene, made so much noise that the *Flaherty* lost con-tact with the U-boat.

Hayter managed to rescue three officers and sixty-six enlisted sailors from the *Frederick C. Davis*, although three died after being pulled on board. Thirteen officers and 179 enlisted sailors were lost.

Still eluding the barrier force, U-boat skipper Just was as good a captain as Nazi Germany had ever produced. A former member of the Luftwaffe, he had joined the undersea service in January 1941 and served on U-156 through July 1942, making three war patrols that sank seventeen ships and damaged four others. Now captain of U-546, Just was into his third war patrol with a crew of fifty-eight. As one of the Seewolf group, the boat got past the First Barrier Force and was attempting to escape the clutches of the second.

For twelve hours, U-546 endured every type of surface antisubmarine tactic the Americans could come up with. A dozen destroyers took turns working over the boat. Nevertheless, the sub persevered, often going deep to get below depth-charge range. But the sub was nearing the limit of its endurance. Surfacing was inevitable. At 1810 the *Pillsbury* reported the U-boat coming up. Noises from its main pumps were easily picked up on hydrophones. The *Flaherty*, coached by the *Pillsbury*, moved in and lobbed more hedgehogs. One ruptured the pressure hull and split open batteries in the boat's keel, unleashing deadly chlorine gas. Commander Just had no choice but to surface.

At 1836 the *Flaherty* sounded the alarm to prepare for action: "Sub is coming to surface, stand by guns!" Two minutes later, U-546 broached and simultaneously launched a single torpedo at *Flaherty*. It missed. Captain Firth was incensed. "That stinker fired a torpedo at me!" he radioed Hall before returning fire with two torpedoes. Both missed. Destroyers let loose with deck guns, ripping apart the U-boat's conning tower to ensure that there would be no escape. Captain Just and his crew jumped overboard as the stern of the U-boat sank, cantilevering the bow out of the water vertically before sliding back into the abyss. The Americans rescued thirty-three of U-546's crew, including the skipper, who defied all attempts at interrogation. Under armed guard, the captives were taken to Argentia for what would prove to be rough treatment to determine what they knew about a rocket attack on American cities.

The Second Barrier Force went back to work seeking the whereabouts of the three remaining Seewolf submarines—U-805, U-853, and U-858. The destroyers patrolled southwesterly at a slow five knots in an attempt to make them and their carriers bait for the U-boats so that they would reveal themselves. Admiral Ingram also ordered the *Mission Bay* group from the First Barrier Force to deploy back to sea from Argentia to extend the reach of the barrier.

Nearly two weeks passed with no sub sightings. Then on 6 May at 0413, USS *Farquhar* (DE-139) made contact with what mistakenly was thought to be a Seewolf boat. It was U-881, a boat sent to fortify the Seewolf group. Sonar tracking indicated that it was preparing to attack *Mission Bay*. *Farquhar* made a determined charge to prevent that, dropping a pattern of thirteen depth charges over the U-boat at 0431. Nine explosions proved a quick end to the submarine and its crew of forty-four.

"Moby Dick"
U-853, Atlantic Ocean
5 May 1945

No one knows whether sub skipper Helmut Fromsdorf knew the end was coming for the Third Reich. The twenty-four-year-old captain was making his first war patrol. His snorkel-equipped U-853, one of the three remaining Seewolf boats, had made the treacherous, five-week crossing of the Atlantic from its base in Norway to reach the Gulf of Maine on 1 April. His orders were to attack coastal vessels, and he had carried them out on 23 April by putting a torpedo into USS *Eagle Boat 56* (PE-56) near Portland, Maine. The 430-ton ship, which had been towing targets for U.S. Navy bombers, sank quickly with the loss of fifty-four of the sixty-seven-man crew. The next day, USS *Muskegon* (PF-24) located U-853 by sonar and dropped depth charges over the target. The boat escaped.

Fromsdorf stayed on the offensive and in the late afternoon of 5 May prepared to attack the 5,353-ton, fully loaded coal freighter *Black Point* in seas off Rhode Island. Either the boat captain had no intention of surrendering, or he had no idea the war was nearly over, that Adolf Hitler had committed suicide on 30 April, that Berlin was being battered by twenty Russian armies backed by 6,300 tanks and 8,500 aircraft, and that German grand admiral Doenitz, commander of the U-boat navy, had become the de facto president of all that was left of the Third Reich.

U-853, as a last vestige of the once mighty undersea fleet, was one of the more famous submarines of the Atlantic war. The boat's former captain, Helmut Sommer, was known in the German submarine fleet as "the Tightrope Walker" for his bravado and ability to make narrow escapes. The boat on its first patrol in late May 1944 attempted to sink the *Queen Mary*, which was loaded with American troops and supplies. The luxury cruise liner put on the speed and outran the submarine, which had surfaced in the ship's wake in an attempt to overtake it. When the liner radioed for help, three British warplanes zoomed in and attacked, causing slight damage to the sub. U-853 returned fire, hitting all three planes and forcing them to return to their carriers, where one of the aircraft had to be jettisoned overboard as a total loss. A few weeks later, the sub surfaced near the carrier *Croatan* and its barrier force in the mid-Atlantic. U-853's radio transmissions to a base station on the coast of France were intercepted by the *Croatan* and traced back to their source. The carrier's six destroyers headed for the scene, having already sunk two other U-boats. But U-853 could not be found. A two-week search proved fruitless despite daily weather reports broadcast from the U-boat. The *Croatan* shipmates began referring to the sub as "Moby Dick," after the albino whale hunted by Captain Ahab in Herman Melville's iconic novel. On 17 June the sub again surfaced for its daily meteorological broadcast, this time a mere thirty miles from the *Croatan*. FM-1 Wildcat fighters flew off the carrier and within minutes strafed the submarine. Gunfire killed two and wounded a dozen others, including U-boat skipper Sommer, who sustained numerous bullet and shrapnel wounds. The captain gave the order to dive and saved the boat, which returned to its base at Lorient, France, where Sommer was relieved of command.

Now, a year later, his executive officer, Fromsdorf, was in command. Coming off the sinking of the patrol boat on 23 April, the new skipper prepared for a submerged attack on *Black Point* on 5 May. The collier was making its way slowly westward toward the entrance to Rhode Island Sound, the ship's destination after a voyage from Norfolk, Virginia. At 1739, U-853 fired a single torpedo that hit the ship's starboard side, aft of the engine room. The explosion killed thirteen sailors. Others abandoned the ship before it rolled over and sank. A nearby freighter issued an SOS. Eleven Navy and Coast Guard ships arrived two hours after the sinking and set up a barrier force to find the U-boat.

Inexplicably, Fromsdorf had not used the commotion of the coal hauler going down to mask a getaway. Rather, he submerged to the seabed and remained there. Overhead, barrier vessels began echo ranging as the U-boat began moving away to the north among the many wrecks littering the ocean floor. At 2014 USS *Atherton* (DE-169) made contact and dropped thirteen magnetic charges over the boat's position. One detonated. The destroyer followed up with a hedgehog attack. When no telltale debris floated to the surface to indicate the U-boat's demise, the surface force resumed its sonar search.

Just before midnight, the *Atherton* again located U-853 about four thousand yards east of its previous location, lying prone on the sea floor a hundred feet down, its propellers at a dead stop. No doubt, the sub had incurred much internal damage from the numerous hedgehog explosions. Another withering attack from the *Atherton* ripped at the U-boat. Oil and air bubbled to the surface as well as bits of wood. For twenty minutes, the destroyer circled and then lobbed more hedgehogs, hoping to split the submarine's pressure hull. More oil spillage, air bubbles, and debris, including a pillow, a life jacket, and a small wooden flagstaff, floated to the surface. The attack was so violent that it knocked out the destroyer's dead-reckoning tracer. Thus, the Coast Guard frigate *Moberly* (PF-63) moved in to renew a sonar sweep. To the disbelief of those in the barrier force, U-853 not only was intact but had turned south at four to five knots. At 0200 *Moberly* focused another hedgehog attack on the boat, whose speed dropped to two knots before it came to a halt, grounded on the bottom.

With the morning light, evidence that "Moby Dick" had met its doom appeared in large pools of oil on the ocean's surface dotted with life jackets, canvas escape lungs, and other debris, including Captain Fromsdorf's hat and the boat's chart table. At 0600 Navy blimps *K-16* and *K-58* from Lakehurst, New Jersey, arrived to fix the position of the sub with smoke and dye markers and to photograph the scene. The blimps also lowered sound buoys, which detected possible survivors. The "rhythmic hammering on a metal surface," however, was lost as destroyers renewed attacks on the submerged hulk, using it for target practice. At 1230 as most of the barrier force left for Boston, a diver sent down to examine U-853 discovered the boat's side torn open and bodies strewn about inside. The war in the Atlantic had finally ended. It was 6 May.

The next day, Admiral Doenitz ordered all U-boat forces to halt operations, return to bases, or surrender to the Allies. In quick order, U-805 and U-858—the two remaining Seewolf boats—plus U-234, U-873, and U-1228 surfaced, ran up black flags as directed by the U.S. Navy, and awaited barrier forces to effect surrender. It would be a moment of supreme triumph for all those in the Tenth Fleet, especially Admiral Ingram and Rear Admiral McCann, who worked so tirelessly to defeat the Seewolf threat.

"Heroic Fight That Knows No Equal"
Tenth Fleet Headquarters, Washington, D.C.
15 June 1945

On the day the Tenth Fleet was dissolved, there was no pomp and circumstance for what the "fleet with no ships" had accomplished. After all, the war with Japan still raged. Still, Rear Admiral McCann's direction of the fleet and Admiral Ingram's scheme for barrier forces proved decisive against the Seewolf subs, one of the great successes of World War II. Six of the seven submarines that set out from Norway to create havoc off the coast of the United States never made it. McCann and Rear Admiral Low before him had accomplished what Fleet Admiral King set out to do: eliminate the undersea navy thrown at the Allies by German grand admiral Doenitz, which had seemed on the verge of triumph until the Tenth Fleet was born in 1943. The factor that made the Tenth most effective was the breaking of the German naval code, which allowed the Allies to decipher movements of U-boats in the Atlantic. This intelligence enabled the U.S. Navy to position its barrier forces in the right place at the right time to deliver a death knell. Doenitz, in ordering the U-boat surrender, acknowledged the valor of his sub sailors and their desire to keep fighting. "I will hear no more of this 'heroes death' business," he said. "It is now my responsibility to finish." Of the remaining German submarines, the crews of 181 surrendered to the Allies. Crews of 217 others scuttled the boats rather than turn them over. The embittered skippers of U-530 and U-977, unwilling to quit the fight, stayed on the run for two months before they reached the neutral port of Mar del Plat in Argentina on 9 July. Officers and enlisted submariners were given sanctuary, but their boats were turned over to U.S. naval authorities. Doenitz, in looking back at the war in the Atlantic, described it as "a heroic fight that knows no equal." It was a battle of technological breakthroughs that first favored one side, then the other, but it was ultimately won by the Allies. Out of 39,000 officers and enlisted submariners who went to war in U-boats, only 7,000 returned alive.

The biggest mystery to be resolved for McCann in the aftermath of the war was whether Seewolf subs were carrying missiles. Captured crew members and officers interrogated at a Marine Corps brig in Argentia confirmed that there were none on board, that the subs' only intent was to make a final offensive strike against U.S. coastal shipping. Skipper Fritz Stienhoff of U-873 and his crew had been among the last taken into custody after they surrendered off Portsmouth, New Hampshire. Stienhoff previously commanded U-511 during submerged rocket trials in the Baltic; his brother also was involved in rocket research in Germany. Whether the U.S. Navy knew this is unclear. Stienhoff and his men were transported to Charles Street Jail in Boston, where the captain committed suicide on 19 May.

As the Tenth Fleet faded from view, the war in the Pacific continued unabated. For Rear Admiral McCann, historic new horizons were ahead. First up: taking command of a Navy task force that would deliver President Harry S Truman to the Berlin Peace Conference.

CHAPTER 14

Terribly Cruel

St. Mawgan Airfield
Cornwall, England
2 August 1945

Fog so thick you couldn't see the runway had settled over St. Mawgan Airfield, the primary landing strip for the port city of Plymouth in Cornwall, England. Rear Admiral Allan R. McCann, U.S. ambassador John G. Winnant, Navy admiral Harold R. Stark, and British major general Alec W. Lee had arrived at the airfield at midmorning in a cavalcade of vehicles that McCann had mustered for the forty-mile drive from the port to greet Harry S Truman upon his return from the bombed-out ruins of Berlin. The president, top officials from his administration, and the White House press corps and photographers were inbound on four transports on the last stage of an eight-hundred-mile flight from Berlin. Truman was anxious to get back to Plymouth, where McCann's Navy Task Force 68 remained at anchor in the harbor to return the president to Washington. Truman was in a hurry; the top secret he had been carrying—the explosion of an atomic bomb over Japan—soon would rivet world attention.

Truman's mission—to attend a seventeen-day conference in Potsdam, Germany, to map out plans for postwar central Europe—had begun on 7 July, when the heavy cruiser USS *Augusta* (CA-31), the presidential flagship, led by the light cruiser USS *Philadelphia* (CL-41), McCann's flagship, stood out from Norfolk, Virginia, for Antwerp, Belgium. There the president, Secretary of State James F. Byrnes, Fleet Adm. William D. Leahy, and the rest of Truman's delegation debarked in a forty-car caravan for Brussels, where they boarded planes for Berlin. In suburban Potsdam, Truman met with British prime minister Winston Churchill and Soviet premier Joseph Stalin to formalize the division of Germany and Austria and their capitals into four occupation zones. During the talks, on 26 July, the leaders issued the Potsdam Declaration, which set the terms for a surrender by Japan. The president was triumphant about the outcome. Stalin had agreed to rush his armies west across Siberia, declare war on Japan, and then invade. "He'll be in the Jap War on August 15th," noted Truman in his diary. "Fini Japs when that comes about."

The president believed that the Russians, not the Americans, would take the brunt of casualties in what most thought would be a bloody invasion tantamount to what had occurred for Americans at Iwo Jima. Although estimates indicated that as many as 35 percent of American troops would die during an invasion of Japan, Truman ordered the Joint Chiefs of Staff to move ahead with plans for Operation Olympic, a 1 November 1945 invasion of Kyushu, the southernmost of the four main Japanese islands. Key members of Truman's administration, including Admiral Leahy, had staunchly opposed the president's effort to persuade the Soviets to invade. They worried that Stalin would use the occasion to extend his postwar influence on Japan and Asia. Backwater intelligence further revealed that Japan had made contact with the Soviets in hopes of reaching a peace accord in which the two countries would divvy up control of territories conquered by Japan in Asia.

On 16 July news of the successful explosion of a Manhattan Project test atomic bomb in New Mexico altered Truman's view. "Believe Japs will fold up before Russia comes in. I am sure they will when Manhattan appears over their homeland," he wrote in his diary on 18 July. He added, "We have discovered the most terrible bomb in the history of the world. . . . Thirteen pounds of the explosive caused the complete disintegration of a steel tower 60 feet high, created a crater 6 feet deep and 1,200 feet in diameter, knocked over a steel tower 1/2 mile away and knocked men down 10,000 yards away. The explosion was visible for more than 200 miles and audible for 40 miles and more."

On 24 July a top-secret U.S. Army weather forecast communiqué informed Truman of specific dates the first A-bomb could be detonated over Japan: "Some chance August 1 to 3, good chance August 4 to 5 and barring unexpected relapse almost certain before August 10." On 25 July the president had decided to proceed against a military target. "Even if the Japs are savages, ruthless, merciless and fanatic, we as the leader of the world for the common welfare cannot drop this terrible bomb on the old capital [Kyoto] or the new [Tokyo]," the president concluded. A warning in the form of the Potsdam Declaration demanded Japan's unconditional surrender. But it did not mention the existence of the atomic bomb. Rather it included the ominous warning, "The alternative for Japan is prompt and utter destruction."

With the Potsdam conference winding down, McCann made a continuous round of official calls in Antwerp that included having lunch with the burgomaster, attending the symphony at the city's opera house, and attending a state dinner at the governor's palace. He also toured the countryside, visited an orchid nursery, and boarded a canal boat for a ride around the city in what he later called a "busman's holiday" in a letter home. Finally, the admiral and his task force sailed from Antwerp to Plymouth to await Truman's return. Dense fog at St. Mawgan now threatened to delay the president's return to the *Augusta* and to leave McCann and his welcoming party empty-handed. As the president's plane neared Plymouth, the pilot got word that St. Mawgan was closed. Informed that a smaller landing field called Harrowbeer, about ten miles outside Plymouth, was clear, Truman decided to put down there to the surprise of onlookers. While awaiting transportation to the port, he left his plane to pose for still and motion picture photos with three young officers of the British Women's Auxiliary Air Force on duty at the airfield—Section Officer Eira Buckland Jones, Cpl. Clarice Turner, and Leading Aircraft Woman Audley Bartlett. The president and others then boarded vehicles to make the short trip to Plymouth, where he hastened to board the *Augusta* just before noon. Meanwhile, McCann and others at St. Mawgan beat a fast track back to Plymouth, where they too boarded the *Augusta* ten minutes behind Truman.

Anchored near the *Augusta* was the royal battle cruiser *Renown* with King George VI on board. The king, who had invited the president to London but was politely turned down, wanted to meet Truman and invited him to the cruiser. The president couldn't blow off a quick courtesy call, so he, Secretary Byrnes, Admiral Leahy, and Admiral McCann boarded a royal barge for the *Renown* and lunched with the ruler. The king returned the call later that afternoon for a brief visit. At 1549 the *Augusta* and the *Philadelphia* got under way, setting a course for Newport News, Virginia, at twenty-six knots, the maximum speed McCann's flagship could maintain without refueling.

"Greatest Thing in History"
After Mess Hall, Heavy Cruiser *Augusta*, Atlantic Ocean
6 August 1945

Four days into the voyage home, the president and Secretary of State Byrnes awaited news from Japan as they lunched with enlisted sailors. Truman, coatless but wearing his iconic bow tie, knew he might be interrupted at any time with the bulletin from Washington relayed by McCann in the *Philadelphia*. A few minutes before noon, Capt. Frank H. Graham, the *Augusta*'s map room watch officer, walked in and passed a brief message to the president. It was from the Navy Department. An Army B-29 had dropped an atomic bomb on the military port of Hiroshima a few hours earlier under perfect weather conditions. The devastation was more than had been expected. Truman turned to the captain and shook his hand. "This is the greatest thing in history," the president beamed.

Admiral McCann (top left) arrives on British admiral Sir John Leatham's barge for lunch with King George VI on the battle cruiser HMS *Renown* in Portsmouth Harbor in England on 2 August 1945. Also on the barge (from left to right) are U.S. Secretary of State James Byrnes, Adm. William D. Leahy, Admiral Leatham, and President Harry S Truman. Truman had just flown to Portsmouth from Potsdam, Germany, where the partition of postwar Germany was decided. McCann's Navy task force had been waiting at Portsmouth to return Truman to the United States on board the heavy cruiser USS *Augusta* (CA-31).

Harry S Truman Presidential Library, Independence, Missouri

Task force commander McCann from his flagship, the light cruiser USS *Philadelphia* (CL-41) seen here, led a speedy voyage home for Truman after Potsdam. En route, Admiral McCann relayed news to the president that an atomic bomb had exploded over Hiroshima.

Naval History and Heritage Command, Washington Navy Yard, Washington, D.C.

Ten minutes later, a second report arrived, this time from Secretary of War Henry L. Stimson in Washington. Truman looked at it, leaped from his seat, read it to Byrnes, and exclaimed, "It's time for us to get on home!" Turning to the crew, the president called for quiet as he stood facing them, clutching the two dispatches in his hand. He announced the attack on Japan with a powerful new weapon, 20,000 times more explosive than a ton of TNT. Loud applause and whoops punctuated the room. Truman adjourned to the *Augusta*'s wardroom where he informed the ship's officers who were dining there of the attack. Jubilant, they and the president expressed hope that the bombing might bring the Pacific war to a quick end.

Nearing the American coastline, the task force listened in on radio broadcasts from Washington on which narrators read Truman's prearranged statement announcing the detonation of the atomic bomb. In the press release, the president referred to the Potsdam Declaration as an early warning to the Japanese. "Their leaders promptly rejected that ultimatum," he noted. "If they do not now accept our terms they may expect a rain of ruin from the air, the like of which has never been seen on this earth. Behind this air attack will follow sea and land forces in such numbers and power as they have not yet seen and with the fighting skill of which they are already well aware."

Later that day, Truman convened a conference with the White House press corps in the *Augusta*. He discussed in detail the months of research and development it took to create the bomb, then posed for newsreel cameras, and said defiantly, "The Japanese began the war from the air at Pearl Harbor. They have been repaid many fold."

Truman relaxed the rest of the day, enjoying a boxing match on the ship's well deck and entertainment provided by the *Augusta*'s orchestra. Meanwhile, McCann steered a steady, fast pace toward the United States.

"It Will Probably Be Used against Us"
Newport News Naval Shipyard, Virginia
7 August 1945

The *Augusta* moored at Pier No. 6 at the Army Embarkation Dock, Newport News Naval Shipyard, after a record run from Plymouth, averaging 26.5 knots and spanning 3,230 miles in 5 days. Truman, describing the trip as "delightful," congratulated Rear Admiral McCann on a "highly satisfactory and efficient" trans-Atlantic mission. An hour later, the president and his party departed by train for Washington. The next day, Stalin declared war on Japan and sent his armies sweeping across Manchuria. When Japan still hedged on surrender, Truman ordered a second atomic bomb attack, this time on the port city of Nagasaki on 9 August. That same day, the president rebuffed U.S. Senator Richard Russell's plea to drop even more atomic bombs and renew conventional weapon attacks: "I know that Japan is a terribly cruel and uncivilized nation in warfare but I can't bring myself to believe that, because they are beasts, we should ourselves act in the same manner. For myself, I certainly regret the necessity of wiping out whole populations because of the 'pigheadedness' of the leaders of a nation and, for your information, I am not going to do it until it is absolutely necessary."

On 10 August Japan agreed to surrender on a single condition: that the nation be allowed to keep its emperor. Truman conceded that point. On 14 August Japan formally accepted the terms. World War II ended the next day with Emperor Hirohito's radio address to Japanese citizens.

As the full extent of the destruction of Hiroshima and Nagasaki and the loss of 200,000 lives set in, some in the administration began to doubt the wisdom of dropping the bombs. Admiral Leahy was among the early doubters. He noted in a diary entry dated 8 August, "There is a certainty that it [the atomic bomb] will in the future be developed by potential enemies and that it will probably be used against us."

As these events in Japan and Washington played out, Allan McCann returned to the Navy Department, unaware that by 18 December he would be promoted to command of the entire Pacific submarine force and to help deny Russian access to a great discovery in Japan.

"War against All Humanity"
Sasebo Harbor, Japan
1 November 1945

Lt. Thomas O. Paine edged in for a closer view as a strange-looking submarine that dwarfed Navy fleet boats approached its mooring at Sasebo Harbor, a Japanese naval base near Nagasaki on the island of Kyushu. Paine couldn't wait to get on board the I-402. He, like other submarine combat veterans of the Pacific war, couldn't believe what was before his eyes: a lofty conning tower set oddly off center on the port side astride an enormous sea-tight hangar door. An eighty-five-foot-long catapult rose sharply from the door to the bow like the dorsal fin of a barracuda. From the moment their existence was discovered by the U.S. Navy at the close of World War II, the Japanese submarines I-400, I-401, I-402, I-13, and I-14 had inspired awe among intelligence experts, who were shocked that the subs had gone undetected. The vessels, manned by as many as 220 officers and crew, were the largest undersea craft in the world, designed as submersible aircraft carriers. They rivaled the size of an American escort destroyer at 400 feet long with hulls 40 feet high. The I-400s displaced 5,900 tons and could go around the world without refueling. They were snorkel-equipped for subsurface running on diesel propulsion and carried 12-foot-wide pressurized hangars containing aircraft with folding wings and tails plus detachable floats. The subs were capable of cruising at nearly 400-foot depths and diving in under a minute. Upon surfacing, they could roll out three planes and fully assemble and launch them by catapult within fifteen minutes. Manned by two pilots, the Aichi M6A1 *Seiran* float bombers could deliver 1,764 pounds of explosives or torpedoes to targets as far away as 650 miles. The boats also were armed with eight torpedo tubes, all in the bow. Like the Seewolf sub threat that Allan McCann had faced, the mammoth Japanese subs and their aircraft had come along too late and in insufficient numbers to alter the course of the war. Now the boats were arriving in this harbor as prize captives of a U.S. Navy anxious to inspect them.

Lieutenant Paine, who as National Aeronautics and Space Administration (NASA) administrator would eventually direct the Apollo moon landing program, climbed with wonderment from a whaleboat onto the hull of I-402, where he was greeted by stone-faced Japanese crew members who escorted him below. "When you walked aft through the port hull your experience told you that you were inspecting an entire submarine," he later noted.

> You passed through a torpedo room with four tubes, chiefs quarters, radio shack, capacious wardroom . . . , large control room with conning tower trunk in the overhead, engine room with two 1900 HP [horsepower] diesel engines, motor room with a 1200 HP electric motor, and crew compartment with raised wooden decks varnished like a dance floor. . . . You had to remind yourself that welded to the large submarine you'd just inspected were two other big hulls. You'd only checked a third of your boat and had better keep going because every compartment in all three hulls required manning, rigging for sea, maintenance, etc. I kept a very wary eye on the enormous hydraulic door opening into the hangar; you can imagine the devastating effect of a loss of buoyancy and a 115-foot-long free water surface so high above her metacenter (shades of HMS M-1).

The Japanese had modeled the I-400s after England's 300-foot-long M-class experimental undersea aircraft carriers produced after World War I. The Royal Navy gave up on the prototypes following the accidental sinking of the M-1 when flooding through the hangar door doomed its entire crew of sixty in 1925.

The I-400s came along in 1943 in hopes of giving Japan a means of taking the war to the American mainland. Their initial mission was a direct response to the firebombing of Japanese cities by American aircraft. As sketched out by Vice Admiral Ozawa, Operation PX was to use the carrier subs to unleash bacteriological warfare on densely populated cities on the West Coast of the United States and some Pacific possessions. The idea was for submarine-launched aircraft to take aloft rats and mosquitoes infected with bubonic plague, cholera, typhus, and other deadly militarized germs and float them down over targeted areas. The mission was scrubbed on 26 March 1945 by Army general Yoshijiro Umezu, who concluded, "Germ warfare against the United States would escalate to war against all humanity."

Conventional bombing raids on San Francisco, Washington, and New York were considered but never actuated. Rather, an attack with torpedo bombers on the great Gatun Lock of the Panama Canal was given the go-ahead. The thinking was that if the lock could be destroyed on the Atlantic side of the waterway, it would drain the lake behind it and deny passage of military cargo headed to the Pacific. The submarines and aircraft prepared for the mission by attacking a full-scale mock-up of the lock built in Toyama Bay on the west coast of Honshu. In June, as the ability of the Japanese navy continued to deteriorate, the plan changed to sub-launched suicide torpedo bomber attacks on U.S. carriers gathering at Ulithi Atoll south of Japan. Planes were repainted to disguise them as American combat aircraft.

Japanese Submarine Squadron 1—I-400 and I-401 carrying three aircraft each plus I-13 and I-14 with two aircraft each—were nearing the atoll on 15 August when Emperor Hirohito's radio broadcast from the Imperial Palace ended the war. The sub commanders complied with orders to surface, hoist black flags of surrender, and return to their home ports. Worried about the repercussions of being found with planes with false American markings, the sub commanders ordered the aircraft catapulted into the sea. All torpedoes and bombs were disposed of overboard, along with charts, codes, logs, and secret documents. In late August U.S. Navy warships intercepted the mysterious I-boats east of Honshu. American submarine veterans commanded by some of the top boat skippers in the war against Japan—among them Hiram Cassedy, William B. Sieglaff, and John S. McCain Jr.—later took control of the boats.

By mid-November Japanese submarines of all classes were grouped together in Sasebo Harbor to await possible scuttling. However, three aircraft carrier subs—I-400, I-401, and I-14—plus Japan's two experimental fast-attack subs, I-201 and I-203, were to be spared. The latter could make nineteen knots submerged, which was far faster than any American fleet submarine. Approximately 4,500 storage batteries lined their keels, compared to 256 in fleet subs. The I-200s also had rubberized coatings on their hulls to make them less detectable to sonar and radar. Most distinctive were their streamlined designs, similar to future nuclear subs, with slimmed down conning towers, retractable deck guns, and other adaptations that made them the fastest undersea vessels in the world. The decision was made to sail all five to Pearl Harbor for further study and deny access to the Russians, who were pressing the United States to share any technological secrets as called for in the peace treaty. The Truman administration's belief was that the subs' unique design might aid the Navy in developing future submarines.

With the I-boats about to cast off for Hawaii, Lieutenant Paine reported for duty as executive officer and navigator of the I-400 under the command of Joseph M. McDowell. Operating with a skeletal crew of forty, the squadron of giant submarines departed Sasebo on 11 December.

"Dispose of All Captured Japanese Submarines"
Submarine Base, Pearl Harbor, Hawaii
6 January 1946

Rear Admiral McCann, who succeeded Vice Adm. Charles Lockwood on 18 December as commander of the U.S. Pacific submarine fleet, was among a large dockside crowd when the I-400 entered Pearl Harbor and headed for the submarine base. For the admiral, matters had come full circle from that moment five years earlier when he watched in disbelief from the submarine ten-der *Pelias* as Japanese aircraft wreaked massive destruction in a surprise attack on Battleship Row. Also struck by the irony of the moment was I-400 skipper McDowell, who was on the bridge of the sub when crew members dipped the boat's American and Japanese ensigns in solemn salute as the vessel passed the sunken hulk of USS *Arizona* and headed for the sub base. As soon as I-400 moored, the high command, including McCann, came on board for a look. Like most submarine officers with engineering backgrounds, the admiral found the many nuances of the craft intriguing. The submarines soon went into dry dock, where for the next six months they were carefully scrutinized by a variety of naval experts to learn as much as possible. During that period, Russian scien-tists expressed increasing annoyance at the United States for not allowing them access to any of the captured submarines, especially the giant ones that for a time had been on public display in Hawaii. Still, the Navy resisted, wary of the developing Cold War between the two countries and not wanting to hand Stalin any advantages.

Orders to "dispose of all captured Japanese submarines by sinking" were issued on 26 March 1945 and announced at the Submarine Officers Conference in Washington. Twenty boats being held in Japan, including the I-402, were packed with explosives and blown up in the Sea of Japan. However, discretion was given to McCann at Pearl to do the same at a later date in waters around Hawaii.

Lieutenant Paine had urged "anyone who would listen" to refit the I-400 for submerged running. He wrote, "I was convinced that we should find out how such a huge submarine handled submerged, how her automatic trim sys-tem works, what lessons her Japanese naval constructors had incorporated into her design from their long experience with big submarines, and all the other things I felt she could teach us." That wish, however, was not carried out.

"Very Sickening"
USS *Trumpetfish* (SS-425), off Oahu
4 June 1946

Rear Admiral McCann was on board to witness the destruction of the world's last submersible carrier. I-400 had been towed to its burial grounds in waters 2,500 feet deep off Oahu. Its sister ships had preceded it, each sent to the bot-tom by American submarines. Navy lieutenant commander Allen B. "Buck" Catlin, submarine division commander, described hauling each of the Japanese subs to a designated point twenty miles off the coast: "I would take each one of them out there and then we would leave with a small boat and the American submarine would come in," he recalled. On 21 May USS *Caiman* (SS-323) torpedoed I-203, sending it to the bottom. On 23 May USS *Queenfish* (SS-393) torpedoed I-14 and I-201. On 31 May USS *Cabezon* (SS-334) torpedoed I-401. To Catlin, seeing the I-200 boats succumb was startling: "The most amazing thing with those I-201 and I-203 boats. They were thin skinners, and when the torpedo hit, after the explosion, they had just disappeared."

Now it was I-400's turn. At noon, the final curtain was to be drawn on the last vestige of Japan's once proud submarine fleet. The *Trumpetfish* had trailed after I-400 to its final resting place. Embarked in the submarine were three top officers who had played a significant role in the war against Japan. Capt. Elton W. Greenfell was former commanding officer of USS *Gudgeon* (SS-211) in 1941, when she became the first submarine to depart on war patrol from Pearl Harbor. Cdr. Lawson "Red" Ramage, one of the most famous sub skippers of the war, was former commanding officer of USS *Parche* (SS-384) and earned a Medal of Honor for a daring shootout with a Japanese convoy in 1944. Joining Greenfell and Ramage was Rear Admiral McCann, one of the architects of the U.S. submarine offensive in its earliest days.

With I-400 in range, *Trumpetfish*'s skipper, Cdr. D. B. Bell, took aim and fired three Mark 18-2 electric torpedoes at the huge submarine target. Successive explosions battered the boat, but it seemingly withstood them all. The carrier submarine remained afloat for some time but then slowly slipped below the waves and disappeared.

Charles Alger, a U.S. Navy submarine chief who filmed the destruction, couldn't help feeling bad about it: "It was very sickening, the moment of the explosion. But like any good sailor, a job is done, and we've done it."

Time would march on for McCann. In just a few months it would take him full circle again—positioning him to complete an age-old quest that had defied all earlier attempts, including one in 1931 that he had participated in.

CHAPTER 15

UNDER ICE

Navy Electronics Laboratory
Point Loma Peninsula, San Diego
1 May 1947

Waldo Lyon was in need of an advocate. As director of the Navy Electronics Laboratory's Submarine Studies Branch, the thirty-three-year-old physicist had spent months working closely with Canadian oceanologists in British Columbia to understand the nature of cold Arctic sea currents and how sonar scanning devices might be used to navigate under ice. Lyon needed a diesel-powered submarine to test the reliability of the acoustic technology he and his staff of 150 had developed to make diving under polar ice possible. There wasn't much support for the project, however. Navy higher-ups—even in the submarine community—weren't interested in the Arctic given other strategic concerns in the postwar world. Furthermore, experience with submarines did not auger well for future attempts to penetrate ice fields.

In January 1946 USS *Sennet* (SS-408) had participated in Rear Adm. Richard E. Byrd's Operation High Jump in the Antarctic to test various types of naval vessels under frigid conditions. Traveling on the surface, the *Sennet*, with Lyon on board as a research scientist, followed the Coast Guard cutter *Northwind* (WAGB-282) into the ice pack off Scott Island and conducted excursions under the edge of the ice fields there, according to XO Max Duncan. The sub, under the command of Capt. J. B. Icenhower, took a battering as the ice broken up by the cutter closed in on the *Sennet*, at the tail end of a line of ships following the *Northwind*. With the sub unable to continue, the *Northwind* connected a tow line to the boat and reversed course for an eighty-mile run to open seas. The experience was harrowing. "There were icebergs all over the place, and

USS *Sennett* (SS-408) was unable to proceed through the ice pack off Antarctica and had to be taken under tow by USS *Northwind* (WAGB-282) in January 1947. It was a harrowing experience for Navy scientist Waldo Lyon, who was pioneering forward and upward scanning sonar to map the underside of floating ice to make submarine passage possible.

Naval History and Heritage Command, Washington Navy Yard, Washington, D.C.

they were huge, running miles in dimensions and depths to the order of 1,200 feet or more in draft," Lyon recalled. On the way out, slabs of ice scrapped the sides of the boat, "making a shrieking, screeching sound, something like finger nails across a blackboard, only a thousand times worse." It took nearly three full days to reach open water, and by then all the paint of the hull had been scraped clean, leaving shiny steel. Lyon had hoped to test a modified fathometer pointed upward to measure the thickness of ice while submerged. However, the device flooded out and could not be used.

At the other end of the Earth, two events later that summer raised doubt about submarine operations in the Arctic. In one, famed World War II sub skipper Lawson "Red" Ramage led four submarines from the Pacific Fleet to the Northeast Cape of Siberia, where they practiced cold-water maneuvers by darting about the peripheries of the ice pack. The hostile conditions mortified Ramage, who concluded that the Arctic would never be useful for undersea operations. He predicted that Russian submariners would get lost if they tried to navigate the ice wilderness. Meanwhile, the Atlantic Fleet sub USS *Atule* (SS-403) attempted to dive below sea ice in Nares Strait off the southwest coast of Greenland. The boat didn't get far. Her periscope shears smashed into an ice pinnacle; the shears were damaged, and the sub was forced to turn back.

All this conspired to threaten Lyon's desire to test new equipment that theoretically could make it safe for submersibles to navigate below Arctic ice, chart the underside of the canopy, measure its thickness, and find thin areas where submarines could safely surface to recharge air and batteries before continuing. To the physicist, the strategic threat posed by the Soviet Union in the Arctic was a matter the Navy could not ignore. He was mindful of the experience of German submarines at the mouth of the St. Lawrence River in World War II. The U-boats were able to attack surface craft and then hide below cold-water layers that sonar could not penetrate. The possibility of Soviet submarines developing the means to navigate the Arctic Ocean and mask their presence so close to American territory was worrisome.

What was needed was someone high up in the Navy hierarchy who would embrace what Lyon and his fellow scientists were pioneering. To them, that person was likely Allan McCann, the new commander of the Pacific submarine fleet.

Those at the lab learned that the rear admiral had led a submarine squadron to the Bering Sea in the summer of 1946 out of his own curiosity about anomalies posed by ice and cold sea on undersea craft. "They didn't do too much other than find out it was cold and miserable on a submarine," Lyon said. Scientists at the Navy lab also learned that McCann in 1930 had been the Navy's junior officer involved in the transfer of the antiquated submarine *O-12*, rechristened the *Nautilus*, to Australian explorer George Hubert Wilkins for his ill-fated attempt to sail beneath the Arctic ice cap. Norwegian oceanographer Harald Sverdrup, the chief scientist on board the *Nautilus*, provided Lyon with insights on McCann. Sverdrup had formed a bond with the American physicist after becoming director of the Scripps Institute of Oceanography in the late 1930s. He told Lyon that McCann was disturbed by Wilkins' attempt to convert the *O-12* into an upside-down sled. Wilkins thought the *Nautilus* should dive below an ice field, become positive buoyant, and slide around under the ice on rails attached topside. To McCann, that seemed incredibly risky—and it turned out to be so.

McCann's elevation to ComSubPac now put an Arctic mission within the realm of possibility for Lyon. "I had my experience in the south [Antarctica], knowing what the problem was, and then asking McCann, it was a natural for us to get together," he recalled. From a distance, the admiral seemed a kindred spirit: a military man with the temperament of a scientist—patient, persistent, and inquisitive about pushing limits to overcome challenges. He had shown

ComSubPac Allan McCann and his wife, Katheryne, at a reception in Pearl Harbor in 1946. Having succeeded Vice Adm. Charles Lockwood, McCann provided full support for an attempt to sail submarines under the Arctic ice cap.

Courtesy of McCann family (Edie Sims)

that in development of the McCann rescue chamber, which spared the lives of the *Squalus* survivors in 1939, and in his earlier involvement and interest in Wilkins' *Nautilus* expedition. But would the admiral lend Lyon a submarine for his grand experiment?

To Lyon's surprise, McCann agreed not only to loan the scientist a submarine but also to provide an entire task force under the command of Capt. Lucius Chappell, former skipper of the *Sculpin* during the war. McCann assigned USS *Boarfish* (SS-315), then operating out of San Diego, as the vessel to be outfitted with specialized electronic gear to attempt history's first dive under polar ice. "Admiral McCann always did things up in a good way," said Lyon. "He meant that we make a study and so he said, 'Well, we'll put everything on and I'll even go myself.'"

Hell's Bells
Adak Island, Alaska
15 July 1947

The admiral and the physicist arrived separately by plane at the big Navy base on Adak Island in Alaska, where they joined Task Force 17.3, sent ahead by McCann. McCann planted his flag on board the 500-foot-long sub tender *Nereus*, the most modern in the Navy and named for the mythical Greek "Old Man of the Sea." The ship, a floating hotel and repair ship for submarines, also was to serve as an oceanographic research vessel for the many scientists who had joined the expedition. The *Nereus* and the submarines, seemingly tiny slivers alongside the tender, would sail north from Adak on Operation Blue Nose, whose name was derived from the longtime naval moniker for those who crossed the Arctic Circle.

Adak, a remote island near the western extent of the Aleutian Island chain and a southern gateway to the Bering Sea, proved a harsh introduction to the Arctic environment. Weather was routinely cold and foggy with high winds. Shelter was provided by Quonset huts, often mired in mud. There are no trees on the 274-square-mile island, a forbidding place covered by tundra and mounted by two active volcanoes that often puff smoke. In July and August, cloud cover blocks out the sun most days. Rainfall is abundant, with measurable amounts falling almost every day of the year.

In this rather grim setting, McCann's task force prepared for its bold mission. Accompanying the tender were the four submarines promised by the admiral—Cdr. N. D. Cage's USS *Caiman* (SS-323), Cdr. O. C. Cole's USS *Cabezon* (SS-334), Cdr. H. B. Dodge's USS *Chub* (SS-329), and Cdr. J. H. Turner's *Boarfish*. With the task force and its full complement of officers, enlisted sailors, and scientists gathered together, excitement permeated the air in anticipation of fulfilling a quest imagined by Jules Verne and unsuccessfully pursued by Wilkins in the *Nautilus*. Despite nearly a century of exploration, little was known about the Arctic Ocean other than that it was cloaked by a floating ice cap, which connected the Atlantic with the Pacific. And it was deep. Arctic explorer Robert Edwin Peary in 1909 had tried to determine how deep. He and his small team hauled a spool of piano wire to the area of the North Pole, carved a hole in the ice, and lowered one end of the wire, affixed with a metal weight, into the mysterious sea below. When the spool ran out at nine thousand feet, the weight still hadn't reached the bottom, which, it was later discovered, was still another eight thousand feet down. "There was very little information," said Lyon. "The chart of the Arctic Ocean at that time just shows a big bowl, just a big basin and nobody knows anything about it."

Adak Island, nine hundred miles due south of Bering Strait, was chosen for the jumping-off point for Blue Nose because of analyses made by Lyon and others in San Diego. The physicist had met often with Sverdrup to determine what he knew about the area north of the strait. Lyon recalled, "I was always in continual contact for everything I could get out of Sverdrup as far as that area is concerned—the type of sonar conditions to be expected, the entire story of the environment, what happened to the sea ice, how it grew, what it was like, anything I could get as far as information was concerned." Sverdrup knew much. His research came from an unprecedented six-year voyage across the top of the world on the oak-hulled sailing ship *Maud*, built as an icebreaker in Norway in 1916. Sverdrup had been the scientific director of the expedition, which was helmed by Arctic explorer Roald Amundsen. Between 1918 and 1924, the ship had forged a drift path from the Northeast Passage in the Atlantic following circular Arctic currents, which eventually landed it in Nome, Alaska. En route, Sverdrup filled extensive logbooks with data about the Arctic's meteorology, magnetics, atmospheric electricity, physical oceanography, and tidal dynamics, particularly in the Chukchi Sea, just north of Bering Strait and named for the indigenous people of the northeastern tip of Siberia. The data not only plotted conditions likely to be encountered on the surface but also the depth and nature of the seabed.

To Lyon, the Chukchi seemed ideal for attempting the first dive under ice. The sea was relatively shallow—90 to 180 feet deep—with an unusually flat, soft mud floor and no rocky outcropping to impede submarine operations.

On 17 July Operation Blue Nose got under way. The *Nereus*, in league with her submarines, followed the International Date Line north from Adak for nearly two weeks. Along the route, Navy Electronics Laboratory scientists and graduate students, such as Walter Heinrich Munk and Donald W. Pritchard, who in years ahead would become famous oceanographers, took seabed core samples, hauled in plankton, measured sea temperatures, and dropped scores of Nansen bottles to take samples so that they could measure salinity, dissolved oxygen, and other components of seawater.

In the *Boarfish*, Lyon and his assistants practiced using specialized electronics they had devised, which were critical to the success of the mission. A key component was the boat's sonar sound head, mounted on the deck forward and known by the acronym QLA. Late in the war scientists in the lab had invented the sound head to enable Navy submarines to get past minefields guarding harbors in Japan. Known as "Hell's Bells" to submariners for the alarm sent up when mines were detected, the device continually transmitted a conical beam of sound pulses forward of the boat. Any solid object, such as a mine, caused a return pulse. A monitor on board the boat would present what was detected, how far away it was, and its direction. The virtual plot, interpreted by the QLA operator, would guide the sub safely past any obstruction. For Operation Blue Nose, the thinking was that QLA should be able to detect hanging ice pinnacles and deep drafts of icebergs as the *Boarfish* proceeded submerged. Using the data, the captain could plot safe passage. Lyon arranged for lab researcher Art Roshon, who invented QLA, to be on board the sub to ensure accurate interpretations of sonar plots. Melting polar ice results in clouds of warm and cold water, a mix that can affect a sonar beam, which is sensitive to temperature changes. Misinterpretation of QLA imagery could be disastrous for a submarine under a sheet of heavy ice. "It's like looking through the atmosphere on days over a hot pavement, and you will see an image wandering around," explained Lyon. "Well, the ocean does the same thing for you. You must understand the ocean, and what the temperature and density layers do to what you're seeing. The picture that you may see ahead of you may not be directly ahead of you. It may be off here somewhere by bending."

The *Boarfish* also had a fathometer in the keel to measure the sub's distance to the bottom. An additional echo sounder invented by Lyon was positioned topside to measure the space between the boat and the underside of the ice. Theoretically, the *Boarfish*'s electronic eyes could see forward, topside, and below—everything needed for under-ice travel.

"We All Had a Look"
Nereus, Arctic Circle
30 July 1947

The task force passed through Bering Strait, crossed the Arctic Circle, and entered the icy Chukchi. The subs followed the tender, which skirted east in open water along the ice floe. Lyon and McCann on the bridge of the *Nereus* surveyed the scene, looking for a place to make the historic dive. The task force continued trolling eastward until a serpentine river of seawater stretched northward in the limitless, fractured ice field. "Then came the decision," recalled Lyon. "Are we going to do this or not—that is, go under the ice?"

With the *Nereus* setting her anchor, McCann and Lyon decided to make a personal inspection of the ice up close. The admiral ordered the ship's whaleboat lowered, and he and Lyon boarded it. They were joined by Art Roshon, *Boarfish* skipper Turner, his officers, Electronics Laboratory science director Eugene C. LaFond, and a few others. "We took the small boat and wandered around the ice, just to see what it was all about before going under in the submarine," said Lyon.

The boat worked its way north about twenty miles. Lyon measured the height of the ice in order to estimate its maximum draft. "That gave us some idea, by seeing what the thickness of the ice was above the water, and trying to guess how much it was below the water—we could get a picture of what it looked like," explained the physicist. "We all had a look. Based on that, then, it gave us some picture of the ice and it looked like we should try it."

By Lyon's calculations, there would be plenty of room for the *Boarfish* to pass beneath the ice. The decision was cast: go for it.

"Running Back and Forth"
Boarfish, Chukchi Sea
1 August 1947

The whaler made its way back out of the ice pack and came alongside the *Boarfish*. Lyon, Roshon, Turner, and the others boarded the sub. McCann joined them, making the *Boarfish* the task force flagship for the historic dive. Roshon manned the QLA sonarscope in the conning tower, while Lyon and others settled into the forward torpedo room to monitor recordings from the keel and topside fathometers.

The *Boarfish* began her dive with extreme caution at three knots near the surface so that Commander Turner could view approaching ice through the periscope. Down below, Lyon studied echo soundings that revealed a depth of 140 feet to an extremely flat seabed—"the flattest area there is in the world," in the physicist's view. The submarine took up fifty feet of that depth, leaving ninety feet, divided above and below the vessel. Step-by-step procedures were followed as the *Boarfish* slowly descended. With both the QLA and echo rangers working properly, Turner lowered the periscope back into its housing. The *Boarfish*, now dependent on Lyon's equipment, proceeded forward, suspended thirty feet off the ocean floor and leaving sixty feet between the top of the conning tower and the surface to avoid thickening ice.

Lyon and his fellow scientists were totally engaged. They determined that the ice generally descended thirty feet, giving a safety margin of thirty feet for the 300-foot-long sub as she passed. Sonar detected blocks of ice that looked dangerous. "We were seeing on the screen other stuff that looked much thicker so we'd avoid that," recalled Lyon. Roshon, in the conning tower, provided McCann and the skipper with continuous interpretations of the QLA data. Reports of fathometer data also came in over the ship's phone system from Lyon. The trip was nerve-racking for the skipper, who was responsible for the safety of the multi-million-dollar vessel. McCann came on board for the first dive in part to relieve Commander Turner of responsibility if something went wrong. But unspoken tension remained high. "The commanding officer did a lot of running back and forth to see what was happening in the forward torpedo room, seeing what was going on, interpretation, and the same thing was happening to Admiral McCann, who was running back and forth too," said Lyon.

The submarine's run continued until it reached four miles. After an hour below ice, the skipper decided to take the *Boarfish* up for a look through the

Dr. Waldo Lyon (right) and Cdr. William R. Anderson observe the thickness of the overhead ice on sonar equipment on board USS *Nautilus* (SSN-571) in August 1958. Lyon served alongside flag commander Admiral McCann on board USS *Boarfish* (SS-315) to perfect his upward scanning sonar during the historic initial voyage by a submarine under the Arctic ice cap in 1947.

Naval History and Heritage Command, Washington Navy Yard, Washington, D.C.

periscope. The view included chunks of ice all around, some as close as ten feet. The sub continued its ascent, breaking surface. There uncharted ice "skidded over the bow," Turner noted and bent an antenna stanchion. In his later assessment, the skipper suggested that the QLA needed improvements; it had failed to detect ice blocks three feet high, ten feet long, ten feet wide, and more than seven tons in weight. The commander warned that surfacing without a more precise QLA reading "is not recommended if one desires to keep his periscope."

The voyage had gone relatively well. The *Boarfish* easily avoided ice while submerged. McCann, confident the sub faced no imminent peril in successive dives, left the boat to return to the *Nereus*. The big ship and the rest of the submarine squadron spread out to undertake various experiments, including dragging the bottom, catching biological samples, and recording the sea's bathymetry. In the meantime, the *Boarfish* completed two additional under-ice dives, the longest of which was twelve miles, and Lyon's equipment recorded ice pinnacles extending fifty feet below the surface. The sub encountered no difficulties and avoided collisions with floating ice. McCann, Lyon, and the people from the Navy lab were euphoric. "That told us, 'Okay, we go from an open sea with the sonar equipment and avoid the ice, in the summertime, and see what we're traveling under, clear the bottom and avoid what's ahead of us, and go in and come out," said Lyon, sizing up the significance of the dives.

McCann asked Lyon to report the results of both the Chukchi Sea expedition and his experience in Antarctica at an upcoming conference of Atlantic and Pacific Fleet commanders. The *Boarfish* had proved beyond doubt that submarines could navigate successfully below ice fields and that improvements in QLA would better track smaller ice obstacles. Lyon urged the Navy to continue the research he had begun. "I believe the problem of submarine adaption to polar seas has been formulated and that the submarine shows promise of unusual tactical advantage," he concluded.

Back in San Diego, scientists pondered a return trip to the Arctic. The next step seemed obvious—with McCann's help.

"Measure a New Ocean"
USS *Carp* (SS-327), Chukchi Sea
1 September 1947

One year after the *Boarfish*'s historic dives, USS *Carp* (SS-327) arrived in the Chukchi, intending to push the envelope. The previous March McCann, as ComSubPac, had given his full backing to a follow-up mission. The admiral was quite satisfied with the achievements of Operation Blue Nose and, in correspondence with Lyon, agreed that there was wisdom in launching another exploration. Because the admiral was about to be relieved of command in August, to return to Washington, he couldn't go along. However, he had assigned the *Carp* to make the next dive and ordered USS *Blower* (SS-325) to go along as a communications escort.

At the Mare Island Naval Shipyard in San Francisco Bay, the *Carp* had been equipped with a QLA capable of projecting a wider sonar beam and fathometers of the type the *Boarfish* had carried to the Arctic. The objective was for the *Carp*, with Lyon and other scientists on board, to dive under the ice and find a polynya. Cdr. J. H. Palmer would position the boat directly beneath the open water and make a stationary ascent to the surface without striking ice. If that could be accomplished, it would prove that diesel subs could extend their range, using polynyas to surface, recharge batteries, and keep going.

McCann was relieved of command on 9 August by Rear Adm. Oswald S. Colclough, who immediately ordered Palmer to avoid undo risks and to safeguard the ship and its equipment. The skipper, realizing the danger of surfacing amid ice, had his crew repeatedly practice the technique of stationary ascents all the way from San Francisco to the Chukchi.

On 3 September, the boat reached the ice pack and dove. Using the improved QLA, Palmer located several ice-free lakes and set a course for one of them. Over the next eight days, the *Carp*, traveling sixty miles beneath the ice, completed fourteen ascents into various lakes without damage to the submarine.

Lyon and his fellow scientists returned to San Diego triumphant. In a report to directors of the Navy lab, Lyon urged that another fleet boat be prepared for more experiments in 1949. A follow-up request to Admiral Colclough dated 3 December stressed the critical nature of continuing what McCann had started. "The all important objective is to measure a new ocean—determine its oceanography and undersea physics," Lyon argued. "The objective can be met by present sonar equipment and an experimental Fleet submarine modified for the Arctic Ocean."

Colclough, not a fan of McCann's vision or enthusiasm for further Arctic adventures, rejected the overture. He left it up to Lyon to arrange his own resources for any additional experiments. Colclough stuck to his position for the next few years. But it wouldn't last. In 1952 a McCann ally—Rear Adm. Charles Momsen—relieved Colclough. Momsen went to work on all kinds of experimental projects. Among them: perfecting under-ice submarines, forerunners of the nuclear subs that would revolutionize operations in the Arctic.

As for McCann, he returned to Washington for brief duty on the General Board of the Navy Department before he relieved Rear Adm. Lee H. Thebaud as naval inspector general (IG). As IG in 1949 he would land right in the middle of an explosive scandal that would rock the admiralty in Washington.

CHAPTER 16

NIBBLED TO DEATH

Shipway No. 11
Newport News, Virginia
18 April 1949

*A*t 0845 a "tower whirler" crane went into action, lofting into the air the hopes of the postwar Navy. The gigantic red machine lofted a thirty-foot-long steel plate, three feet wide and one inch thick, into midair. Swinging out over the graving dock at the Newport News shipyard, where the iconic World War II carriers USS *Midway* (CV-41) and USS *Coral Sea* (CV-43) had been built, the crane lowered the steel slab to the floor of Shipway No. 11, where workers helped position it. The crane repeated the action for much of the day, laying nearly a hundred plates end to end so that they could be welded together. Capt. W. T. "Water Tight" Jones, the resident supervisor of naval construction at the shipyard, was the highest-ranking officer present. He was joined by a half-dozen reporters and photographers plus a few junior officers down from Washington to supervise the filming of a documentary about the soon-to-be largest aircraft carrier in the world.

Under threatening skies, the shape of the keel began to emerge, giving a hint of how colossal USS *United States* (CVA-58) would be. The $189 million supercarrier, the forerunner of a new class of five such vessels, would displace 65,000 tons and have a flight deck that stretched 1,090 feet, nearly the length of four football fields. With a beam of 190 feet, it was too big to sail through the Panama Canal. No matter. The warship was designed to launch fleets of aircraft—124 fighters and two dozen 100,000-pound bombers capable of long-range nuclear bombardment to deter any enemy from a preemptive strike. To the Navy, the *United States* would be key to the service going forward. But it would be at great cost. The carrier's task force of thirty-nine ships would bring the total price tag to $1.265 billion.

The keel laying at the Newport News Shipbuilding and Dry Dock Company should have been a festive occasion for the Navy, possibly attracting the secretary of the Navy, the chief of naval operations (CNO), and members of the General Board, now including Rear Adm. Allan McCann, who was assigned the previous September. But the Navy had given no special attention to the event, not even confirming what day it would occur. The plan for the vaunted carrier—approved by President Truman in 1948 and funded by the Naval Appropriations Act of 1949—had been under attack for months in a war of

Keel laying of the Navy's supercarrier USS *United States* (CVA-58) gets under way on 18 April 1949. U.S. defense secretary Louis A. Johnson ordered construction halted just five days later as he endorsed building B-36 bombers for the Air Force as a cheaper alternative to the carrier. The move initiated what was to be called the "Revolt of the Admirals."

Naval History and Heritage Command, Washington Navy Yard, Washington, D.C.

words between the Navy and the new Air Force, created by the 1947 Unification Act. The Navy adamantly opposed downgrading its aviation capability coming off its overwhelming triumph against Japan in World War II. Yet major political and military figures—President Truman and Gen. Dwight D. Eisenhower, Army chief of staff, among them—wondered why the service was investing in a supercarrier for strategic bombing when the Air Force's B-36 intercontinental bomber served the same purpose. Truman and Eisenhower envisioned the Air Force, Army, and Navy in a peaceable kingdom of mutual support of one another's noncompeting missions, which had been left undefined by the Unification Act. Eisenhower worried that the country couldn't afford the Navy acting as an independent force. Unless unification measures took hold under civilian control, he told Congress, "someday we're going to have a blowup."

Truman made a stab at resolving the situation. In 1948 he directed the Navy and Air Force to come to a compromise at meetings in Key West, Florida, and Newport, Rhode Island. The meetings broke down over who would hold the atomic trigger. James V. Forrestal, appointed by Truman as the nation's first defense secretary, didn't help matters. He supported the supercarrier, opposed unification, and questioned the creation of the Air Force. He subsequently lost influence with the administration, especially after he gave only cursory support to Truman's reelection bid in 1948. Declining health and mental distress led to his resignation in March 1949 and suicide two months later in a leap from the sixteenth floor of the National Naval Medical Center in Bethesda, Maryland. The president replaced Forrestal with Louis A. Johnson, an Air Force booster and assistant secretary of war from 1937 to 1940. Johnson was also the chief fund-raiser during Truman's successful reelection campaign.

Johnson set a bold course, launching a major review of all military procurement programs. Fixing attention on the supercarrier, he wanted a consensus from military leaders on whether to build it. Adm. Louis E. Denfeld, CNO, said it was critical "in the interest of national security." But Gen. Omar N. Bradley, Army chief of staff, and Gen. Hoyt S. Vandenberg, Air Force chief of staff, strenuously opposed it as a duplication of what the B-36 could accomplish. Eisenhower, chair of the Joint Chiefs, sided with Bradley and Vandenberg.

Amid this backdrop, reporters who had gathered in Newport News witnessed a rather somber keel laying. As Walter Waggoner of the *New York Times* put it, "The super-carrier is the issue over which the Air Force and the Navy have fought with such vigor. The Air Force and its supporters in Congress argue that the B-36 can deliver the atomic bomb at an altitude beyond the range of enemy fighter planes. They say, further, that the atomic bomb has made the Navy and its aircraft carriers all but obsolete."

"Does Away with the Navy"
The Pentagon, Arlington, Virginia
23 April 1949

Defense Secretary Johnson ordered all work halted on the Navy's *United States* just five days after the keel laying. His decision was announced in a two-sentence memorandum released to the news media. Johnson instructed Navy Secretary John L. Sullivan to discontinue construction at once "at the least possible cost to the Government." He coupled his move with a gag order—Consolidation Directive No. 1—to prevent overt criticism of his decision by either retired or active-duty military personnel.

In scuttling the carrier, Johnson had not consulted Sullivan, who was in Corpus Christi, Texas, attending a Reserve Officers Association convention. The Navy secretary immediately returned to Washington to tender his resignation. Sullivan accused the defense secretary of being the first American in history to "prevent the development of a powerful weapon." Johnson promptly named a new secretary of the Navy—Francis P. Matthews, an Omaha lawyer who backed the defense secretary's point of view. Johnson pointed out that for

U.S. Navy Secretary Francis P. Matthews backed the decision to cancel construction of USS *United States*, initiating wide controversy within the Navy, particularly among Navy airmen.

U.S. Naval Institute photo archive

the $190 million cost of a single supercarrier, the nation could buy dozens of B-36 bombers manned by far fewer personnel. His ultimate plan, he told confidants, was to scale back the Navy into a convoy-escort force. As he would make clear later in the year, "There's no reason for having a Navy and Marine Corps. General Bradley tells me that amphibious operations are a thing of the past. . . . That does away with the Marine Corps. And the Air Force can do anything the Navy can do nowadays, so that does away with the Navy."

Shock waves over Johnson's decisiveness reverberated in the Navy as the internecine war between the Navy and Air Force continued behind the scenes. The Navy insisted that the B-36 was too slow and couldn't fly high enough to avoid enemy aircraft. To settle the issue, U.S. Representative Carl Vinson, Democratic chair of the House Armed Services Committee, recommended a mock duel eight miles above the earth between the bomber and Navy fighter planes. The Navy offered up seven McDonnell Banshees out of Norfolk to take the challenge before it was even formally authorized. "The Navy had sent fighters up to intercept Air Force planes and 'shoot them down' with cameras to show their weakness," explained Navy captain Max Duncan, then on the staff of the commander in chief, U.S. Atlantic Fleet, in Norfolk. "One of the pilots was on the staff with me. He kept avoiding being found and sent to Washington for grilling. He delivered the movies he took and then vanished." Before those movies could be made public, the Joint Chiefs voted against the idea of a mock intercept. In a public memorandum signed by Admiral Denfeld, the Joint Chiefs concluded that it would "serve no useful purpose" and could lead to "serious misinterpretation on the part of the public."

"Strange Proceedings"
U.S. House of Representatives, Washington, D.C.
25 May 1949

A nine-page, unsigned letter leaked to various officials around the capital landed with a thud before members of the House Armed Services Committee, which was about to move unification of the services a notch closer to completion. The mysterious document implied that Defense Secretary Johnson and Secretary of the Air Force Stuart Symington had a financial interest in the $500 million program to build the B-36. It alleged that "influence at the right spots" had procured contracts for B-36 builder Consolidated-Vultee Aircraft Corporation, which was controlled by Floyd Odlum, one of the richest people in America, who had contributed heavily to Truman's reelection. The document accused Odlum of wanting to establish "a huge aircraft combine" and said that Symington would resign to run the business after Congress authorized more funds for B-36s. The memorandum noted that Symington was a "frequent visitor" to Odlum's Palm Springs, California, home. It also reported that Johnson, until three days after his nomination as secretary of defense, was a director and Washington counsel for Consolidated. In addition, the letter charged that the world's largest bomber did not meet minimum performance goals. The six-engine Peacemaker couldn't fly high enough and did not have the 10,000-mile range without refueling claimed by the Air Force. Numerous other problems were noted, including a history of catastrophic engine fires, electrical failures, and inaccessible fuel and oil leaks.

Was the B-36 deficient? Were there improprieties in the procurement process? Who leaked the document? Who wrote it? Where did the allegations arise? Given the timing of the leak, suspicion pointed directly at the Navy. The motive seemed clear: Johnson's cancellation of the *United States*.

Representative James E. Van Zandt, ranking Republican member of the committee and a captain in the Naval Reserve, demanded a thorough investigation of "these strange proceedings" in procuring the B-36. A week later the committee voted unanimously to proceed. Chair Vinson vowed, "This is not going to be a whitewash." He set the scope of the inquiry as follows: "All phases of the B-36 bomber including, specifically, all facts relating to when this bomber was purchased, why it has been purchased, how it was purchased, any cancellations of other aircraft procurement that may have resulted from such purchases, and any and all other collateral matters that such inquiries may develop."

"Ugly, Dirty Rumors"
Navy Department, Pentagon, Arlington, Virginia
9 June 1949

With the messy fight between the Navy and the Air Force out in the open, Rear Admiral McCann moved from a position on the General Board to that of naval IG. In his new job, he faced the prospect of being pulled into the burgeoning interservice fight. At age fifty-two, he wasn't altogether surprised at his selection as the Navy's fourth IG. In the twilight of his illustrious career, his record of impartiality and scrupulous attention to detail made him an ideal choice as the so-called conscience of the Navy. The mission of IG, as established in May 1942 by former secretary of the Navy Frank Knox, was to investigate any challenge to the Navy's integrity and make an objective, candid analysis of the situation for the commander in chief, U.S. Fleet. A main function was vigorous investigation of top echelon officers accused of abusing their authority or engaging in perceived unethical conduct—behavior the anonymous letter seemed to portend.

The Armed Services Committee set a two-step agenda for its public hearings into what Van Zandt called the "ugly, dirty rumors" contained in the memorandum. At hearings in August, the panel would attempt to establish whether the B-36 was a substandard weapon and had been procured unethically. At follow-up hearings in October, the committee would examine the roles and missions of the aviation wings of the Air Force, Navy, and Marines to determine whether cancelling the *United States* was justified. For his part, Secretary Symington emphatically denied all charges, branding them "lies" in a letter to the committee. He urged the group to "trace them to their source." Meanwhile, in a narrow vote of 13–12, the committee decided to shelve any further action on military unification until the inquiry was complete.

Fear in the Navy of Johnson's draconian budget cuts heightened in July. His fiscal 1951 budget proposed downsizing from eight large carriers and 1,557 aircraft to four carriers and 690 planes. Shocking as the decision appeared, CNO Denfeld did not complain, preferring to see how things played out.

"I Wrote It"
House of Representatives, Washington, D.C.
24 August 1949

Surprise witness Cedric R. Worth sat before the Armed Services Committee in a packed hearing room and admitted under oath that, yes, he had authored the anonymous document that had started the investigation of the B-36. Saying he was bound to lose his job as civilian special assistant to the undersecretary of the Navy, he confessed, "I wrote it." Brig. Gen. Joseph F. Carroll, director of Air Force Special Investigations, had fingered Worth, a World War II Navy veteran and former Hollywood scriptwriter. During his voluntary testimony, Worth said the information came from multiple sources and was distributed clandestinely without anyone's knowledge in the Navy: "I was greatly concerned. I felt that the defenses of this country were going in the wrong direction. I believed the defenses were being materially weakened by propaganda which was untrue." During two days of testimony, Worth admitted he could not verify his charges, that they were conclusions he'd drawn based on material he had seen.

Worth's dramatic appearance overshadowed earlier appearances by General Bradley and Gen. Curtis LeMay, who defended the B-36. "It is the best bomber available at this time for its purpose. We are not spending too much money on it," Bradley told the committee. LeMay testified that he was so confident in the B-36 that, if called on in an emergency, "I will order my crews out in those airplanes, and I expect to be in the first one myself." Other Air Force witnesses laid out a methodical, step-by-step defense of the bomber's development and procurement, successfully refuting all allegations.

At the end of the August hearings, the committee concluded it found "not one scintilla of evidence [to] support charges that collusion, fraud, corruption, influence, or favoritism played any part whatsoever in the procurement of the B-36 bomber." The panel also made it clear that Defense Secretary Johnson and the Air Force's Symington retained "unblemished, impeccable reputations." Navy Secretary Matthews suspended Worth pending a formal naval investigation.

"Rank Gossip"
Navy Department, Pentagon, Arlington, Virginia
6 September 1949

A Navy court of inquiry convened in open hearing to determine whether others had knowingly aided Cedric Worth in leaking information and allegations about the B-36 procurement process to Congress. Cdr. Thomas D. Davies, a Navy pilot who had set a record-breaking long-distance nonstop flight in 1946, testified that he had relayed much of the information, including unsubstantiated stories that he heard about the B-36, to Worth. But Davies said he took no part in preparing the letter, nor did he know that Worth was writing one.

Under blistering questioning from court examiner Capt. Sanford B. D. Wood, Davies said that he could not vouch for the reliability of the information he had given to Worth. Demanded Wood, "It was rank gossip, wasn't it?" The pilot replied, "Yes, sir."

In a related development, the Navy accepted Worth's resignation from the service.

"Accessory to a Crime"
Georgetown, Washington, D.C.
10 September 1949

Few were more agitated about how the Navy had lost face in the B-36 hearings than Capt. John G. Crommelin, staff member under the Joint Chiefs. One of the Navy's greatest combat pilots, he stood before reporters at his white-brick home on Thirtieth Street NW to level blistering criticism at the Defense Department at the risk of his court-martial.

In thirty years as a distinguished naval commander and fighter pilot, Crommelin saw ferocious combat in the South Pacific on board USS *Enterprise*. As chief of staff in USS *Liscome Bay* (CVE-56), he survived her sinking in the Makin Island campaign in 1943 by crawling out of a hauser hole while badly burned. After he was treated in Pearl Harbor, he returned to duty. A native of Montgomery, Alabama, he was the oldest of five brothers. Four were Navy pilots; two died in combat. After the war, Crommelin commanded the carrier USS *Saipan* (CVL-48) with new jet fighters, which he flew.

Like other Navy aviators, "Bomb-Run John" viewed cancellation of the *United States* with bitterness and considered the ascendancy of the Air Force a death knell for naval aviation. What irked him most was Secretary of the Navy Matthews' and CNO Denfeld's inaction on the issue. It made him sick to his stomach, he said. When he was not called to testify before the naval court of inquiry looking into the Worth matter, he told associates in the Pentagon that he might take action on his own. Rear Adm. Joseph L. Howard, a staff member in the Navy's Op-23 public relations research group, said the captain believed that officers should do whatever was necessary to spread the message. Op-23, a high-level clearinghouse for matters of unification for the CNO and other senior Navy officers, had always gone about its duties beneath the radar. News reporters long viewed the office with suspicion because of its lack of public access. Adm. Arleigh Burke, who headed Op-23, urged Crommelin to work within channels as the Navy prepared witnesses for the upcoming Armed Services Committee hearings. Adm. Arthur Radford, commander of the Pacific Fleet, who had been recalled to help prepare the Navy's case, also urged Crommelin to "hold your horses." But he would not do so.

The captain decided to act amid rumors that CNO Denfeld had been reappointed for another two-year term on the condition that he minimize naval aviation in favor of antisubmarine and surface-ship operations. At his home in Georgetown, Crommelin let loose. "I just can't stand it any longer," he announced in a prepared statement. The Navy, he said, was "being nibbled to death" by Pentagon brass operating like "a Prussian General Staff system of the type employed by Hitler." Secretary of Defense Johnson and other military policy makers were "emasculating the offensive potential of the United States Navy" by cancelling the supercarrier, he said; Johnson planned a "gradual reduction of naval aviation and the absorption of its remnants after a period of time by the Air Force." He added, "I'm finished. This means my Naval career. But I hope this will blow the whole thing open and bring on another Congressional investigation. . . . They'll say I'm nuts. I'm not nuts. Up to now I've felt like an accessory to a crime."

Crommelin's sensational accusations initiated five days of suspense within the Pentagon, characterized by *New York Times* reporter Hanson W. Baldwin as "the revolt of naval aviation." Many came to the captain's defense privately. Retired Fleet Admiral Halsey did so publicly, praising him for his willingness to jeopardize his career for the Navy.

At first it seemed Captain Crommelin might dodge punishment. Within days he became director of naval aviation personnel, which put him on the admiralty track. However, when Secretary Matthews realized what the Navy chiefs had done, he countermanded the appointment by demoting Crommelin to the lesser post of deputy CNO for air. As Matthews put it in a cryptic public

Adm. Arleigh A. Burke headed Op-23, the Navy's public relations information group in the Pentagon. The office was long suspected of fanning dissent over the Truman administration's decision to cancel the supercarrier in favor of Air Force airpower.

Naval History and Heritage Command, Washington Navy Yard, Washington, D.C.

announcement, "Captain Crommelin in a statement of his views concerning unification obviously disqualified himself."

As September wound down, Matthews, in company with Admiral Radford, met in the Pentagon with attorneys for the House Armed Services Committee. The secretary urged the committee to suspend further hearings. Radford, however, disagreed. Navy witnesses were fully prepared to be heard, he said. In a follow-up meeting with Chair Vinson at his office on the afternoon of 3 October, Matthews again urged that the hearings be shelved. However, Radford and others at the meeting were just as adamant that they go on. The Navy secretary, upset at the challenge to his authority, nevertheless refrained from saying anything.

"Arleigh, It's a Raid!"
Navy Department, Pentagon, Arlington, Virginia
29 September 1949

A column written by Jack Norris in the *Washington Post* sent a shock wave through the office of the Navy secretary. Norris quoted an informant who claimed that Matthews was trying to keep the admirals from testifying in public before the House Armed Services Committee. Matthews, infuriated, was determined to ferret out who was behind the leak and summoned Rear Admiral McCann to his office around noon on 29 September 1949. He ordered the IG to begin an investigation at once. "I don't mind being criticized for mistakes that I have made but I don't like to be accused of unworthy purposes or unworthy motives," he later confided to columnist C. B. Allen. "In an organization, a Military organization, you have to have discipline, you have to have order, and there are certain things that have to be respected and observed." Just as McCann was gearing up his investigation, someone told the secretary that the leak might have come from Op-23, the outfit run by Arleigh Burke. Matthews called the IG and ordered him to make a beeline for Burke's office.

Cdr. Snowden Arthur, an Op-23 staffer, happened to be cruising the corridors of the Pentagon when he ran into a Navy lieutenant. "They're gonna raid you. The IG's headed toward you," the lieutenant warned. Arthur sprinted back to his office, where he and Burke quickly pulled the most damning evidence that the Op-23 office had been promoting dissent over unification from files and stuffed it inside a briefcase. Two staffers—Sam Shaw and Admiral Howard—helped. Sensitive papers listed the names of allies in the Air Force and Army who agreed with the need for Navy airpower.

Commander Arthur, briefcase in hand, ducked into a separate office, with its own door to the corridor, just as McCann entered through the main door to the office suite. "I heard the Inspector General come in and say, 'Arleigh, it's a raid!' And boom, I took off like a catapult," Arthur later recounted. He bolted down the corridor until he ran into a friend who agreed to hide the briefcase in his safe in another office.

Meanwhile, McCann stood resolute before Admiral Burke. "You looked at that man [McCann] and you knew something was afoot," recalled one of the office staffers. "And he says, 'Arleigh, I want to talk to you for a moment out in the hall.' So they went out in the hall and closed the door." Momentarily, Burke reentered the office alone, "pissed off as hell," said Howard. Shaw described the scene: "The man was just about to burst. The first thing he said was, 'Sam, how many people have left to go home?'" Shaw gave him a number. "Get 'em all back," Burke demanded.

Within minutes, the IG's aides arrived to assist him. With the entire Op-23 office staff reassembled, McCann and his staff sifted through records as Marines stood guard at the doors to make sure no one left the office suite. For more than nine grueling hours, until 0300, the investigation proceeded. Sandwiches were brought in. Anyone who needed to go to the restroom was escorted by a Marine. One by one, McCann engaged each Op-23 staff member in a tense interrogation similar to one conducted in the Star Chamber, recalled one of them. As the hours dragged on, mental fatigue set in. McCann, cool and deliberative, wanted to know about Op-23's contact with reporters and the

Rear Adm. Allan McCann, as Navy inspector general, raided Burke's office to uncover suspected leaks of documents detrimental to Navy Secretary Matthews during the "Revolt of the Admirals."

U.S. Naval Institute photo archive

daily work done in the office. He gave no indication what the investigation was about, although Burke and others deduced that the *Post* article was the cause, that McCann at Matthews' directive wanted to know who disclosed to the *Post* that the Navy secretary wanted to stop the admirals from testifying.

The investigation of Op-23 ultimately did not turn up anything incriminating; the informant was not identified. Later, however, Adm. John Dale Price, Denfeld's vice CNO, was revealed as the guilty party.

"False Bill of Goods"
The Pentagon, Arlington, Virginia
3 October 1949

An article on the 3 October front page of the *Washington Times-Herald* with the headline "Navy Big Brass Blasts Defense Setup" provided another jolt to Secretary Matthews. Copies of classified letters written by three admirals critical of the Defense Department had been secretly smuggled to an Associated Press reporter in the darkened stairwell on the sixth floor of the National Press Building in Washington. One letter written by Vice Adm. Gerald F. Bogan, commander of the First Task Fleet in the Pacific, said Navy morale had fallen "almost to despondency" owing to a belief that the country was being "sold a false bill of goods" in its dependency on the Air Force for its nuclear deterrence. Bogan asserted that morale "is lower today than at any time since I entered the commissioned ranks in 1916." He also declared that there was no unity in the Department of Defense, that "it would be sheer balderdash to assume that there has been anything approaching it among the Secretariat, the Joint Staff, or the high command of the three services. Bickering is still the rule. Unanimity is non-existent." A second letter, an endorsement of what Bogan wrote, was from Admiral Denfeld; it said that a "Navy stripped of its offensive power means a nation stripped of its offensive power." The third missive, an endorsement by Admiral Radford, claimed that a majority of Navy officers supported Crommelin's views and that he was in "hearty and complete" agreement with the captain. The disclosures were like a red-hot rod skewering Matthews and his support of Defense Secretary Johnson's desire to downgrade naval aviation.

In the end, the source of the letter leak proved to be a friend of United Press International bureau chief Jim Austin: Captain Crommelin. McCann summoned the unrepentant captain to his office, suspended him from duty, and confined him to house arrest in Georgetown. The kerfuffle in the Navy had one fallout: Vinson was determined to air the resolution of the matter promptly— in public.

"Fancy Dans"
House of Representatives, Washington, D.C.
6 October 1949

Navy Secretary Matthews led off what was to become twelve days of public hearings on unification and military strategy before the Armed Services Committee. He told the panel that morale was good in the Navy and accused a "minority" of naval aviators of being opposed to unification. That conclusion drew loud guffaws from some naval officers gathered in the hearing chamber. The secretary, prior to his remarks, had appealed to the committee to prevent Admiral Radford from testifying. What he had to say, Matthews argued, might harm national security. Later in the day the committee heard what the admiral had to say privately and then voted to let him speak publicly the next morning. Radford attacked the Air Force's position that B-36 bombers would ensure cheap and easy victory in war. "The type of war we plan to fight must fit the kind of peace we want," he told lawmakers. "We cannot look to the military victory alone, with no thought to the solution of the staggering problems that would be generated by the death and destruction of an atom blitz." He said that the B-36 was "slow, expensive, very vulnerable," with a single purpose; the country, however, should favor small, fast bombers and agile, fast fighter jets.

In succeeding days, Navy technical experts and flag officers detailed the performance flaws of the B-36, including the difficulty of dropping a bomb on a military target from 40,000 feet without harming civilians. Relying on the B-36 could lead to "the random slaughter of men, women and children in enemy country," as one put it. Senior wartime leadership also testified about the rationale behind maintaining the Navy's strategic mission; among these leaders were Fleet Adm. Ernest J. King Jr., Fleet Adm. Chester Nimitz, Fleet Adm. William Halsey, Adm. Raymond Spruance, Adm. Thomas Kinkaid, and former Marine Corps commandant Gen. Alexander Vandegrift. *Time* magazine termed their testimony "the Revolt of the Admirals."

One last Navy witness was scheduled to appear. CNO Denfeld would present the closing statement. Secretary Matthews pressured him to toe the line of drawing down naval aviation set by Defense Secretary Johnson. Many believed Denfeld would do exactly that, given that he had been virtually mute about the issue for months. He wrestled with his testimony for several days, putting off his boss, who wanted to jointly work out what Denfeld would say. Realizing his distress, his wife Rachel asked over breakfast, "Louie, are you going to stand up and be counted or aren't you?" He replied, "I am."

On the evening of 12 October, Arleigh Burke and Admiral Radford, among others, helped Denfeld draft his statement. The following afternoon he went before the committee and stunned spectators. "As the senior military spokesman for the Navy, I want to state forthwith that I fully support the broad conclusions presented to this committee by the Naval and Marine officers who have preceded me," he began. He discussed the effect of budget cuts on the Navy and Marines and the channeling of more money into the B-36 program. "Limitations are imposed without consultation, and without understanding of the Navy's responsibility in defense of our maritime nation," he told the committee. He stressed that the Navy was not of secondary importance in the atomic age and argued that cancellation of the *United States* was "another exemplification of the improper operation of unification." As he put it, "Fleets never in history met opposing fleets for any other purpose than to gain control of the sea—not as an end in itself, but so that national power could be exerted against the enemy."

The next morning the *New York Times* proclaimed, "Denfeld Sees Navy Gravely Imperiled by Chiefs' Decisions." Matthews was livid. He termed the CNO's statement "an attack against the President and civilian control and economy. . . . They really have gone below the belt this time." Within days he fired Denfeld. He also abolished Op-23 in his belief it had aided insubordination.

After the Navy's presentation, Air Force rebuttal witnesses testified. Secretary Symington and Gen. Hoyt S. Vandenberg reiterated that there was no need for a Navy with strategic bombing responsibilities. There was only one possible enemy—Soviet Russia—and it had no navy of any consequence. General Bradley, the chair of the Joint Chiefs, testified that the Navy may have harmed national security through its testimony. As he put it, "this is no time for 'fancy Dans' who won't hit the line with all they have on every play unless they can call the signals." The problem, he said, was that the Navy had rejected unification from the beginning and continued to oppose it in any form.

The committee concluded that the dispute between the Air Force and Navy really came down to disagreements "on the art of warfare. Service prejudices, jealousies and thirst for power and recognition have had only a bare minimum of influence on this controversy." However, the committee agreed, "Military air power consists of Air Force, Navy and Marine Corps air power, and of this, strategic bombing is but one phase."

To observers, the Navy seemed to have won over supporters in Congress during the hearings. Admiral Radford was optimistic. In writing to an associate, he noted, "The Navy is not in a horrible mess, but just coming up out of a deep pit, and we have good times ahead." Although Navy appropriations continued to be limited, the outbreak of the Korean War in 1950 emphasized the versatility of Navy carriers, fighters, and bombers operating off the coast. Naval performance in the war would lay the foundation for congressional approval of the *Forrestal*-class of supercarriers and long-range attack aircraft that would be intrinsic in future conflicts.

As for McCann, his investigation of Op-23 would be the final footnote in his long and remarkable career, which touched several historic events. On 1 May 1950 he retired with a promotion to vice admiral of the U.S. Navy.

CHAPTER 17

HOMECOMING

"Explore Their Limits"

North Adams, Massachusetts

10 October 1960

*T*en years after his retirement, Allan McCann returned to his hometown in the picturesque Berkshire Mountains. He had come and gone from North Adams throughout his naval career and maintained a home on Cherry Street. Whenever he was in town, the local newspaper inevitably noted the event. Thus, in the fall of 1960 the *North Adams Transcript* reported his brief stopover for lunch with relatives. "Adm. McCann, veteran of the Pearl Harbor attack, inventor of the McCann Bell submarine rescue device and commander of a 1947 submarine cruise under the polar ice cap, with Mrs. McCann, has been visiting her sister, Mrs. Walter Ridley of Foxboro," the newspaper reported. The article also reminded readers that the admiral had been Navy IG before he retired. Yet, the article included no interview with McCann, no quotes to relay to readers any sense of the drama that dotted his service to the country. He preferred not to discuss a career that brought him international fame for the epic rescue of the *Squalus* survivors off the coast of New England in 1939.

For the vice admiral, North Adams was a kind of firmament during his thirty-seven years in the Navy. There he met and married his bride, Katheryne Gallup, daughter of the town's mayor. In those early days, the city rode the crest of prosperity derived from rapid industrialization—its "golden age," as local historian Paul W. Marino put it. But by the fall of 1960, the blush had faded. North Adams' cotton and wool mills, which once ruled the textile world, had relocated to the South and then overseas. Its renowned shoe factories moved out as well. In 1942 the closure of the Arnold Print Works, the largest textile print factory in the world, resulted in 3,200 employees losing their jobs. But the greatest shock came in 1958, two years before the admiral's visit, when Mill Number Four of the Berkshire-Hathaway Company closed. The closure was the final epitaph for the 150-year-old textile manufacturing industry of western Massachusetts. It was a bitter shock and forced the layoff of another thousand workers in a city of 20,000. The fast-flowing Hoosic River would no longer power the mills, and rail traffic through the wondrous Hoosac Tunnel would slow to a trickle. The year that Mill Number Four shut down also saw the end of regularly scheduled passenger train service. The railroad itself would declare bankruptcy by 1971. North Adams had become a museum, hanging on to its former glory through the mansions of former mill owners and its Gothic Revival churches, which gave the city at the foot of 3,500-foot Mount Greylock its distinctive skyline of steeples.

By the 1960s the tether that bound the McCanns to the city had frayed. Entering retirement, they sold their home. They, like many other older Americans, found life more to their liking in Winter Park, Florida. Developed in 1887 as a winter retreat for wealthy northerners, the city north of Orlando had become one of the state's most beautiful, with abundant parks, lakes, brick-lined streets, spectacular homes, museums, and fine shops lining Park Avenue. The McCanns lived a quiet life and became active in the local garden club. Their declining health, however, convinced them to relocate to Laguna Beach, California, to be close to daughters Barbara and Lois, who had married Annapolis graduates from the class of 1943, Capt. Miles R. Finley Jr. and Capt. David B. Maher, respectively. During the admiral's lifetime, he enjoyed the blessings of his three daughters, nine grandchildren, and six great-grandchildren. One, David B. Maher Jr., also graduated from the Naval Academy.

"All Hands Bury the Dead"
Pacific Ocean off San Diego, California
13 March 1978

Vice Admiral McCann passed away at age eighty-one on 22 February 1978 at the Balboa Naval Hospital in San Diego. His body was cremated, and the ashes were taken on board the diesel submarine USS *Sailfish* (SSR-572) to be scattered at sea.

Preceding McCann in death was George Hubert Wilkins, the great Australian explorer whom McCann had helped to convert Navy sub *O-12* for the first attempt to sail beneath the Arctic ice in 1931. In 1958 Wilkins' ashes were taken on board USS *Skate* (SSN-578), which surfaced at the North Pole. There crew members scattered his remains at his request. Likewise, the cremated remains of Dr. Waldo Lyon would be scattered at the North Pole by the crew of USS *Hawkbill* (SSN-666) in 1998.

The *Sailfish*, under Cdr. George R. Waterman, came to rest at 1000 hours on the surface off Point Loma, separating San Diego Bay from the Pacific Ocean. The officer of the deck barked out, "All hands bury the dead." With the crew, including a firing party and bugler, mustered on deck, an honor guard brought up the urn bearing the admiral's remains and placed it on a stand. Waterman, presiding over the burial, briefly summarized Admiral McCann's career. His Navy awards included the Legion of Merit with Gold Star in lieu of the second Legion of Merit; the Bronze Star Medal; the Commendation Ribbon; the Victory Medal; the Atlantic Fleet Clasp (USS *Kansas*); the American Defense Service Medal, with Fleet Clasp; the Asiatic-Pacific Campaign Medal; European–African–Middle Eastern Campaign Medal; and the World War II Victory Medal. Beyond the medals and ribbons, his lifetime would be remembered for his role in events that once commanded world headlines: involvement in the successful rescue of trapped crew members from the submarine *O-5* in Panama in 1923; command of submarines searching for the downed pilots of the Dole Derby air race from California to Honolulu in 1927; service as naval liaison officer in the conversion of the former *O-12* into the *Nautilus*, the first submarine to navigate under the Arctic ice cap in 1931; service as a naval engineer who perfected the submersible chamber that saved the crew of the sunken USS *Squalus* off the coast of New Hampshire in 1939; service as the lieutenant commander who directed gunnery counterattacks from the tender *Pelias* in Pearl Harbor the morning of the surprise attack in 1941; command of submarines holding the line against the enemy from Australia in 1942, while the Navy rebuilt from losses at Pearl Harbor; command of USS *Iowa*, the Navy's most potent battleship, during the Battle of Leyte Gulf; deployment to the Navy's Tenth Fleet as tactical commander in the last Battle of the Atlantic against Nazi U-boats in 1945; service as commander of the task force that conveyed President Truman to Europe for the Potsdam Conference, responsible for informing the president of the atomic bomb explosion over Hiroshima in 1945; flag command of the first submarine to successfully venture under the polar ice cap in 1947; and service as the Navy IG during the so-called Revolt of the Admirals in 1949.

For the *Sailfish* crew, that moment off Point Loma had special significance. The submarine, built at the Portsmouth Naval Shipyard in Portsmouth, New Hampshire, in 1953, was named after a predecessor that had been scrapped after the war. That boat, the USS *Sailfish* (SS-192), was a veteran of all four years of Pacific combat during World War II, had engaged the enemy repeatedly, and, in one astonishing attack in the middle of a typhoon in 1943, had single-handedly sunk a Japanese carrier. No one at the time believed the *Sailfish* would make it back from the war. Even the Japanese referred to it as a "ghost ship," doomed to perish. But she did, outliving her legacy as the former *Squalus* (SS-192), the submarine that sank off New Hampshire, whose survivors were rescued from 240 feet down by the McCann rescue chamber.

Now, in the stillness off Point Loma, the honor guard of the modern *Sailfish* opened the urn and scattered the admiral's ashes downwind. Scripture and prayers were offered, followed by the command, "Firing party, present arms." Gunfire from three volleys shattered the calm. Then "Taps" was played and a wreath was laid in the vice admiral's memory.

The Navy presented a letter and photos of the burial at sea to McCann's wife, Katheryne, and her family. McCann's son-in-law, retired Navy captain Miles R. Finley Jr., expressed the family's gratitude in a letter to Commander Waterman and the crew of the *Sailfish*. "Along with COUNTRY and NAVY, the SUBMARINE FORCE occupied a prominent and constant place in his mind and heart," Finley wrote of the admiral. "Therefore you can understand the appropriateness of the beautiful Burial at Sea ceremony conducted by you from your ship—a submarine—on 13 March 1978 at 1000 off Point Loma, San Diego, California, a landfall and a point of departure for Admiral McCann many times in past years."

"McCann"
Cartagena, Spain
30 May–10 June 2011

Seventy-two years after the McCann submarine rescue chamber brought about the miraculous rescue of otherwise doomed crew members trapped in the *Squalus*, history of another sort was made off the Mediterranean coast northeast of Cartagena, the Spanish port city. It occurred during the triennial exercise Bold Monarch, sponsored by the International Submarine Escape and Rescue Liaison Office of the North Atlantic Treaty Organization (NATO). The office coordinates rescue efforts throughout the world and monitors the whereabouts of more than a thousand commercial vessels that could be chartered in an emergency.

For Bold Monarch 2011, thirteen NATO and non-NATO nations were on hand to practice rescue techniques. Four diesel submarines—one each from Spain, Portugal, Turkey, and Russia—were "disabled" on the ocean floor some two-hundred-plus feet down. The object was to find them and then employ a variety of exotic rescue systems from Italy, the United States, Russia, and Sweden and one jointly owned by Norway, France, and Britain to "save" those who were trapped. Dozens of support vessels included designated "mother ships" from Norway, Italy, Spain, and France, from which the rescue devices were deployed. Over a hectic period of forty-eight hours, the exercise involved two thousand participants and observers from the United States, the United

The Italian naval submarine rescue vessel ITS *Anteo* (A-5309) lofts its McCann rescue chamber above the deck of the Italian submarine ITS *Salvatore Todaro* (S-526) during an exercise to ensure that the chamber can seal properly to the boat's forward escape hatch. This check with the bell designed by Vice Adm. Allan Rockwell McCann, USN, in the early 1930s is done every time an Italian sub returns to service after an overhaul. The *Todaro*, a U212A-class diesel-electric submarine, was commissioned in 2006.

Courtesy of Cdr. Bruno Rocca, Diving Operation and Training, Diving Department, COMSUBIN—Italian Navy

Kingdom, Russia, China, Australia, Canada, Pakistan, India, Norway, Italy, Israel, Sweden, Spain, Singapore, France, Chile, Brazil, Japan, Peru, South Korea, and the Netherlands—some of the fifty nations operating 440 submarines worldwide.

The multiple phases of rescue included first-responder parachute teams from Italy, Russia, and the United Kingdom deployed by Italian aircraft to locate each sub. Subsequently, specialist divers and hyperbaric medical teams from

France, Greece, Italy, the Netherlands, Spain, Sweden, and the United Kingdom would assemble on a variety of specialized rescue ships and chartered vessels, prepared for action to facilitate the "rescue" of 150 survivors, some "injured."

For the current exercise, SSK *Alrosa*, a Kilo-class diesel submarine of the Russian Black Sea Fleet, had come to rest on the Atlantic seabed 195 feet down, where the crew awaited rescue by the U.S. Navy's Submarine Rescue Diving and Recompression System (SRDRS). It had been eleven years since the *Kursk* tragedy, in which 118 Russian submariners succumbed to a slow death at a depth of 350 feet in the Barents Sea as the Russian government refused assistance from foreign navies. "The Russians learned many lessons after that," Capt. David Dittmer of the U.S. Navy told reporters. "When a Russian auxiliary sub with seven men on board became entangled in lines and stuck on the Pacific Ocean floor in 2005, they did ask for help, and a British remote vehicle was sent to cut them free. They were just one hour short of their oxygen running out. Now the Russians have changed further and are very enthusiastic to participate." The captain added that submariners are a family: "We all understand that we have an enemy in common: the sea."

In fact, submarine accidents at depths where rescue is possible are not all that rare. In 1950 HMS *Truculent* sank following a collision with a merchant ship near the British shore. All seventy-two crew members escaped, but fifty-seven were swept out to sea and lost. In 1989 the Russian submarine *Komsomolets* sank after a fire broke out. Thirty-four of the sixty-nine crew members who got off the boat later died from hypothermia before rescue arrived. In 2005 the U.S. nuclear sub USS *San Francisco* (SSN-711) rammed an uncharted peak in the South Pacific. The crash killed one crew member and injured twenty-four. Loss of life was avoided in other incidents. In 2002 the British sub *Trafalgar* hit the seabed off the Isle of Skye. In 2008 HMS *Superb* struck an underwater pinnacle. In 2010 the new British sub *Astute* ran aground.

The Navy's SRDRS employs a three-part rescue apparatus that can quickly be assembled on a rescue vessel. The first element is the launch and recovery system (LARS), an A-frame crane assembled on the deck of the host ship. Second, a pressurized rescue module (PRM), looking much like the original McCann chamber, is lofted over the side from the crane and descends to the stranded submarine following a cable previously connected by advance divers between the ship and the stranded sub's rescue hatch. PRM, once reaching the hull of the boat, makes a watertight seal around the escape hatch of the sub after and then is undogged to take survivors on board. Once the PRM returns to the surface, it docks with the third component of the Navy's rescue apparatus, a mobile submarine decompression system (SDS). Survivors transfer to the pressurized SDS chamber, where they undergo a slow decompression to prevent the painful and potentially deadly bends.

The SRDRS, based out of Naval Base Coronado in San Diego, under the command of the Navy's Deep Submergence Unit, is designed as a "flyaway" rescue system. On short notice it can be loaded on board a transport plane and then flown anywhere in the world. It can be assembled on various types of military or charter vessels in a matter of two hours. Gone is the nomenclature "McCann" for the rescue chamber. It has been replaced by the acronym PRM and is sometimes referred to informally as the "Falcon," after the Navy tug that carried the original McCann rescue chamber to the site of the *Squalus* disaster in 1939.

During World War II, Admiral McCann's original chamber and a few others produced during the 1930s stood by in both the Atlantic and Pacific but were never needed. Only once after 1939 was one used in a real emergency—the sinking in 1953 of the Turkish submarine TCG *Dulupinar* after it was rammed by a freighter in the Dardanelles Strait. Trapped in the sub were 81 crew members at a depth of 278 feet. Although a McCann chamber was brought to the scene, swift currents and the pronounced list of the submarine foiled rescue attempts and the submariners perished. Still, the very existence of the chambers and their spinoffs in other countries offers comforting hope of rescue to submariners throughout the world. Modern versions of the chamber, like those used in Bold Monarch, are very much like McCann's original concept and are capable of descending to more than eight hundred feet, withstanding currents, and linking up to submarine rescue hatches with a trim of as much as forty-five degrees.

In the spring of 2011 off Cartagena, the imminent docking of the Navy's SRDRS with the *Alrosa* in inner space was viewed by many with the same sense of détente as the docking of the Russian spacecraft *Soyuz* with the U.S. *Apollo* in outer space in July 1975. Upon arrival from San Diego, SRDRS was brought on board the chartered vessel HOS *Shooting Star*, which delivered it to the target zone over the *Alrosa*. The PRM was deployed over the side. A select group rode in the rescue chamber down along the descent line to the sub's forward rescue hatch. On contact, the chamber made a hydrostatic, watertight seal with the *Alrosa*. The SRDRS operator broadcast "Lima, Lima, Lima" on low frequency into the surrounding sea, the sound clearly discernible to those in the sub. "Lima" was the prearranged code word for a successful mating between the Russian boat and SRDRS.

One of the first to pass through the hatch into the *Alrosa* was MM2 Joel Rivera, a sailor assigned to the Deep Submergence Unit and forward attendant for SRDRS. "I never thought I'd be able to walk around on a Russian submarine," Rivera marveled, adding, "As a submariner I will be more comfortable going back to submarines knowing all these countries are willing to help if something goes wrong."

The coupling of old adversaries—the Russian submarine with the U.S. Navy's rescue system—was a highlight of ten days of joint force practice with search-and-rescue equipment from various navies. The exercise involved the Italian navy's rescue vessel *Anteo*. Ship commander Diego Priami was to descend in a rescue chamber to the *Alrosa*, where he would be exchanged for the submarine's sonar officer. Said Priami, "When you go out to rescue someone, you take risks. We train in exercises such as Bold Monarch 2011 to reduce those risks." A guest observer who would also make the trip down to the Russian sub was Israeli navy commander Roy Perry, skipper of the submarine INS *Tekuma*. "All these nations come together to explore their limits and see what they can do together," he said. "As a submariner, we always see the ship from the inside. This is a great opportunity to see it from the outside."

Three times the Italians successfully mated with the *Alrosa*. Each time they carried down a variety of dignitaries and journalists. None could miss the reminder of what had come before, off the coast of New Hampshire in 1939. Written in bold, black letters across the midsection of the brilliant yellow rescue chamber was a name recognizable to submariners around the world. It meant salvation had arrived. It was a single word: "McCann."

Notes

For those interested in a time line of Vice Adm. Allan Rockwell McCann's life, I recommend that compiled by Jeff Scism, found at http://ibssg.org/mccann/. The U.S. Navy's official Admiral McCann biography can be found at http://www.history.navy.mil/faqs/faq99-11.htm.

Chapter 1. Robot Bombs

The quotations from Admiral Ingram throughout this chapter can be located in "Robot Bomb Attacks Here Held 'Probable' by Admiral," *New York Times*, 9 January 1945. Edward Thomas's warning to Manhattan citizens about a submarine attack on page 6 and La Guardia's quotation about war production on page 6 can be found in Associated Press, "Robot Bomb Hits on City Predicted," *New York Times*, 9 January 1945. Albert Speer's radio broadcast from Germany in December 1944 threatening U-bomb attacks on the United States on page 2 can be found in various sources, including Duffy, *Target, America*. The news of the Seewolf boat offensive causing brief "chaos" in Washington on page 8 is found in Farago, *Tenth Fleet*. Commander Giambattista's quotations on page 10 are from Youngblood, *Hunter Killer*.

Chapter 2. Peculiar Place

The quote from the P. J. Boland Overcutting and Company advertisement on page 14 comes from Wohl, *North Adams Massachusetts Old Home Week*. Nathaniel Hawthorne's view of the early settlement of North Adams on page 14 is from his *Passages from the American Note-Books*. The description of how explosives were used to create the Hoosac Tunnel on page 16 is found in Byron, *Pinprick of Light*. Descriptions of the rigorous education that young McCann experienced at Drury Academy on page 18 come from the *Drury Academy 1909 Year Book*.

Chapter 3. Luckiest Class

The quotation from McCann's letter to his father on page 22 is found in "Luckiest Class in Annapolis," *North Adams Evening Transcript*. President Wilson's quote declaring U.S. neutrality in World War I on page 22 is found in Love, *History of the U.S. Navy.* Wilson's quotations on page 24 are from Wilson, *War Messages.* McCann's wedding, mentioned on page 26, is described in "Lieut. McCann Takes a Bride," *North Adams Evening Transcript.* The testimony of those who survived the fire on board the submarine USS *O-5* at the Brooklyn Navy Yard beginning on page 28 comes from the official Naval inquiry of 5 October 1918 on file at the National Archives and Records Administration, Washington, DC. Adm. Charles L. Lockwood's view of the prototypical submarine sailor found on pages 31–32 comes from Lockwood, *Through Hell and Deep Water.* The axioms used in the training of submarine sailors on page 32 are drawn from "Spritz's Navy," *Polaris*, December 1987.

Chapter 4. Awful Mess

The quote by the captain of the SS *Abangarez* on page 37 is found in Olive, *Panama's Canal.* Diver Sheppard Shreaves' quotes recalling his rescue of sailors trapped in USS *O-5* in Limón Bay, Panama, starting on page 39 come from Grigore, "The O-5 Is Down!" U.S. Naval Institute *Proceedings*, February 1972. Grigore's article is also the source of trapped submariner Lawrence Brown's recollection of his rescue on page 41.

Chapter 5. Worlds to Conquer

San Francisco newspaper headlines on page 43 are from the *New York Times*; these headlines were reprinted in newspapers across the country. The dialogue between James D. Dole and Harry McConaughty on pages 43–45 is drawn from Forden, *Glory Gamblers.* The discussion of the U.S. Navy's magnetic exploder on its torpedoes, including the quotation by Capt. Thomas Hart on page 47, is drawn from Blair, *Silent Victory.* Mildred Doran's quotations on pages 50, 52, and 53 are from Forden, *Glory Gamblers.* The quotes from pilot Martin Jensen in *Aloha* on page 54 come from Burlingame, "The Dole Derby," *Honolulu Star Bulletin*, 12 January 2004. Goebel's "two goals" comment on page 54 is from Forden, *Glory Gamblers.* Goebel's comments on winning the race on page 55 can be found in Burlingame, "The Dole Derby," *Honolulu Star Bulletin*, 5 January 2004. Mrs. Jensen's comment to her husband on his overdue landing on page 56 is from Forden, *Glory Gamblers.* The Morse code messages sent from the doomed *Dallas Spirit* on page 57 come from Forden, *Glory Gamblers.* The message from the downed *Miss Doran* on page 58 comes from "Aeronautics: Flights, Flyers," *Time*, 3 September 1928.

Chapter 6. Utterly Helpless

Unless otherwise cited, the quotations in this chapter are from Maas, *The Rescuer.* Quotes by Lt. Allan McCann, beginning on page 67, are from McCann, letter to Walter Welham, 26 January 1962, MS VF 27, Nimitz Library, U.S. Naval Academy.

Chapter 7. Mad Scheme

Sir George Hubert Wilkins' quote on page 74 comes from Leary, *Under Ice*. Jules Verne's congratulatory note to Simon Lake on page 74 is also from Leary, *Under Ice*. Simon Lake's quote about drifting "through the streets of Atlantis" on page 79 is found at "Nautilus," Simon Lake Submarine Web Site, www. simonlake.com/html/nautilus.html. The quote about the "suicide club" on page 80 is from "Nautilus Trip to Pole No Suicide Club, Says Lake," *The Day*, 12 May 1931. *Nautilus* captain Sloan Danenhower's quote about a worst-case scenario for the sub on page 80 is from "Commander of Nautilus Tells of Unique Plans," *Syracuse American*, 1 March 1931. The quote about the *Nautilus* expedition being a "mad scheme" on page 80 comes from L. Cameron Mae Donald, letter to Wilkins, n.d., *Nautilus* Exhibition, Ohio State University Library. Lake's quote distancing himself from the expedition on page 80 is from Nelson, *Sabotage in the Arctic*. *Nautilus* engineer John R. Janson's quote defending his decision to leave the boat on page 80 is also from Nelson, *Sabotage in the Arctic*. The quotes from Wilkins' diary on page 82 are from Nelson, *Sabotage in the Arctic*, as is the quote from Wilkins' dispatch to Hearst on page 82. Finally, Naval Examining Board's finding of no fault for the officers and crew of the failed *Nautilus* mission on page 83 is from Nelson, *Sabotage in the Arctic*. McCann's commendation from the Bureau of Construction and Repair on page 83 is from "Citation Copies Received," *North Adams Evening Transcript*, 1 January 1932.

Chapter 8. Desperate Hours

Oliver Naquin's quote about the smell of diesel fumes on page 86 is from LaVO, *Back from the Deep*. The quotes on pages 87 and 88 from crew members of the *Squalus* come from Barrows, *Blow All Ballast!*, the seminal account of the tragedy and rescue. The quote from CE Lawrence Gainor on page 88 comes from personal interviews, as recounted in LaVO, *Back from the Deep*. The quote from Adm. Cole on page 89 is from Barrows, *Blow All Ballast!* The conversation between Wilkins and Naquin on page 90 comes from Maas, *The Rescuer*. Lt. Cdr. Charles Momsen's quote recalling the *Squalus* sinking on page 91 is drawn from Momsen, "Rescue and Salvage of U.S.S. *Squalus*." Master Diver Squire's quote about the race by automobile to New Hampshire on page 92 is from LaVO, *Back from the Deep*. Carl Bryson's quote about plans to escape the *Squalus* by Momsen lung on page 92 is from a personal interview as recounted in LaVO, *Back from the Deep*. The quote from a *Penacook* sailor about hooking the *Squalus*

on page 93 is from LaVO, *Back from the Deep*. The *Falcon* captain's warning to
trapped *Squalus* crew members on page 93 is from Barrows, *Blow All Ballast!*
Donato Persico's quotes on pages 95 and 97 are from personal interviews, as
recounted in LaVO, *Back from the Deep*. McCann's quotes beginning on page
95 illustrating his pivotal role in the rescue of *Squalus* survivors comes from
McCann, letter to Walter Welham, 26 January 1962, MS VF 27, Nimitz Library,
U.S. Naval Academy. Momsen's "sea monster" quote on page 96 is from Maas,
The Rescuer. Momsen's "eyes of the outside world" quote on page 98 is from
Momsen, "Rescue and Salvage of U.S.S. *Squalus*." Badders' quote about bringing up more survivors than recommended on page 99 is from LaVO, *Back from
the Deep*, as is the quotation from McDonald's efforts to calm the survivors
on page 101. Momsen's welcome to *Squalus* captain Oliver Naquin on surfacing on page 103 is from Barrows, *Blow All Ballast!* as are Preble's quote praising
Lawrence Gainor on page 104 and Maness' "never any doubt" quote on page
104. Treadway's speech to Congress praising McCann for the *Squalus* heroics on
page 104 is from "McCann's Name Wins Applause," *North Adams Transcript*, 27
May 1939. The quote from a *Squalus* crew member watching the unsuccessful
first salvage attempt to raise the submarine on page 106 is from LaVO, *Back
from the Deep*. President Roosevelt's commendation of McCann and others on
page 107 is from Barrows, *Blow All Ballast!*

Chapter 9. Unbelievable

The quote regarding Navy commander Gene Tunney's physical fitness program on page 109 comes from Tunney, "It's More Fun to Be Fit," *Reader's Digest*,
February 1942. War plans for the eventuality of conflict with Japan on page 110
come from "War Plan Orange," GlobalSecurity.org, May 7, 2011, http://www.
globalsecurity.org/military/ops/war-plan-orange.htm. Eakin's quote describing
the initial bombing run on Pearl Harbor by Japanese aircraft on page 111 is
from Hayes, "Two Survivors Recall Pearl Harbor Attack at Jersey City Event,"
Jersey Journal, 7 December 2009. Seaman Hewett's "ringside seat" quote on
page 112 is from Guinta, "Pearl Harbor: 60 Years Later," *St. Augustine Record*,
7 December 2001. The quote from McCann on page 111 is from Blair, *Silent
Victory*. The quotes from Edward Gaulrapp on pages 112 and 114 come from
"Edward Dutch Gallrupp, Pearl Harbor Survivor, Shares Memories of Attack,"
CNR Hawaii Newspapers, 7 December 2007. Lt. Bernard Clarey's recollections
of the attack on page 112 come from a recollection on file at the USS *Bowfin*
Submarine Museum and Park, Pearl Harbor, HI. Quotes about the carnage
at Pearl Harbor beginning on page 114 come from "Chronology of the Attack
from the Deck Logs of the Vessels Moored at Pearl Harbor, December 7, 1941,"
NavSource Naval History, October 2003, www.navsource.org/Naval/logs.htm.

Winston Churchill's quote on page 116 comes from Havighurst, *Britain in Transition*.

Chapter 10. Dead Issues

Unless otherwise cited, the quotations in this chapter are from Blair, *Silent Victory*. Sieglaff's quote on page 118 comes from Holwitt, *"Execute against Japan."* Slade Cutter's quotes on pages 119, 121, and 122 are from LaVO, *Slade Cutter*. The quote from Claude Braun on pages 120–21 is from LaVO, *Back from the Deep*. Daubin's assessment of Parks' patrol on page 122 is from the official war patrol report of the USS *Pompano*. Longstaff's quote recommending a thorough investigation of the Mark 14 torpedoes on page 133 and Pace's quote on page 133 are from the USS *Tinosa*'s Submarine War Patrol Report, Part 2, Historic Naval Ships Association, http://issuu.com/hnsa/docs/ss-283_tinosa_part2?e=1149954/2755142. Lockwood's quote about "shaking hands with Saint Peter" on page 134 is from Maas, *The Rescuer*.

Chapter 11. Bermuda College

Winston Churchill's quote about the war in the North Atlantic on page 137 is from volume 10 of Morison, *History of United States Naval Operations in World War II*. The German communique declaring a U-boat triumph on page 137 is from Werner, *Iron Coffins*. The quote by Karl Doenitz declaring a German victory in the Battle of the Atlantic on page 137 is from Farago, *The Tenth Fleet*. So are King's quote demanding a concentrated effort to thwart U-boats on page 137, the description of Low on page 138, and Low's quote about employing enough carriers and aircraft in the Atlantic Ocean on page 139. King's quote about the urgency of building an antisubmarine effort on page 140 is from volume 1 of Morison, *History of United States Naval Operations in World War II*.

Chapter 12. Kurita's Blunder

Unless otherwise cited, the quotations in this chapter are from Cutler, *The Battle of Leyte Gulf*. George Graham's quote on page 148 is from an interview conducted by the author. Vice Admiral Kurita's "meat for the enemy" quote on page 151 and his follow-up quote on page 151 are from Thomas, *Sea of Thunder*. Vice Admiral Ozawa's quote on page 153 is drawn from Woodward, *The Battle of Leyte Gulf*. Admiral Halsey's quote about the power of aircraft carriers on page 155 and his boast after the Pearl Harbor attack on page 155 come from Wukovits, *Admiral "Bull" Halsey*. The quote from *Iowa* crew member Sims on page 156 comes from an interview conducted by the author. Admiral Kurita's quote about breaking into Leyte Gulf on page 158 and Admiral Halsey's quote on page 165 admitting his "gravest error" come from Wukovits, *Admiral "Bull"*

Halsey. Japanese navy minister Admiral Yonai's quote on page 165 summarizing the outcome of the battle is from volume 12 of Morison's *History of United States Naval Operations in World War II*.

Chapter 13. Operation Teardrop

The quote from the unidentified escort carrier commander noting few contacts with U-boats on page 169 is from Youngblood, *Hunter Killer*. Admiral King's decision to begin demobilizing the Tenth Fleet on page 169 is from Farago, *The Tenth Fleet*. Admiral Ingram's reference to stopping "a phalanx of snorkel boats" on page 170, the *Croatan* flight leader's quote about how hard pilots tried to find U-boats on page 172, and the story of the "Fightin' Freddy" beginning on page 172 are from volume 10 of Morison's *History of United States Naval Operations in World War II*. The story of "Moby Dick" beginning on page 175 is from Farago, *The Tenth Fleet*. German admiral Doenitz's quote ending the U-boat war on page 177 is from Levine, *D-Day to Berlin*. The admiral's quote on page 178 evaluating the U-boat war is from volume 10 of Morison's *History of United States Naval Operations in World War II*.

Chapter 14. Terribly Cruel

President Truman's quotes expressing enthusiasm that the Soviet Union would join the war against Japan and about the atomic bomb on page 180 are from *The Diary of Harry S Truman*. The intelligence report to Truman on weather conditions in Hiroshima on page 180 is also from *The Diary of Harry S Truman*, as is the quote about Truman's decision to proceed with the atomic bombing of Hiroshima on page 180. The quote from the Potsdam Declaration on page 180 is from Rigdon, "President's Trip to the Berlin Conference." President Truman's "greatest thing in history" quote on page 182 and his "time to get on home" quote on page 183 also come from Rigdon, "President's Trip to the Berlin Conference." Truman's statement released to the press after the dropping of the atomic bomb on page 183 is from the Eben A. Ayers Papers. Truman's quote in defense of the Hiroshima bombing on page 184 is from *Public Papers of the Presidents, Harry S. Truman, 1945*. Truman's quote congratulating Admiral McCann on page 184 is from Rigdon, "President's Trip to the Berlin Conference." The quote from Truman rebuffing Senator Russell's plea to drop more atomic bombs on page 184 is from Truman, letter to Richard Russell, 9 August 1945. Admiral Leahy's prediction that the atomic bomb would be used against the United States in the future on pages 184–85 is from Leahy, *I Was There*. Thomas Paine's discussion of Japanese I-boats captured at the end of World War II on pages 185, 186, and 188 is from Paine, *The Transpacific Voyage of His Imperial Japanese Majesty's Submarine I-400*. Japanese general Umezu's quote about the possibility of germ warfare on page 186, the order to dispose of all captured Japanese subs on page 188, and Catlin's quote about the destruction of captured Japanese I-subs on page 188 are also from Paine, *The Transpacific Voyage*. Charles Alger's quote expressing remorse at the scuttling of the I-400 on page 189 is from National Geographic's TV documentary *Hunt for the Samurai Subs*, 19 November 2009.

Chapter 15. Under Ice

Unless otherwise cited, quotations in this chapter are from Kitchen, *The Reminiscences of Dr. Waldo K. Lyon*. Information from Duncan about the *Sennet*'s excursion under the Antarctic ice pack on page 190 is from an interview by the author. Lyon's reference to the Arctic Ocean as "a big basin" on page 195 comes from Leary, *Under Ice*. Turner's quotes about chunks of ice breaking over the *Boarfish*'s bow on page 199 and about preserving his periscope on page 199 are also from Leary, *Under Ice*. So is Lyon's quote requesting ComSubPac to continue explorations of "a new ocean" on page 200.

Chapter 16. Nibbled to Death

General Eisenhower's prediction of a "blowup" between the armed services on page 203 is from Wolk, "The Battle of the B-36," *Air Force Magazine*, July 1996. Walter Waggoner's quote about the atomic bomb making the Navy "obsolete" on page 203 is from Waggoner, "Keel Is Laid for Super-Carrier, Issue in Navy-Air Force Dispute," *New York Times*, 19 April 1949. Johnson's instruction to Sullivan regarding the supercarrier on page 204 is from Waggoner, "Carrier Is Halted: Air Force Triumphs in Strategy Fight," *New York Times*, 24 April 1949. Navy Secretary Sullivan's quote criticizing Defense Secretary Johnson for cancelling construction of the USS *United States* on page 204 comes from Lewis, "The Revolt of the Admirals." Defense Secretary Johnson's quote about doing away with the Navy on page 205 is from Barlow, *Revolt of the Admirals*. Duncan's quote about movies taken by a Navy fighter pilot to show how vulnerable Air Force bombers were on page 205 is from an interview by the author. The Joint Chiefs memorandum signed by Denfeld quoted on page 205 is from "Joint Chiefs Bar Duel of Jets, B-36," *New York Times*, 2 June 1949. The memorandum detailing how the B-36 did not meet performance goals (pages 205–6) is discussed in Barlow, *Revolt of the Admirals*. Van Zandt's "strange proceedings" quote on page 206 is from Hurd, "House Study Urged of B-36 Contracts," *New York Times*, 26 May 1949. Vinson's "whitewash" quote on page 206 is from Hurd, "House Unit Sets Full Study of Nation's Air Power Plans," *New York Times*, 1 June 1949. Representative Van Zandt's "ugly, dirty rumors" quotation on page 206 is from Hurd, "House Clears Way for Inquiry on B-36," *New York Times*, 8 June 1949. Symington's letter branding allegations of improprieties regarding the B-36 as "lies" on page 207 is from "Symington Condemns as Lies Charges of B-36 Irregularity," *New York Times*, 4 June 1949. Cedric Worth's testimony on page 207 is from Conklin, "Navy Aide Admits Writing B-36 Note That Led to Inquiry," *New York Times*, 25 August 1949. The quotations from General Bradley and General LeMay on page 207 are also from Conklin, "Navy Aide Admits Writing B-36 Note That Led to Inquiry." The Armed Services Committee's findings that there was "not one scintilla of evidence" that favoritism played a role in the B-36 program on page 207 is from Conklin, "House's B-36 Inquiry Ends with Clearing of Officials," *New York Times*, 26 August 1949. Captain Wood's interrogation of Commander Davies on page 208 is from "'Rank Gossip' Led to Inquiry on B-36," *New York Times*, 7 September 1949. Quotes from Captain Crommelin's prepared statement on page 209 are from "Crommelin Retains 'Bulldog Tenacity' of Wartime," *Evening Star*, 7 October 1949. Navy Secretary Matthews' quote demoting Crommelin on page 210 is from the *New York Times*, 16 September 1949. The secretary's quote defending his order to Admiral McCann to investigate Op-23 on page 211 is from Barlow, *Revolt of the Admirals*. The unnamed lieutenant's warning to Commander Arthur that a raid was imminent on page 211 is also from Barlow, *Revolt of the Admirals*. So are all the quotes from those involved describing McCann's raid on page 211. Vice Admiral Bogan's quotes about Navy morale on pages 212 and 213 are from Associated Press, "Pentagon Crippling Power of Navy, Captain Says, Risking His Career," 10 September 1949. The quotes from Denfeld's and Radford's letters on page 213 are from Barlow, *Revolt of the Admirals*. So are the quotes from Radford's testimony before the House Armed Services Committee on page 213. The "random slaughter" quote on page 214 is from House Armed Services Committee, *Investigation of the B-36 Bomber Program*. Rachel Denfeld's "stand up" quote on page 214 is from Barlow, *Revolt of the Admirals*, as is Admiral Denfeld's testimony before the House Armed Services Committee on page 214. Secretary Matthews' quote expressing anger at Denfeld on page 214 and Bradley's "fancy Dans" quote on page 215 are also from Barlow, *Revolt of the Admirals*. The Armed Services Committee's conclusions on page 215 are from House Armed Services Committee, *Investigation of the B-36 Bomber Program*. Radford's "horrible mess" quote on page 215 is from Barlow, *Revolt of the Admirals*.

Chapter 17. Homecoming

Navy captain Finley's quote on page 219 is from a letter in the author's possession. Navy captain Dittmer's quote about Russia joining submarine practice rescues on page 221 is from "Russian and U.S. Navies Cooperate on Submarine Rescue," *Ottawa Citizen*, 10 June 2011. MM2C Joel Rivera's quote on page 222 is also from "Russian and U.S. Navies Cooperate on Submarine Rescue," *Ottawa Citizen*, 10 June 2011. Commander Priami's quote on page 223 is from "Italian ITS *Anteo*," Sorbet Royal, http://sorbetroyal2005.celex.net/photo_album/antco. htm. Perry's quote on page 223 is from Exercise Bold Monarch 2011, "Russian Submarine Participates in NATO Submarine Rescue Exercise for First Time," news release, 2 June 2011.

BIBLIOGRAPHY

In preparing my manuscript over the past three years, the following sources proved most helpful in understanding all the twists and turns of Vice Admiral McCann's remarkable career.

Books

Adams, Henry H. *Witness to Power: The Life of Fleet Admiral William D. Leahy*. Annapolis, MD: Naval Institute Press, 1985.

Alden, John D. *U.S. Submarine Attacks during World War II*. Annapolis, MD: Naval Institute Press, 1989.

Barlow, Jeffrey G. *Revolt of the Admirals: The Fight for Naval Aviation*. Washington, DC: Naval Historical Center, 1994.

———. "The Revolt of the Admirals Reconsidered." *New Interpretations in Naval History*. Edited by William B. Cogar. Annapolis, MD: Naval Institute Press, 1989.

Barrows, Nat A. *Blow All Ballast! The Story of the* Squalus. New York: Dodd, Mead, 1943.

Blair, Clay, Jr. *Silent Victory: The U.S. Submarine War against Japan*. Annapolis, MD: Naval Institute Press, 1975.

Bonner, Kit, and Carolyn Bonner. *USS* Iowa *at War*. St. Paul, MN: MBI Publishing, 2007.

Breuer, William B. *Hitler's Undercover War*. New York: St. Martin's Press, 1989.

———. *Secret Weapons of World War II*. New York: John Wiley & Sons, 2000.

Byron, Carl. *A Pinprick of Light: The Troy and Greenfield Railroad and Its Hoosac Tunnel*. Shelburne, VT: New England Press, 1995.

Campanile, Robert. *North Adams*. Postcard History Series. Portsmouth, NH: Arcadia Publishing, 2007.

Cutler, Thomas J. *The Battle of Leyte Gulf: 23–26 October, 1944*. Annapolis, MD: Naval Institute Press, 2001.

Duffy, James P. *Target, America: Hitler's Plan to Attack the United States.* Guilford, CT: Globe Pequot, 2006.

Ellsberg, Edward. *On the Bottom.* Rahway, NJ: Quinn & Boben, 1928.

Farago, Ladislas. *The Tenth Fleet.* New York: Ivan Orolenky, 1962.

Forden, Lesley. *Glory Gamblers.* New York: Ballantine Books, 1961.

Fukui, Shizsui. *The Japanese Navy at the End of World War II.* Old Greenwich, CT: We, 1947.

Hadley, Michael L. *U-Boats against Canada: German Submarines in Canadian Waters.* Montreal: McGill-Queen's University Press, 1990.

Hammond, Paul Y. *Super Carriers and B-36 Bombers: Appropriations, Strategy, and Policy.* Birmingham: University of Alabama Press, 1963.

Hashimoto, Mochitsura. *Sunk—The Story of the Japanese Submarine Fleet 1941–1945.* New York: Henry Holt, 1954.

Havighurst, Alfred F. *Britain in Transition: The Twentieth Century.* Chicago: University of Chicago Press, 1985.

Hawthorne, Nathaniel. *Passages from the American Note-Books.* Edited by Sophia Hawthorne. Boston: Houghton Mifflin, 1883.

Heinl, Robert Debbs. *Victory at High Tide: The Inchon-Seoul Campaign.* Baltimore, MD: Nautical and Aviation Publishing Corporation of America, 1979.

Herrick, John. *Subsurface Warfare: The History of Division 6, National Research Defense Committee.* Washington, DC: Department of Defense, 1951.

Holwitt, Joel Ira. *"Execute against Japan": The U.S. Decision to Conduct Unrestricted Submarine Warfare.* College Station: Texas A&M University Press, 2009.

Horvat, William J. *Above the Pacific.* Fallbrook, CA: Aero Publishers, 1966.

LaVO, Carl. *Back from the Deep: The Strange Story of the Sister Subs* Squalus *and* Sculpin. Annapolis, MD: Naval Institute Press, 1994.

———. *Slade Cutter: Submarine Warrior.* Annapolis, MD: Naval Institute Press, 2003.

Leahy, William D. *I Was There.* New York: Arno Press, 1950.

Leary, William M. *Under Ice: Waldo Lyon and the Development of the Arctic Submarine.* College Station: Texas A & M University Press, 1999.

Levine, Alan J. *D-Day to Berlin: The Northwest Europe Campaign, 1944–45.* Harrisburg, PA: Stackpole Books, 2007.

Lockwood, Charles. *Through Hell and Deep Water.* New York: Bantam, 1991.

Love, Robert W., Jr. *History of the U.S. Navy*. Vol. 1. Harrisburg, PA: Stackpole Books, 1992.

Maas, Peter. *The Rescuer: The Extraordinary Life of Navy's "Swede" Momsen and His Role in an Epic Submarine Disaster*. New York: Harper & Row, 1967.

———. *The Terrible Hours: The Man behind the Greatest Submarine Rescue in History*. New York: Harper Collins, 1999.

MacIntyre, Donald. *U-Boat Killer*. Annapolis, MD: Naval Institute Press, 1975.

Mauro, James. *Twilight at the World of Tomorrow: Genius, Madness, Murder and the 1939 World's Fair on the Brink of War*. New York: Ballantine Books, 2012.

Morison, Samuel Eliot. *History of United States Naval Operations in World War II*. Vol. 10, *The Atlantic Battle Won*. Boston: Little, Brown, 1990.

———. *History of United States Naval Operations in World War II*. Vol. 12, *Leyte June 1944–January 1945*. Boston: Little, Brown, 1958.

Nelson, Stewart B. *Sabotage in the Arctic: Fate of the Submarine Nautilus*. N.p.: Xlibris, 2007.

Newpower, Anthony, *Iron Men and Tin Fish: The Race to Build a Better Torpedo during World War II*. Westport, CT: Praeger Security International, 2006.

North Adams. Troy, NY: Troy Daily Times Presses, 1890. Reprint, North Adams, MA: North Adams Historical Society, 1998.

Olive, Carl R. *Panama's Canal*. Danbury, CT: Scholastic Library Pub, 1990.

Paine, Thomas O. *The Transpacific Voyage of His Imperial Japanese Majesty's Submarine I-400*. Los Angeles: Submarine Warfare Library, Thomas Paine Associates, 1984.

Rhodes, Richard. *The Making of the Atomic Bomb*. New York: Simon & Schuster, 1995.

Robertson, Terence. *Escort Commander*. New York: Nelson Doubleday, 1956.

Roscoe, Theodore. *U.S. Destroyer Operations*. Annapolis, MD: U.S. Naval Institute, 1953.

Rose, Lisle A. *Assault on Eternity: Richard E. Byrd and the Exploration of Antarctica, 1946–47*. Annapolis, MD: Naval Institute Press, 1980.

Stillwell, Paul. *Submarine Stories: Recollections from the Diesel Boats*. Annapolis, MD: Naval Institute Press, 2007.

Sweetman, Jack. *The U.S. Naval Academy: An Illustrated History*. 2nd ed. Revised by Thomas J. Cutler. Annapolis, MD: Naval Institute Press, 1995.

Thomas, Evan. *Sea of Thunder: Four Commanders and the Last Great Naval Campaign 1941–1945*. New York: Simon & Schuster, 2007.

Vat, Dan van der. *The Atlantic Campaign: World War II's Great Struggle at Sea*. New York: Harper & Row, 1988.

———. *Pearl Harbor: The Day of Infamy—An Illustrated History*. Toronto: Basic Books, 2001.

Werner, Herbert A. *Iron Coffins: A Personal Account of the German U-Boat Battles of World War II*. Boston: Da Capo Press, 2002.

Wilkins, George Hubert. *Under the North Pole: The Wilkins-Ellsworth Submarine Expedition*. New York: Brewer, Warren & Putnam, 1931.

Wohl, Diane. *North Adams Massachusetts Old Home Week, September 5–11, 1909*. Reprint, North Adams: North Adams Historical Society, 1987.

Woodward, Corner Van. *The Battle for Leyte Gulf: The Incredible Story of World War II's Largest Naval Battle*. New York: Skyhorse Publishing, 2007.

Wukovits, John. *Admiral "Bull" Halsey: The Life and Wars of the Navy's Most Controversial Commander*. New York: Palgrave Macmillian, 2010.

Youngblood, William T. *Hunter Killer*. Annapolis, MD: Naval Institute Press, 1983.

Articles

Altonn, Helen. "UH Team Discovers 2 WWII-Era Japanese Subs off Oahu." *Honolulu Star Bulletin*, 21 November 2009.

Associated Press. "American Submarine Skirts Siberia under Polar Floes." 26 August 1947.

———. "Morale of Navy Is Shattered in New Set-Up, Admirals Say." 4 October 1949.

———. "Navy-Air Force Duel with B-36 Is Urged." 19 May 1949.

———. "Pentagon Crippling Power of Navy, Captain Says, Risking His Career." 10 September 1949.

———. "Robot Bomb Hits on City Predicted," as printed in the New York Times, 9 January 1945.

Baldwin, Hanson W. "Unification Is Hurt." *New York Times*, 14 September 1949.

———. "War Plane Orders Face Examination by Congressmen." *New York Times*, 24 May 1949.

Barlow, Jeffrey G. "Moral Courage: Vital to Navy Leadership." *Naval Aviation News*, September-October 1998.

————. "Naval Aviation's Most Serious Crisis?" *Naval History*, December 2011, 39–44.

Bernstein, Barton. "Understanding the Atomic Bomb and the Japanese Surrender: Missed Opportunities, Little-Known Near Disasters, and Modern Memory." *Diplomatic History*, Spring 1995.

Bernstein, Marc D. "'Hell Broke Loose' at Leyte Gulf." *Naval History* 23, no. 5 (October 2009): 24–29.

Burlingame, Burl. "The Dole Derby." *Honolulu Star-Bulletin*, 29 December 2003, 5 January 2004, and 12 January 2004.

CNR Hawaii Newspapers. "Edward Dutch Gallrupp, Pearl Harbor Survivor, Shares Memories of Attack." 7 December 2007.

Conklin, William E. "House's B-36 Inquiry Ends with Clearing of Officials." *New York Times*, 26 August 1949.

————. "Navy Aide Admits Writing B-36 Note That Led to Inquiry." *New York Times*, 25 August 1949.

Danenhower, Sloan. "Commander of *Nautilus* Tells of Unique Plans." *Syracuse American*, 1 March 1931.

Estrada, Larry, "The Arctic Submarine Laboratory: The Navy's Arctic Center of Excellence." *Undersea Warfare*, Summer 2011.

Evening Star. "Crommelin Retains 'Bulldog Tenacity' of Wartime." 7 October 1949.

Grigore, Jules, Jr. "The O-5 Is Down!" U.S. Naval Institute *Proceedings*, February 1972, 54–60.

————. "Submarine Tragedy Sets Stage for Heroes." *Panama Canal Review*, May 1969.

Grover, David. "Search for the Lost Dole Racers." *Air Classics*, August 2002.

Hayes, Melissa. "Two Survivors Recall Pearl Harbor Attack at Jersey City Event." *Jersey Journal*, 7 December 2009.

Holt, Lew. "Submarine Safety—An Insolvable Problem?" *Modern Mechanix*, April 1932.

Hone, Thomas C. "When the Well Runs Dry." *Naval History* 26, no. 2 (April 2012): 43–44.

Hornfischer, James D. "A Warrior's Destiny." *Naval History* 23, no. 5 (October 2009): 30–34.

Hurd, Charles. "House Clears Way for Inquiry on B-36." *New York Times*, 8 June 1949.

———. "House Study Urged of B-36 Contracts." *New York Times*, 26 May 1949.

———. "House Unit Sets Full Study of Nation's Air Power Plans." *New York Times*, 1 June 1949.

———. "Vinson Asks House to Sift Air Orders." *New York Times*, 27 May 1949.

Joint Force Quarterly. "Admiral Louis Emil Denfeld." Summer 1997, 115.

Lynch, Adam. "Kill and Be Killed? The U-853 Mystery." *Naval History* 22, no. 3 (June 2008): 39–43.

New York Times. "Admirals Elevate Crommelin, but Matthews Reverses Them." 16 September 1949.

———. "Halsey Champions Critic of Pentagon, Asks Navy Support." 13 September 1949.

———. "Joint Chiefs Bar Duel of Jets, B-36." 2 June 1949.

———. "'Rank Gossip' Led to inquiry on B-36." 7 September 1949.

———. "Robot Bomb Attacks Here Held 'Probable' by Admiral." 9 January 1945.

———. "Symington Condemns as Lies Charges of B-36 Irregularity." 4 June 1949.

North Adams Evening Transcript. "Citation Copies Received." 1 January 1932.

———. "Former Resident Invents Submarine Rescue Device." 23 June 1931.

———. "Lieut. McCann Takes a Bride." 7 October 1918.

———. "Luckiest Class in Annapolis." 23 March 1917.

———. "'McCann Bell' Proves Worth in Tests." 20 July 1931.

———. "The Other McCann in City's History." 27 October 1995.

North Adams Telegraph. "Allan McCann Commended for Squalus Rescue Work." 18 September 1939, 1–2.

———. "McCann's Name Wins Applause." 26 May 1939, 3.

———. "Navy Gives 13 Nations Plans for McCann Bell." 18 September 1939, 2.

North Adams Transcript. "Adm. McCann Lunches with Relatives Here." 19 October 1960.

———. McCann's Name Wins Applause." 27 May 1939.

Ottawa Citizen. "Russian and U.S. Navies Cooperate on Submarine Rescue." 10 June 2011.

Polaris. "Spritz's Navy." December 1987.

The Day. "Nautilus Trip to Pole No Suicide Club, Says Lake," New London, Connecticut 12 May 1931.

Time. "Aeronautics: Flights, Flyers." 3 September 1928.

Tunney, Gene. "It's More Fun to Be Fit." *Reader's Digest*, February 1942.

Waggoner, Walter H. "Armed Forces News Unified to Stop 'Leaks' and Rivalry." *New York Times*, 18 March 1949.

———. "Carrier Is Halted; Air Force Triumphs in Strategy Fight." *New York Times*, 24 April 1949.

———. "Keel Is Laid for Super-Carrier, Issue in Navy-Air Force Dispute." *New York Times*, 19 April 1949.

———. "Orders from Johnson Stir Action toward Unification." *New York Times*, 1 May 1949.

———. "Unification Measure Shelved until B-36 Inquiry Is Ended." *New York Times*, 13 July 1949.

White, William S. "Navy Sets Inquiry on Letter Release, Congress May Act." *New York Times*, 5 October 1949.

Wolk, Herman S. "The Battle of the B-36." *Air Force Magazine*, July 1996.

Yokelson, Mitchell. "The United States Armed Forces and the Mexican Punitive Expedition, Part 1." *Prologue Magazine* 29, no. 3 (Fall 1997): 334–43.

Internet Sources

Ahern, J. J. "The Nautilus: Low Road to the Pole." American Philosophical Society. 2000. http://www.amphilsoc.org/exhibits/nautilus/history.

Anderson, Charles Robert. "Leyte: The U.S. Army Campaigns of World War II." Transcribed by Patrick Clancey, HyperWar Foundation. Accessed 2 May 2012. http://www.ibiblio.org/hyperwar/USA/USA-C-Leyte/index.html.

Bermuda Online. "American Military Bases in Bermuda from 1941 to 1995." Last modified 22 June 2013. http://www.bermuda-online.org/milquit.htm.

Citizendia.org. "Mark 14 Torpedo." Last modified 2009. http://citizendia.org/Mark_14_torpedo.

City of Winter Park Florida. Accessed 2 May 2012. http://www.cityofwinterpark.org.

Commander, Submarine Force U.S. Pacific Fleet. "Commander, Submarine Squadron Seven." Accessed 2 May 2012. http://www.csp.navy.mil/subssquadrons/CSS7/css7_homepage.shtml.

Day, Deborah. "Harald Ulrick Sverdrup Biography." Scripps Institution of Oceanography Archives, 21 August 2002. http://scilib.ucsd.edu/sio/biogr/Sverdrup_Biogr.pdf

DiCarpio, Ralph. "The Battle of Point Judith." 2003. http://www.desausa.org/de_photo_library/battle_of_point_judith.

Fleetsubmarine.com. Last modified 2008. http://www.fleetsubmarine.com.

"German U-Boat bunkers." Accessed 2 May 2012. http://www.uboataces.com/articles-uboat-bunker.shtml.

Givens, Benjamin M. "Remembrances." Last modified 7 January 2002. http://www.ussoklahomabb37.ussindianabb58.com/remembrances.html.

Gold, Robert Andrew. "Development of a Procedure for the Selection Candidate Vessels of Opportunity in Support of the Submarine Rescue Diving and Recompression System." Master's thesis, Massachusetts Institute of Technology, 2005. http://dspace.mit.edu/bitstream/handle/1721.1/33578/63518235.pdf?sequence=1.

Guinta, Peter. "Pearl Harbor: 60 Years Later." *St. Augustine Record*, 7 December 2001. http://staugustine.com/stories/120701/new_337234.shtml.

Harris, Edward Cecil. "Fixed Aircraft Carriers of the Atlantic Oceans." *Royal Gazette Online*. 12 June 2011. http://www.royalgazette.com/article/20110612/ISLAND09/706119970/0/news.

Historic Naval Ships Association. "Submarine War Patrol Reports." Accessed 2 May 2012. http://hnsa.org/doc/subreports.htm.

MassHumanities. "Coast Guard Cutter Collides with Navy Submarine, December 17, 1927." MassMoments. Accessed 2 May 2012. http://massmoments.org/moment.cfm?mid=361.

Moore, S. Clayton. "The Secrets of Station X." *Go World Travel: Britain's Hidden Weapon*. Accessed 2 May 2012. http://www.goworldtravel.com/travel-london-historic-wwii/.

National Parks Service. "The Battle of Bennington: An American Victory." Accessed 2 May 2012. http://www.nps.gov/history/nr/twhp/wwwlps/lessons/107bennington/107bennington.htm.

Naval Historical Center. "USS *S-4* (Submarine # 109, later SS-109), 1919–1936." 16 October 2005. http://www.history.navy.mil/photos/sh-usn/usnsh-s/ss109.htm.

Naval Inspector General. Accessed 2 May 2012. http://www.ig.navy.mil/.

NavSource Naval History. "Chronology of the Attack from the Deck Logs of the Vessels Moored at Pearl Harbor, December 7, 1941." Last modified October 2003. www.navsource.org/Naval/logs.htm

Office of War Information. "Department of the Navy." *U.S. Government Manual 1945*, 1st ed. Transcribed by Patrick Clancey, HyperWar Foundation. Accessed 2 May 2012. http://www.ibiblio.org/hyperwar/ATO/USGM/Navy.html.

Ohio State University Libraries. "Under the North Pole: The Voyage of the Nautilus." Accessed 2 May 2012. http://library.osu.edu/sites/exhibits/nautilus.

Patterson, Michael Robert. "Jonas Howard Ingram, Admiral, United States Navy." Arlington National Cemetery Website. Last modified 10 December 2006. www.arlingtoncemetery.net/jhingram.

Preston, Andrews. "Diving into the Abyss aboard Britain's World-Leading Submarine Rescue System." *Mail Online*. 15 February 2012. http://www.dailymail.co.uk/home/moslive/article-2016798/Diving-abyss-aboard-Britains-world-leading-submarine-rescue-system.html.

Prinz Eugen.com. "The U-Boat Rocket Program." Accessed 2 May 2012. www.prinzeugen.com/V2.htm.

Reformation Online. "Admiral William D. Leahy, Chairman of the Joint Chiefs of Staff during World War II." Accessed 2 May 2012. http://www.reformation.org/admiral-leahy.html.

Rigdon, William M. "President's Trip to the Berlin Conference, July 6 1945 to August 7, 1945." Harry S Truman Library and Museum. Accessed 2 May 2012. http://www.trumanlibrary.org/calendar/travel_log/pdfs/berlin45.pdf.

"Rocket U-Boat Program." Accessed 2 May 2012. http://www.uboataces.com/articles-rocket-uboat.shtml.

Rodgers, John. "The First Navy Pacific Flight." Hawaii Aviation. Accessed 2 May 2012. http://hawaii.gov/hawaiiaviation/hawaii-aviation-pioneers/john-rodgers.

Shireman, Douglas A. "U.S. Torpedo Troubles." Military.com. Last modified 2000. http://www.military.com/content/MoreContent?file=PRtorpedo.

Simon Lake Submarine Web Site. "Nautilus." Accessed 2 May 2012. http://www.simonlake.com/html/nautilus.html.

Sorbet Royal. "Italian ITS Anteo." Accessed 2 May 2012. http://sorbetroyal2005.celex.net/photo_album/antco.htm.

Team Submarine Public Affairs. "New Submarine Rescue Asset Joins Fleet." Navy News Service. 2 October 2008. http://www.navy.mil/search/display.asp?story_id=40147.

Uboataces. "U-boat Types." Last modified 2012. http://www.uboataces.com/uboat-type-ix.shtml.

Uboat.net. "List of All U-Boat Commanders." Accessed 2 May 2012. http://www.uboat.net/men/commanders/index.html

Valor at Sea. "WWII Anti-Submarine Warfare Tactics: The U.S. Navy Destroyer Operations in World War II." Last modified 2002. http://www.valoratsea.com/destroyer.htm.

"War Plan Orange." GlobalSecurity.org, 7 May 2011, http://www.globalsecurity.org/military/ops/war-plan-orange.htm.

Whittenberger, Kathryn. "Russian Submarine Works with U.S. Sub Rescue System for First Time." Navy News Service. 9 June 2011. http://www.navy.mil/search/display.asp?story_id=60904&page=2.

Other Sources

Donald, Mae Cameron. Letter to Sir George Hubert Wilkins, *Under the North Pole: The Voyage of the Nautilus* exhibition, Ohio State University Library.

Doyle, W. T. "Statement of Lieutenant W. T. Doyle, USN; USS *Squalus* Survivor." Naval History and Heritage Command, Washington Navy Yard, Washington, DC.

Drury Academy 1909 Yearbook, North Adams Historical Society, North Adams, MA.

Eben A. Ayers Papers, Harry S Truman Library and Museum, Independence, MO.

Exercise Bold Monarch 2011. "Russian Submarine Participates in NATO Submarine Rescue Exercise for First Time." News release, 2 June 2011.

Finley, Miles R. Letter to George R. Waterman, 1 May 1978. In author's possession.

House Armed Services Committee. *Investigation of the B-36 Bomber Program.* 81st Cong., 1st sess. Washington, DC: Government Printing Office, 1949.

Inquiry into the Fire on Submarine USS *O-5*, 5 October 1918. National Archives and Records Administration, Washington, DC.

Inquiry into the Sinking of Submarine USS *O-5*, 23 October 1923. File #12992, General File of the Secretary of the Navy, 1897–1926, File 26835–2545, National Archives and Records Administration, Washington, DC.

Leahy, William D. Papers of William D. Leahy. Library of Congress, Washington, DC.

Lewis, Andrew L. "The Revolt of the Admirals." PhD diss., Air Command and Staff College, 1998.

Lyon, Waldo. "Under Surface Profiles of Sea Ice Observed." Presented at the Eleventh Pacific Science Congress, Tokyo, 1966.

Lyon, Waldo K. *The Reminiscences of Dr. Waldo K. Lyon, Director, Arctic Marine Environmental Laboratory, San Diego, California.* January 1971–March 1972. Interviews with Cdr. Ette-Belle Kitchen, USN (Ret.), Naval Institute oral history, Annapolis, MD.

McCann, Allan Rockwell. Letter to Walter Welham, 26 January 1962. MS VF 27, Nimitz Library, U.S. Naval Academy, Annapolis, MD.

Momsen, Charles B. "Rescue and Salvage of U.S.S. *Squalus*." Lecture, Harvard Engineers Society, 6 October 1939. Naval History and Heritage Command, Washington Navy Yard, Washington, DC.

National Geographic. *Hunt for the Samurai Subs.* Aired 19 November 2009.

North Adams Historical Commission. *The Architectural Heritage of North Adams, Massachusetts.* Ithaca, NY: Herschensohn and Reed Associates, Historic Preservation Planners, December 1980.

Preble, Harold C. "Statement of Harold C. Preble, Naval Architect, USS *Squalus* Survivor." Naval History and Heritage Command, Washington Navy Yard, Washington, DC.

Submarine Casualties Booklet. Groton, CT: U.S. Naval Submarine School, 1966.

Surface Ship Operations, NAVEDTRA 10776-A. Pensacola, FL: Naval Education and Training Command, 1978.

Truman, Harry S. *The Diary of Harry S. Truman.* Harry S Truman Library and Museum, Independence, MO.

———. Letter to Richard Russell, 9 August 1945. Official File, Truman Papers, Harry S Truman Library and Museum, Independence, MO.

———. *Public Papers of the Presidents, 1945.* Harry S Truman Library and Museum, Independence, MO.

"USS *Squalus* SS-192: Report of Commander Rescue Operations." Naval History and Heritage Command, Washington Navy Yard, Washington, DC.

Wilson, Woodrow. *War Messages.* S. Doc. No. 5, Serial No. 7264 (1917), 3–8.

INDEX

ABOUT THE AUTHOR

A native Californian, **CARL LAVO** is the author of three previous books for the Naval Institute Press. He is a graduate of the University of Florida, where he was chapter officer/editor of the National Speleological Society. With a life-long interest in underseas explorations, he became an experienced scuba diver while pushing the limits, mapping water-filled caverns and subterranean rivers of Florida. Now living in Bucks County, PA, he and his wife, Mary Anne, have a daughter, Genevieve, son-in-law, Michael, grandson, Dashiell, and granddaughter, Margaux. He is an avid long-distance bicyclist and kayaker.